Folktales Retold

Folktales Retold

A Critical Overview of
Stories Updated for Children

Amie A. Doughty

McFarland & Company, Inc., Publishers
Jefferson, North Carolina, and London

Library of Congress Cataloguing-in-Publication Data

Doughty, Amie A., 1970–
    Folktales retold : a critical overview of stories updated for
children / Amie A. Doughty.
        p.   cm.
    Includes bibliographical references and index.

    ISBN 0-7864-2591-1 (softcover : 50# alkaline paper) ∞

    1. Folklore and children.   2. Folklore — Europe — Classification.
I. Title.
GR43.C4D68   2006
398.083 — dc22   2006006086

British Library cataloguing data are available

Front cover image ©2006 Pictures Now

Manufactured in the United States of America

*McFarland & Company, Inc., Publishers
  Box 611, Jefferson, North Carolina 28640
  www.mcfarlandpub.com*

For Nathan, Eden, Anna, and Alaina

Acknowledgments

This book could not have been written without the help and encouragement of many people. First and foremost, I want to thank Charlotte Amaro, who has been unflagging in her support during the writing process. Not only has she provided invaluable feedback on the entire book, but she has also been a fount of encouragement. Without her help I would not have completed this book. I am privileged to have her as a friend and a colleague.

Other friends and colleagues from Lake Superior State University and beyond have also shown me great encouragement, and I'd like to thank them for their support: Lance Rivers, Eric Gadzinski, Susan Cosby Ronnenberg, Matthew Pifer, Gary Balfantz, Jillena Rose, James Zukowski, Linda McHenry, Laurie DeNeve-Ewing, Karen McClenny, and Susan Kendrick.

I'd also like to acknowledge my family, particularly my parents, John and Elaine Doughty, who have always encouraged my love of reading and who have been a constant source of support in the writing of this book, as they have been all my life.

The Introduction, Chapter 3 ("Cultural and Regional Folktale Revisions in Picture Books,") and Chapter 9 ("Revising the Folktale Tradition") were all presented in an earlier form at the Popular Culture Association national conferences over the past several years, and have been revised for this book.

Table of Contents

Preface

Folklorists such as Antii Aarne, Stith Thompson, and Alan Dundes examine folktales from many perspectives. Most argue that true folktales must be oral, and for this reason folklorists usually study performances and transcriptions of tales in their analyses. Much of their work is comparative, since for them there can be no true single version of a folktale — only many versions of a tale that are passed through time and space. Many folklorists attempt to find trends in the tales to categorize them formally by plot pattern and motif elements. Antii Aarne and Stith Thompson's *The Types of the Folktale: A Classification and Bibliography* is the best known and most widely used of the classification systems. Other folklorists examine single folktales and attempt to trace their development over time and space, looking for the oldest known variations of "Cinderella" or "Little Red Riding Hood" or other tales. Folklorists tend to avoid examination of folktales they consider literary or otherwise contaminated by the compiler, some even calling them "fakelore" (Dundes 260). For many of these folklorists, written folktales are not true folktales.

Literary critics, by contrast, look at folktales of all types, whether transcribed or original, examining them through different theoretical lenses. Usually calling them fairy tales or literary fairy tales, these critics examine the tales' literary merit, the history of their recordings, their authors and compilers, their psychological impact, their reflection of specific cultures, and many other aspects of the tales. There is no shortage of literary criticism of folktales, and, unlike folklorists, literary critics and other scholars focus on specific versions of tales and their authors.

For folklorists, true folktales have no known authors, only different raconteurs who shape the tales to fit their audience. The originator of the tale is long forgotten and not pertinent to the folklorists' purposes. For literary critics, folktales can and often do have original authors and merit their own examination, though textual comparisons are also common among literary critics. The research about folktales by both folklorists and literary critics has been fruitful. From folklorists Aarne and Thompson's classification text to Alan Dundes' many casebooks, including *Cinderella: A Casebook* and *Little Red Riding Hood: A Casebook*, to Vladimir Propp's *Morphology of the Folktale* to psychologist Bruno Bettelheim's seminal study *The Uses of Enchantment* to literary critics Maria Tatar's *The Hard Facts of the Grimms' Fairy Tales* and Jack Zipes' many cultural critiques of folktales to name just a few, there is no shortage of research on oral and literary folktales.

But though folktales have long been examined by both folklorists and literary critics, folktale revisions—texts in which authors consciously reshape traditional folktales—have received little analysis as a separate form. Jack Zipes talks about revisions as an offshoot of literary folktales in *The Trials and Tribulations of Little Red Riding Hood* and the essay "Spells of Enchantment: An Overview of the History of Fairy Tales" from *When Dreams Came True: Classical Fairy Tales and Their Tradition*, among other texts. Other critics discuss folktale revisions in a similar manner. Cristina Bacchilega is one of the few critics to treat the folktale revision as a separate form in her book *Postmodern Fairy Tales: Gender and Narrative Strategies*, which examines folktale revisions from a fairly narrow perspective. Other critics, including John Pizer, Hilary S. Crew, and Claire Malarte-Feldman, have written journal articles about folktale revisions, also from narrow perspectives.

Most of these critics have dealt with folktale revisions written for adults, particularly the literary revisions of Angela Carter, Donald Barthelme, and Robert Coover. Folktale revisions for children, when mentioned, as in some of Zipes' analyses, are contained within analyses of adult revisions, not as a separate area. This tendency is not surprising given the place of children's literature within literary studies. Literature for children and young adults is often seen as inferior, simpler than literature for adults because of its audience. Only recently has children's and young adult literature become the focus of literary criticism of all kinds instead of being limited to psychological and pedagogical examinations.

This study ties together analysis of folktale revisions of canonical

Western European folktales ("Cinderella," "Little Red Riding Hood," "Snow White and the Seven Dwarfs," etc.) and children's and young adult literature, examining ways in which contemporary authors of folktale revisions for children and young adults take a genre long associated with the nursery — the folktale — and rework it into its own distinct form. This form, though it can and perhaps should be seen as an offshoot of the folktale tradition, is also unique, for no matter how authors choose to revise folktales, there is an intertextual element to the tales that ties them together and that distinguishes them from the traditional folktales upon which they are based. Though it is true that folktales were never traditionally meant for the children — and many authors of adult revisions are reclaiming the tales with all of the previously suppressed sex and violence — these tales have become so associated with the nursery, with childhood that it is not surprising that most folktale revisions have been published for that audience. From picture books to poems to short stories to novels, the folktale revision has become a common sight on shelves in the children's section of book stores and libraries. Authors such as Donna Jo Napoli, John Scieszka, Gail Carson Levine, and Susan Lowell, to name just a few, have written numerous folktale revisions, and many authors continue to return to these popular stories and to put their own spin on this genre.

The goal of this book is to examine how many of these authors have approached revising the folktale, from humorous to cultural to feminist to postmodern, and to present an idea of the vast scope of folktale revisions published for children and young adults. Though the focus of the book is on textual revisions in children's literature, sections of the book also examine the folktale revision in film and for adult audiences to show how authors for different audiences approach revising folktales. Hopefully, the analyses here will spark further interest and examination of folktale revisions, whether it is in analyzing specific authors, focusing on specific types of revisions, or turning to folktale revisions based on tales from other traditions. This field remains rich with potential for further studies.

Introduction: Unraveling the Folktale Tradition

In the Author's Note to her book *The Rumpelstiltskin Problem*, Vivian Vande Velde compares the folktale tradition with a game of gossip (sometimes known as telephone), saying,

> In the beginning [fairy tales] were told, not written down. And over time, as the stories were repeated by different people in different situations, they constantly shifted and changed....
>
> That's why we sometimes have completely different versions of the same story. But in some cases, so many details have been lost that the story stops making sense.
>
> That's how I feel about the story of Rumpelstiltskin — it makes no sense [vii–viii].

She continues her Author's Note by detailing the aspects of "Rumpelstiltskin" that make no sense to her: how the miller comes to be talking to a king; why the miller tells the king his daughter can spin straw to gold; why the king believes him; why the miller's daughter cries instead of trying to help herself; why Rumpelstiltskin wants payment for spinning gold and why he accepts such paltry payment; why the miller's daughter agrees to give her child to him on the final night (and why he wants it); why Rumpelstiltskin later gives her a chance to get out of the deal (and why he doesn't renegotiate the deal in his favor); why Rumpelstiltskin is singing his name outside for anyone to overhear; and, finally, why he gets so mad that he stamps his foot and tears himself in two at the end. All of these questions about the story, she says at the end of the

Author's Note, led her to write the versions of "Rumpelstiltskin" in the book. There are six.

Each of the different versions of the tale speculates on answers to the questions by recasting the tale, usually in a humorous light. In the first version, "A Fairy Tale in Very Bad Taste," Rumpelstiltskin is a troll who has a yen for the delights of baby flesh and goes the extra mile in an attempt to procure it by tricking the miller, the miller's daughter, and the king into the events of the traditional tale so that eventually he can claim her child (he doesn't ask her for it during the last night he spins; rather, he decides to "let you know later what you must pay me" [12]). In the end, it is Rumpelstiltskin's own family who betrays his name (the guessing of which he agrees to in a double or nothing bet). This humorous, though, as the title indicates, also grotesque, retelling of the tale does indeed answer Vande Velde's myriad questions, as do all of the additional versions in the book, each accounting for the problems in its own way and altering the plot as necessary to accomplish that task.

Other authors, while not expressing their questions as Vande Velde does in her author's note, clearly address similar questions in their revisions. In many of Donna Jo Napoli's revisions, for example, she addresses the issue of character motivation by developing extended narratives, frequently in first person and often from the point of view of the traditional folktale's antagonist, as she does in *Beast*, a retelling of "Beauty and the Beast," and in *The Magic Circle*, a retelling of "Hansel and Gretel." *Spinners*, a revision of "Rumpelstiltskin" written with Richard Tchen, alternates third person narrative point of view between the miller's daughter and the Rumpelstiltskin character. Each of Napoli's narratives attempts to address issues similar to Vande Velde but in a longer, more developed manner. Traditional antagonists' points of view are also explored in numerous other folktale revisions, from Jon Scieszka's *The True Story of the 3 Little Pigs* to several of the revisions by Alvin Granowsky for the Steck-Vaughn Point of View series to Priscilla Galloway's story "The Name," another "Rumpelstiltskin" revision from her collection *Truly Grim Tales*.

In addition to the questions about antagonists' motives in folktales, contemporary authors also explore the traditional protagonists' points of view particularly in lengthier revisions. Gail Carson Levine's *Ella Enchanted* examines the passivity of the traditional Cinderella character, as does Margaret Peterson Haddix's *Just Ella*. Robin McKinley has written two different "Beauty and the Beast" revisions, *Beauty* and *Rose Daughter*, that explore Beauty's development. Further, some of Donna

Jo Napoli's revisions, including *Zel* ("Rapunzel") and *Crazy Jack* ("Jack and the Beanstalk"), also present the point of view of traditional protagonists (and in the case of Zel of the antagonist and the prince). In the process, each of these authors attempts to answer questions as Vande Velde does, even if these questions are not articulated: Why is Cinderella so passive? What makes Beauty so different from her sisters (and are her sisters really as unsympathetic as the traditional story makes them out to be)? What would happen if a girl were really left alone in a tower for years? Why is Jack such an odd ne'er-do-well?

Some authors take the revisions another step, not only revising tales but also interweaving them. E.D. Baker's trilogy, starting with *The Frog Princess*, revised "The Frog Prince," but it also interweaves aspects of "Little Red Riding Hood," "Hansel and Gretel," and several other folktales as well as original tales. Similarly, Rebecca Lickiss, in *Never After*, focuses most of the novel on a revision of "Sleeping Beauty" but interweaves "The Frog Prince," "Rumpelstiltskin," and "Cinderella" in it. And Jane B. Mason and Sarah Hines Stephens in The Princess School series not only revise the traditional folktales of their four main characters—Snow White, Cinderella Brown, Rapunzel Arugula, and Briar Rose—but also create new stories for them, including making Briar Rose the Beast in *Beauty Is a Beast*, and bring in numerous other folktale characters such as Little Red Riding Hood and Gretel. These revisions question not just specific tales, but the folktale tradition as a whole, reshaping it in unusual ways but producing stories still identifiable as folktales.

Revisions are not limited to prose fiction either. Poets and dramatists have long revised folktales, and folktales have been part of film for almost as long as there has been film, with versions of "Cinderella" and "Beauty and the Beast," among others, being created at the end of the nineteenth century. While Disney is best known for its folktale films, other companies have also produced numerous folktale revisions, as both feature films and as shorts. *Fractured Fairy Tales* from *Rocky & Bullwinkle & Friends* is still well-known, as is Shelley Duvall's *Faerie Tale Theatre*. Recent feature length folktale revisions include *Ever After* and *A Cinderella Story*. Even television series are revising folktales, from the series *Beauty and the Beast* to episodes of *Buffy the Vampire Slayer* ("Gingerbread," "Hush") and *Northern Exposure* ("Survival of the Species"). As with written folktale revisions, film, television, and theater revisions answer questions about the traditional folktales, only in a different manner.

What are readers to make of all these revisions? Why do authors feel compelled to write these new versions? Why does the modern audience question the conventions of traditional folktales enough to write about them? Clearly there is something missing in the tales that compels the authors to write these versions. Can the questions that Vande Velde finds in "Rumpelstiltskin" and that others have found in other tales be attributed to the change in form from an oral form to a written one? In other words, do questions arise from the written versions because there is no physical narrator to present the context of the story and to answer audience questions? If one looks at the revisions written from a first person point of view or with an intrusive third person narrator, one might assume that the answer to the question is "yes" since these revisions put in place a new narrator who takes over the position of the traditional storyteller, even if it is from a participant's perspective rather than the commentator's. But not all of the stories are told from this perspective. In fact a good number of the revisions are made using a third person narrator who is not intrusive, who doesn't comment on the events. Is there something more that leads to the problems then? Has society changed in a way that makes these questions paramount for authors?

This book attempts to answer these questions while exploring ways in which authors of contemporary children's literature revise folktales. The folktales examined are those from the Western European tradition, primarily the Grimm Brothers and Charles Perrault's tales, but also some from English tradition and other French authors. Chapter 1, "The Folktale Revision as a Form," briefly explores the history and background of folktales and folktale revisions and presents definitions of both folktale and folktale revision for this work.

Chapter 2, "Humor in Folktale Revisions," examines how authors employ humor in folktale revisions, with a focus on word and language play and role reversals. Starting with an analysis of purely humorous folktale revisions by Roald Dahl, Jon Scieszka, and Mike Thaler, the chapter then moves to the more serious, novel-length revisions by Tracy Lynn and Gail Carson Levine, among others, in which humor is used to offset the dramatic events of the stories.

Chapter 3, "Cultural and Regional Folktale Revisions in Picture Books," using picture book revisions of first "Cinderella" and then "Little Red Riding Hood" as the primary focus, reveals how some authors revise folktales using different cultural settings from the Wild West to Louisiana to Hawaii. It also compares cultural versions of folktales—the Egyptian, Persian, and Mexican Cinderellas—with cultural revisions in which the traditional European folktale is clearly being reshaped to fit the new cultural setting rather than being a traditional part of that culture.

Chapter 4, "Breaking the Picture Book Rules," explores several ways in which folktale revisions revise not only folktales but also the conventions of the picture book, from the flip books in Alvin Granowsky's Steck-Vaughn Point of View series to Jon Scieszka's *The Stinky Cheese Man and Other Fairly Stupid Tales* in which Jack the narrator is also responsible for the physical construction of the book, something he does not handle well. These revisions are among the most metatextual of folktale revisions.

Chapter 5, "Feminist Folktale Revisions," describes three ways in which authors of folktale revisions address perceived sexism in traditional folktales: by creating new tales with strong female leads; by switching the gender of the traditional main character from male to female; and by revising traditional tales with weak female leads to make them stronger than the traditional characters. Works by Jane Yolen, Mary Pope Osborne, Gail Carson Levine, and Frances Minters, among others, are examined.

Chapter 6, "Postmodern Folktale Revisions," examines the way in which revisions that alter the traditional main character work, starting with revisions that focus on traditional secondary characters such as Cinderella's fairy godmother or animal helpers in *The Youngest Fairy Godmother Ever* by Stephen Krensky and *Cinderella's Rat* by Susan Meddaugh. Then traditional antagonists who are made protagonists, particularly the big bad wolf, are explored, from Scieszka's *The True Story of the 3 Little Pigs* to Margie Palatini's *Bad Boys* to Bob Hartman's *The Wolf Who Cried Boy*.

Chapter 7, "Narrative in Folktale Revisions," studies how contemporary authors, especially those creating novel-length revisions such as Donna Jo Napoli, Margaret Peterson Haddix, and Robin McKinley, alter the traditional point of view of folktales, whether it is by delving deeper into a character's head in third person or by using a first person narrator. The ways in which these tales reflect on the role of storytelling in society and how the "true story" is altered are also explored.

Chapter 8, "Folktale Revisions on Film," moves from written folktale revisions to performed ones. Focusing on film revisions of "Cinderella," the chapter examines how film and theater revisions compare to written ones, particularly in terms of the first meeting of the main characters in traditional romantic folktales. Revisions with more traditional settings such as *Ever After, The Slipper and the Rose,* and *Hey Cinderella* are contrasted with modernized film revisions such as *A Cinderella Story* and *Cinderfella.*

Chapter 9, "Revising the Folktale Tradition," shifts from revisions of individual tales to an examination of how some authors continue to create original folktales in the vein of Hans Christian Andersen and Oscar Wilde. While some revisions of the tales, such as *The Paper Bag Princess* by Robert Munsch, do not make reference to the folktale tradition that they are revising, others, such as the works by E.D. Baker and Rebecca Lickiss, incorporate bits of other folktales into their original stories. Still other authors, such as Vivian Vande Velde in *A Well-Timed Enchantment,* use modern characters placed in a folktale of their own to comment on the tradition as they know it in modern life.

The final chapter, "The Adult Connection," focuses on "Sleeping Beauty" revisions, including *Enchantment* by Orson Scott Card, *Beauty* by Sheri S. Tepper, and *Briar Rose* by Robert Coover, as it examines how folktale revisions for adults compare to the revisions in children's literature. Differences can include more sexualized themes and older main characters, but also the choice of folktale being revised.

Each of the chapters with the exception of Chapter 1 focuses on close readings of specific texts without attempting to be comprehensive. Though each chapter can be read as an individual analysis, together the chapters represent an examination of an ever-increasing manner in which storytellers continue to reweave the folktale tradition.

1

The Folktale Revision as a Form

Scholars of published folktale collections by the Brothers Grimm, Charles Perrault, and others, such as Jack Zipes and Cristina Bacchilega, generally differentiate the terms *folktale* and *fairy tale* by the mode in which a tale is presented: folktales are oral stories; fairy tales are written tales modeled on their oral counterparts, though not necessarily having an oral ancestor. Mary Beth Stein, in her entry "Folklore and Fairy Tales" from *The Oxford Companion to Fairy Tales*, edited by Zipes, writes, "The term folk tale is reserved for any tale deriving from or existing in oral tradition and is generally preferred by folklorists and anthropologists. Literary scholars tend to use the word fairy tale to refer to a genre of prose literature, which may or may not be based in oral tradition" (167). However, she points out that "The words fairy tale can refer to both a category of oral folk tale and a genre of prose literature" (167).

As a category of oral folktale, fairy tales are stories containing magic of some sort, though not necessarily fairies. As Steven Swann Jones notes in his book *The Fairy Tale: The Magic Mirror of the Imagination*, "Since, in English folk tradition, the fairy realm is the embodiment of the magical aspect of the world, its name is used metonymically to refer to all folktales that incorporate the magical and the marvelous" (9). Fairy tales as part of the oral folktale category are also sometimes called wonder tales, magic tales, or *märchen*. Other folktale categories will vary by folklorist, though common ones include animal tales ("The Bremen Town Musicians," "Henny Penny"), cumulative tales ("The Pancake," "The Gingerbread Man"), and noodlehead, numbskull, or simpleton tales

("The Three Wishes," "Jack and the Beanstalk"[1]). Some of the tales can also be cross-categorized.

In terms of written or literary tales, the term fairy tale usually includes all categories of oral folktales that have been retold in writing as well as new tales created to resemble traditional tales. Thus tales such as "The Pancake," which would be labeled as cumulative in its original oral form, would be a fairy tale in written form. The same is true of an animal tale such as "Henny Penny" or "The Little Red Hen." It is true that most of the best-known tales, the "canon" of popular tales in modern times, are magical or fairy tales under the oral folktale category — "Snow White and the Seven Dwarfs," "Cinderella," "Sleeping Beauty," "Beauty and the Beast," etc. — but using the label *fairy tale* as the label for all written versions when the label *folktale* (and its category fairy tale) already exists seems problematic, even though, as Jack Zipes points out in his introduction to *The Oxford Companion to Fairy Tales*, "the average reader is not aware of the distinction between the oral and literary traditions or even cares about it" (xv), let alone the subcategories of the folktale (or even that there are subcategories). Yet for those studying folktales, the distinctions are important, as is the use of consistent terminology.

Zipes himself, in his early work *Breaking the Magic Spell: Radical Theories of Folk and Fairy Tales*, explains his labels of *folktale* for tales from the oral tradition and *fairy tale* for literary tales by using the German terms *Volksmärchen* and *Kunstmärchen* as his basis. *Märchen*, now often used as a synonym for the folktale category called the fairy tale, is actually "the diminutive form of the Old German word *mär* meaning a short story" (Dégh 62). *Volksmärchen* literally means folktale and refers to tales told to and by "folk." Zipes applies this term to oral tales and written transcriptions of oral tales. *Kunstmärchen* Zipes equates to the English term *fairy tale* or *literary fairy tale*, a story that can be gathered from oral tradition and stylized to "feel" more literary or stories that resemble folktales in terms of motifs, form, and style but that have no oral counterpart, such as some of the tales by Hans Christian Andersen and Oscar Wilde. Zipes makes this connection between *Kunstmärchen* and the fairy tale for "historical" reasons in his text to show how this newer form of folktale came to exist despite the possibility of confusion, instead of using a more "correct" translation of "art tale," something that could conceivably be confused with the short story or other literary forms.[2] Yet the use of *fairy tale* instead of *folktale* to distinguish the oral and literary is still problematic because, as Zipes points out in his introduction to *The Oxford Companion to Fairy Tales*, literary tales, once they became easily accessible to a wider public thanks to small, inexpensive printings, "were often read aloud and made their way back into the oral tradition" (xxiii).[3] Similarly, as many critics have shown, the Grimm brothers, arguably the best-known collectors of folktales, edited many of the tales they had recorded into a more literary style and continued to alter them in each edition of their *Kinder- und Hausmärchen* (*Children's and Household Tales*). The Grimms thus represent a combination of oral and written and are therefore difficult to label using terms that distinguish "pure" oral and written versions of tales.[4]

A better approach to labeling folktales is that adopted by Steven Swann Jones. In *The Fairy Tale: The Magic Mirror of the Imagination*, Jones settles on using the term *fairy tale* from the oral category definition of a magic tale and claims that "our conception of the fairy tale genre recognizes three major forms: indigenous oral versions, collected and variously edited versions in print, and original, single-author fairy tales that are not drawn from oral tradition but that closely resemble that narrative genre" (34). This explanation of fairy tales, while it does not take into consideration the interplay between the oral and written, is more consistent in recognizing the continuation of the form, a continuation that exists despite some folklorists' argument that written folktales represent the death (or at least stagnation) of folktales. While Zipes and others who separate the oral and written tales with different names acknowledge a connection between the oral and written tales, that connection is limited by the shift in terminology. However, the term *folktale* can be similarly divided into Jones' "three major forms" and *fairy tale* remain a subcategory of folktales. In this way, the terminology, and the connection between oral and written tales, remains consistent.

In this work, the term used to refer to the stories upon which the texts being examined are based is *folktale*. Though the majority of the folktales discussed in this work fit the subcategory of fairy tale, not all of them do, thus necessitating the use of the term *folktale*. Often reference will be made to "traditional folktales" or "traditional folktale versions." These labels do not generally mean oral versions but the written version(s) that are established, usually the versions written by the Grimms or Perrault. This work examines *revisions* of folktales.

All traditional folktales have undergone (and continue to undergo) some kind of reshaping, even though most modern readers think of them in terms of a specific version read during childhood. For folklorists, however, it is impossible to understand a folktale based on a single version; only through an examination of various versions of a tale can an understanding of it be attempted. As tales are passed through cultures and generations, taletellers shape them to reflect the changes and expectations of the society hearing the tale. Some folklorists insist that once folktales are written down they lose their power because they become fixed. Alan Dundes, for example, has argued in "Fairy Tales from a Folkloristic Perspective" that "Once a fairy tale or any other type of folktale ... is reduced to written language, one does not have a true fairy tale but instead only a pale and inadequate reflection of what was originally an oral performance complete with raconteur and audience" (259). The problem for folklorists such as Dundes is that the written texts that have become popularized seemingly reduce the folktale to a single version and this problem leads Dundes to say, "The folkloristic approach to fairy tales begins with the oral tale — with literary versions being considered derivative" (266). Dundes' use of the word "versions" here is interesting, for though it is easy to understand why people would think written folktales have only one version, this is no more true than of oral tales. Even the Grimms themselves presented different written versions of their tales with new editions of their collection.

In contemporary literature, different versions or retellings of folktales continue to be published in several ways. One way, for English (or other translated) versions of Grimm and Perrault, among others, is through new translations. Different translators will offer subtle differences in translations of tales that reveal different interpretive possibilities of the texts. For example, in the Grimm brothers' "Cinderella" (sometimes called "Aschenputtle") something as small as the rhyme the pigeons (sometimes doves) call out as the prince rides off with the first sister can vary greatly. In *Grimm's Complete Fairy Tales* published by Doubleday, the poem reads:

> *There they go, there they go!*
> *There is blood on her shoe;*
> *The shoe is too small,*
> *— Not the right bride at all!* [85, emphasis in original].

Jack Zipes translates this same passage in *The Great Fairy Tale Tradition: From Straparola and Basile to the Brothers Grimm* as

> Looky, look, look
> at the shoe that she took.
> There's blood all over, and the shoe's too small.
> She's not the bride you met at the ball [471].

This same passage in Joanna Cole's *Best-Loved Folktales of the World* reads

Prithee, look back, prithee, look back,
There's blood on the track,
The shoe is too small,
At home the true bride is waiting thy call [73].

Even taking into account how difficult it can be to translate poetry does not explain some of the differences in these translations, particularly the final line in each one. Cole's translation presents Cinderella as passive ("waiting thy call"), while both the Doubleday and Zipes translations focus just on pointing out the mistaken identity, Zipes' with the added detail of the ball as the original meeting place. This is a small passage of a much longer folktale, and though the plot of the story remains the same, the translators all present the text in a slightly different manner, retelling the story in their own way and thus creating a new version, a retelling, of the tale, similar to the way an oral teller would have reworked a tale, albeit in a different medium.

Another way in which new versions or retellings of folktales are created in print is in picture books. As with versions that are not illustrated, the text portion of these tales is often retranslated or adapted by an author and/or illustrator. In this form, though, the more important variation is in the illustrations, for each illustrator has a different conception of the story, and the many varied picture book versions of traditional tales show this difference. James Marshall, for example, illustrates his folktales as cartoons, unrealistic and humorous, while Trina Schart Hyman creates realistic illustrations with meticulous detail to reflect the region from which the tale comes. Thus her illustrations for *Little Red Riding Hood*, retold from the Grimm tale "Little Red Cap," abound with German folk patterns in the borders. Each illustrator has a different style and vision of the traditional tale, and thus each picture book is a new version of the traditional tale.

Revisions of folktales, however, are versions of folktales, usually written, that take traditional tales, often well-known ones, and alter them in a much more elaborate manner than retellings. Though still part of the folktale tradition, revisions, unlike retellings, are more consciously reacting to the very tradition they belong to, and a great number of revisions are intertextual, something not true of traditional folktales and retellings. Some critics, such as Jack Zipes, treat revisions as literary fairy tales while others treat them as a separate entity. Cristina Bacchilega in *Postmodern Fairy Tales: Gender and Narrative Strategies*, for example, calls them "contemporary transformations of fairy tales" (3) then later defines them as "Literary and non-literary contemporary nar-

ratives which rewrite and revise 'classic' fairy tales" (4), defining classic
fairy tales as "a *literary* appropriation of the older folk tale, an appropriation which nevertheless continues to exhibit and reproduce some
folkloric features" (3, emphasis in original). Others label folktale revisions fractured fairy tales. In her definition "Fractured Fairy Tales" from
The Oxford Companion to Fairy Tales, Ruth B. Bottigheimer calls them
"traditional fairy tales, rearranged to create new plots with fundamen-
tally different meanings or messages" and contrasts them with fairy tale
parodies: "the two serve different purposes: parodies mock individual
tales and the genre as a whole; fractured fairy tales, with a reforming
intent, seek to impart updated social and moral messages" (172). Though
this definition and comparison makes sense, the name *fractured fairy tale*
is hard to dissociate from the cartoon series (subsequently made into a
book) of the same name. These cartoon shorts, which appeared on *Rocky
& Bullwinkle & Friends*, are parodies and are what people generally associate with the label *fractured fairy tales*. Further, even if the label *fractured fairy tale* weren't already loaded, parodies would have to be
considered a type of fractured fairy tale, for parodies can, and often do,
"impart updated social and moral messages" as the non-parodies do,
just in a different manner. The term *folktale revision* works better than
fractured fairy tales because it reflects what these authors are doing —
revising the folktale tradition. *Revision* also encompasses both parodies
and non-parodies.

Though the folktale revision has become extremely popular in the
past thirty years or so, it is by no means a new form. Jack Zipes, in *The
Trials and Tribulations of Little Red Riding Hood*, presents a poem by
Robert Samber called "The Moral" that reflects on the wolf's role in the
traditional folktale "Little Red Riding Hood." This revision was published in 1729, barely thirty years after Charles Perrault published his
traditional version in 1697. And John Pizer, in "The Disenchantment of
Snow White: Robert Walser, Donald Barthelme and the Modern/Post-
modern Anti-Fairy Tale," mentions Georg Büchner's "pithy grandmother's tale" in *Woyzeck*, arguably a retelling of "The Seven Ravens"
from the Grimms and written in 1836, twenty-four years after the
Grimms published their collection (330).

Folktale revisions exist in many media and forms, from the expected
short prose narrative to novel-length narratives to poems and plays to
musicals and films and advertisements. What ties together these diverse
folktale revisions is the way in which they are responding to the folktale
tradition. While often the revisions can stand by themselves as stories,

it is at the intertextual level that they work best. It might not be necessary, for example, for a reader to know "Cinderella" to enjoy *Ella Enchanted* by Gail Carson Levine or *Just Ella* by Margaret Peterson Haddix, but knowing the traditional folktale will certainly enhance the reading by offering a point of contrast that adds humor and poignancy to the novels. Other revisions rely on the intertextual connection: Roald Dahl's "Cinderella" from *Revolting Rhymes* begins "I guess you think you know this story" (5); Jon Scieszka starts *The True Story of the Three Little Pigs* "Everybody knows the story of the Three Little Pigs" (1); and Alvin Granowsky takes the comparative nature of folktale revisions to the limit in his Steck-Vaughn Point of View Stories. Each of these flip books contains a retelling of a traditional tale on one side and a revision of the same tale in first person on the other side of the book. It is this intertextuality that truly sets the folktale revision apart from the retelling, whether the revision can stand alone or not. The folktale revision interacts with the tradition from which it springs.

In contemporary children's literature, folktale retellings are still far more prevalent and popular than revisions, but over the past thirty years or so, revisions have become increasingly popular, whether they are literary, such as revisions by Robin McKinley and Donna Jo Napoli, or series fiction, such as the Princess School series by Jane B. Mason and Sarah Hines Stephens or Gail Carson Levine's Princess Tales. The rise in popularity of these revisions may in fact spring from the problems Dundes and others find with the writing down of folktales. While the written versions undoubtedly undergo changes with new retellings, they are still always based on one or two original texts and thus do not evolve in the same way that oral tales would since they remain attached to a version from a specific point in time. The world of written folktales is too unrealistic for many modern readers, and authors of revisions seem to be taking great liberties with the traditional texts as they alter the folktale to reflect modern sensibilities, making characters seen as weak stronger (especially females) or explaining that weakness; filling in perceived plot holes or explaining other historically-bound elements inexplicable to the modern reader; and dealing with issues of suspension of disbelief. These alterations, in fact, show the way in which the folktale tradition in writing is now starting to resemble the oral tradition from which it came, with the new authors bringing to their own cultures new versions of traditional folktales that may better speak to them than the traditional folktales do. No single folktale revision is definitive, just as no single version of an oral folktale is definitive. It is in the comparison that understanding of the form comes clear.

Each of the following chapters works from that framework: that understanding folktale revisions requires comparison of many different revisions and their intertextual relationship to the traditional tale upon which they are based. Though it is impossible to discuss all folktale revisions here, of course, it *is* possible to come up with an understanding of how this form connects to the folktale tradition from which it comes and how it acts as a continuation of that same tradition.

2

Humor in Folktale Revisions

Julie Anne Peters, in her brief article "When You Write Humor for Children," discusses eight different methods of making children's literature funny: surprise, exaggeration, word and language play, role reversal, nonsense, slapstick, satire, and adolescent angst. Though Peters' article is primarily about how to include humor in children's literature, her comments can naturally be applied to the analysis of humorous children's texts, something she does as she explains each of the eight methods. Given the popularity of humorous children's literature, it should be no surprise that some authors of folktale revisions choose to create humorous ones.

Though the majority of folktale revisions retain the dramatic (if not melodramatic) tone of traditional folktales, some authors, including Roald Dahl, Jon Scieszka, Vivian Vande Velde, and Mike Thaler, choose to revise the tone of folktales, making them humorous in nature. These humorous revisions are generally brief in nature, either picture books or short stories. When humor appears in short novels, such as Gail Carson Levine's Princess Tales series or Donna Jo Napoli's *The Prince of the Pond: Otherwise Known as De Fawg Pin*, it is usually accompanied with a matching serious tone, even if the humor dominates. Novel-length revisions, including The Princess School series by Jane B. Mason and Sarah Hines Stephens, *Snow* by Tracy Lynn, and *Ella Enchanted* by Gail Carson Levine, though usually maintaining a serious tone, may contain humorous elements to balance the dramatic main stories. The most common devices mentioned by Peters used to evoke humor in folktale revisions are word and language play and role reversal, though the other devices are occasionally used as well.

The six folktale revisions that make up Roald Dahl's *Revolting Rhymes* are made humorous first and foremost because of their form — narrative poems written in rhymed couplets. This format is fast-paced and the content naturally enhances the humor of the form. "Goldilocks and the Three Bears," for example, begins,

> This famous wicked little tale
> Should never have been put on sale.
> It is a mystery to me
> Why loving parents cannot see
> That this is actually a book
> About a brazen little crook [29].

The point of view presented, very sympathetic toward the bear family, is made humorous through the description of Goldilocks as a "brazen little crook," presenting a role reversal, and this humor is underscored by the quick-paced rhymes. The humor at the expense of the traditional protagonist continues as the narrator implores the readers, "Now just imagine how you'd feel" (29) if all of the traditional events of the Goldilocks story had occurred to them.

The narrator then gives a brief introduction to the bear family and continues to explore the role reversal, presenting Papa Bear as refined while retaining elements of juvenile humor in Papa Bear's final comment extolling the virtue of a good walk: "It makes your appetite improve / It also helps your bowels to move" (30). Shortly after the bears go for a walk, Goldilocks is introduced, and the name calling continues. From his opening "brazen little crook," the narrator moves on to calling Goldilocks a "little toad" and a "nosey thieving little louse" (30). A short time later, she becomes "some delinquent little tot" (30), then a "little skunk" (33), a "revolting little clown" (33), and a "little beast" (34). She is also compared to a freak (32). Throughout, the narrator continues to address the audience and encourage them to understand the bears' natural ire over Goldilocks' uncouth behavior, going so far as to list the four crimes of which she is guilty, beginning with breaking and entering. To cement the humor — and to contrast the traditional story with the new interpretation — the narrator shows disgust that "The little beast gets off scott-free" in the books, commenting,

> Myself, I think I'd rather send
> Young Goldie to a sticky end.
> "Oh daddy!" cried the Baby Bear,
> "My porridge is gone! It isn't fair!"
> "Then go upstairs," the Big Bear said,

"Your porridge is upon the bed.
"But as it's inside mademoiselle,
"You'll have to eat *her* up as well" [34].

Quentin Blake's final illustration for the poem is of a well-dressed Baby Bear, his parents looking on, dabbing his mouth with a napkin. Goldilocks' clothes are shown ripped and strewn around him. This surprise ending, though only in the narrator's mind, is a third device that Dahl uses to create humor.

Many of the other revisions in *Revolting Rhymes* are similarly violent and show a role reversal for one character or another. In Dahl's revision "Little Red Riding Hood and the Wolf," it is the antagonist who receives the violence he usually inflicts, but in this case it comes from a different party. The wolf and Little Red Riding Hood exchange the traditional dialog until the last one, when Little Red comments "*what a lovely great big furry coat you have on*" (38, emphasis in original) and confuses the wolf, who is expecting the traditional question about his big teeth. Instead of being victimized by the wolf, Little Red Riding Hood "whips a pistol from her knickers" and shoots him (38), later showing the narrator her "lovely furry WOLFSKIN COAT" (40). In "The Three Little Pigs," however, it is the pigs who are not so lucky. After the first two pigs, considered fools by the narrator, are killed and eaten by a new wolf, the third pig, "bright and brainy" (44), calls Red Riding Hood for help defeating the wolf. Happy to oblige, she once again shoots the wolf to add a second coat to her collection. However, she is not content with that, for as the narrator points out,

Ah Piglet, you must never trust
Young ladies from the upper crust.
For now, Miss Riding Hood, one notes,
Not only has *two* wolfskin coats,
But when she goes from place to place,
She has a PIGSKIN TRAVELLING CASE [47].

For these paired folktale revisions, Dahl has kept the humorous tone with his language use and irreverent reference to characters (and alteration of their roles to some degree), but he has also used surprise turns in the endings to add to the humor of the tales. These poetic revisions of folktales are funny and creative.

Mike Thaler's Happily Ever Laughter series of picture books, illustrated by Jared Lee, also presents revisions in a humorous fashion. He doesn't use Dahl's poetic form to create the humor; instead, he uses prose to present his reversals of characters or character traits and his word and language play. In the case of his "Cinderella" revision, *Cinderella Bigfoot*, Thaler keeps the shoe as the important article for identifying Cinderella, but rather than the dainty foot of tradition, Thaler reverses the tradition so that Cinderella has feet so big that "When she stood up, she looked like a seaplane."[1] Toward the end of the story we learn that her feet are "size 87, triple A." It is the king and queen in this version who decide not to invite Cinderella to the ball because she has a tendency to leave her shoes around town and inviting her "just wouldn't be safe" according to the queen. Thaler further mocks the folktale convention of wicked/ugly stepfamilies, writing, "Cinderella lived with her beautiful stepmother and her three beautiful stepsisters, Weeny, Whiny, and Moe. She also had a beautiful stepcat, a stepdog, and a stepladder." The final "steps," especially the stepladder, focus on the absurdity of traditional folktale treatments of stepfamilies while simultaneously playing on words.

The next character to come under scrutiny is the fairy godmother, whom Thaler turns into Elsie the "Dairy Godmother." She convinces Cinderella to go to the ball, complete with a pair of glass sneakers, though Cinderella is forced to take the bus to get there. Like the Cinderella of the traditional tales, Thaler's Cinderella is stared at as she enters the ballroom, but only because she's "funny-looking." This makes her a good match for "Prince Smeldred, who was quite funny looking himself." Not surprisingly, their dancing is not graceful, and Cinderella steps on his feet continuously. The grace of the traditional folktale heroine is reversed here. And as with traditional versions, Cinderella leaves behind a shoe on her flight from the party, only in this version it's so big that it "blocked the doorway." When Prince Smeldred tries to find Cinderella, he is forced to use a "'toe' truck." This pun, one of many in the revision, enhances the humor. When Cinderella finally tries on the shoe and the prince asks her to marry him, she replies, "Only if you'll marry *me*," whereupon "they rushed out the door to live happily ever after." The story ends with Cinderella's stepmother, in nearly the final pun, saying, "it's going to be hard to fill Cinderella's shoes," followed by Elsie's ending adage, "The shoe must go on." The end of the story is particularly funny thanks to its wordplay compared to previous sections of the story, in which the humor comes more from the altered characterizations.

The textual humor is further enhanced by the illustrations, cartoons depicting the Land of Make Believe's funny-looking population. The busy illustrations often come with dialog balloons, such as when

Cinderella is in ballet class and bangs her head on the ceiling or when the king and queen are seen making out dance party invitations. Thaler's *Schmoe White and the Seven Dorfs* is similarly absurd, though it follows the traditional version of "Snow White and the Seven Dwarfs" less closely than "Cinderella" was followed, ending as it does with Schmoe White being poisoned by lipstick. She wakes when the prince kisses her, but then he "dies," so she kisses him awake, and they end up in a continual loop of kissing the other awake. When the Dorfs, a rock and roll band, tire of waiting for their lead singer to wake up, they break up the band and "started a baseball team with seven shortstops." There is less punning in this revision, but once again the story's altered characters and accompanying illustrations make a humorous story.

Like Thaler's revisions, Jon Scieszka's are in picture book format. His best known revision is perhaps *The True Story of the 3 Little Pigs*, but he has written several others, including *The Frog Prince Continued* and *The Stinky Cheese Man and Other Fairly Stupid Tales*. The humor in each of these revisions varies. In *The True Story of the Three Little Pigs*, the humor lies partly in the reversed point of view. Alexander T. Wolf (Al for short), recounting the story in a mostly deadpan manner, is humorous in certain places, particularly when he urges the reader to "Think of it [the dead pig] as a big cheeseburger just lying there" for him to eat after the first house is blown in by his sneeze. Use of the phrase "Wolf's honor" when the second pig dies adds to the humor. And like Dahl in "Goldilocks and the Three Bears," when Al encounters the third pig, who is very rude to Al, Scieszka uses name calling in a way that not only enhances his point of view (and the antagonistic nature of the pigs), but that also shows humor. The third little pig is called a "rude little porker" after telling the wolf, "Get out of here, Wolf. Don't bother me again." Part of the humor also lies in Lane Smith's illustrations, from the hand drawn page declaring "This is the real story" using various elements related to the tale, from straw to twigs to fur to a pig's snout to create the letters in a manner similar to a ransom note, to the two pictures of pig bottoms sticking out of the rubble of the first two houses, to the picture of the newspaper—*The Daily Pig*—detailing the "facts" about Al's arrest. This paper also includes a headline about Little Red Riding Hood. The final picture, showing Al holding out a cup with the label "Pig Penn" on it, ends the story visually on a humorous note. The humor of *The True Story of the Three Little Pigs* lies most, however, in the presentation of a familiar story from such a different and somewhat absurd point of view.

Scieszka's book *The Frog Prince Continued* brings humor to the revision in a different manner. Beginning where the traditional story "The Frog Prince" ends, this book moves swiftly into how unhappy the Frog Prince and his Princess really are. The Prince is miserable mostly because the Princess does not like any of his residual froggy mannerisms—sticking his tongue out, hopping on the furniture, and having a "horrible, croaking snore." The initial humor of the narrator's revelation that the couple is not living happily ever after (something that the narrator seems reluctant to reveal because it reverses the expectations of the traditional folktale version's ending) gives way to the humor of the Prince's mannerisms. From there the humor comes as the Prince, deciding, after the Princess tells him "Sometimes I think we would both be better off if you were still a frog," that he wants to be a frog again, goes off into the forest "looking for a witch who could turn him into a frog."

In the forest, he encounters three different witches from three different folktales. First is one from "Sleeping Beauty" who wants to stop him from waking Sleeping Beauty too early. The second is the stepmother from "Snow White and the Seven Dwarfs" who, afraid he will wake Snow White, tries to get him to "eat the rest of this apple." He refuses because he "knew his fairy tales (and knew a poisoned apple when he saw one)" and escapes, running into the third witch, this one from "Hansel and Gretel." She invites him to dinner to talk about helping turn him into a frog, but his folktale knowledge helps him escape again. All three of these encounters are humorous partly because in each is the running language gag of the Prince introducing himself as the Frog Prince and the witches commenting that he doesn't look like a frog. This same gag continues when the Prince bumps into Cinderella's fairy godmother, who offers to help him and accidentally turns him into a frog-like carriage. His return home once the spell wears off at the stroke of midnight contains a lovely, seemingly-serious reconciliation between the Prince and Princess, but Scieszka undercuts the drama with humor by, on the final page, having the Frog Prince kiss the Princess and them both turn into frogs, after which "they hopped off happily ever after."

Steve Johnson's illustrations naturally complement the humorous tone of the story, particularly when the Frog Prince meets up with the witches and fairy godmother. Sleeping Beauty's witch is shown with a remote control of "Nasty Spells" while Snow White's witch is at a beauty parlor called "The Fairest" and shown reading a copy of "Hague." And the apple the Frog Prince can tell is poisoned is shown dripping with a green substance. Further, the Hansel and Gretel witch is shown planting a garden of popsicles and ice cream cones, and Cinderella's fairy godmother appears to be practicing her carriage transformation before visiting her charge. Each of these pictures, though dark in their color tones, underscores the humor of the story effectively and places the emphasis on the character, removed from her usual story, interacting with the Frog Prince in his new story. The continued search for happily ever after offers Scieszka and Johnson a place to question the seriousness of the traditional tales.

Many of the humorous picture books like Scieszka's and Thaler's naturally rely on the combination of text and illustrations to make the humor work. Babette Cole's picture book *Prince Cinders*, a retelling of "Cinderella" with a male character in the Cinderella role, uses a surprising transformation to carry the humor — Cinders becomes a gorilla in a bathing suit — but it is the illustrations that truly make the revision humorous. After the transformation, the text reads, "Prince Cinders got big and hairy, all right" without going into the details of his transformation. The picture on the page, the focal point while the text is in the lower right hand corner, shows the giant gorilla, who almost seems to stretch the boundaries of the page, wearing a crown and a red and white striped bathing suit that covers his entire torso. Cole is combining word play with her illustrations. Other images are equally humorous, though this one is the best example of how the image acts as the vehicle for the humor rather than the text.

Falling for Rapunzel, another humorous picture book revision, by Leah Wilcox and illustrated by Lydia Monks similarly needs the humor of the pictures of the prince covered in successively odd things to complement the humor of the miscommunication between him and Rapunzel. Each time the prince calls for something to help him reach Rapunzel, she cannot hear him well enough to understand what he is asking for. Thus when he calls for her to "throw down your hair," she thinks he's asking for underwear and throws it to him. The accompanying image shows the prince with a pair of pink panties on his head, his horse with yellow bloomers. From that point he tries various synonyms—"curly locks," "silky tresses"— or other things he could climb —"a rope," "twine," and "a ladder"— all to no avail. In fact he ends up with socks, dresses, a cantaloupe (which lands on his head), a swine, and finally, pancake batter. With his final request, he calls for her braid and gets her maid, with whom he falls in love. At the end, as the happy couple rides off, Rapunzel comes out the back door, thinking, "I hope if they come back for more, they'll think to knock on my back door," playing the humor a step further. And like Dahl in *Revolting Rhymes*, Wilcox uses rhyming couplets throughout the tale to quicken the rhythm and enhance the humor of the word play.

Illustrated tales, while primarily the ones that are humorous, are not the only types of revisions that employ humor. By the same token, the majority of folktale revisions whose main tone is humorous are short in length, illustrated or not. Vivian Vande Velde's collections of short revisions *Tales from the Brothers Grimm and the Sisters Weird* and *The Rumpelstiltskin Problem* contain a combination of humorous and serious tales, though the majority of them are humorous. Though *Tales from the Brothers Grimm and the Sisters Weird* opens with "Straw into Gold," a serious retelling of "Rumpelstiltskin" that contains little humor,[2] and also includes the story "Twins," a disturbing, primarily serious, retelling of "Hansel and Gretel," the majority of the thirteen revisions employ humor as the driving tone. For example, Vande Velde, like Dahl, recasts Goldilocks as a criminal and her one-page revision "All Points Bulletin," written in the form of a police all points bulletin, details her crimes—breaking and entering, theft, vandalism — and declares her armed and possibly dangerous (36). "Rapunzel" is retold in "And Now a Word from Our Sponsor" as a hair care ad promising hair "Strong enough to climb up" (71). The humor in both of these revisions lies in the way Vande Velde recasts the tales into different rhetorical forms— the all points bulleting and the advertisement — while retaining elements that clearly identify the tales on which the revisions are based.[3]

Another of Vande Velde's short revisions, "Rated PG-13," recounts "Fairy tale endings you're not likely to see" (77), including "the Gingerbread Man turns out to be carnivorous and eats the fox" and "Snow White and Sleeping Beauty simply refuse to get out of bed" (78). Vande Velde boils the tales down to surprise endings in this revision, playing off the traditional ends in a humorous vein. Other revisions are presented in a much more traditional short prose format but with a very humorous tone. The story "Frog," for example, a retelling of "The Frog Prince," presents Sidney, the middle brother of three princes who had "heard enough fairy tales about three sons setting off down the road and meeting a strange old woman and the first two sons were always rude and got into trouble" that he "always did his best to be polite to everybody, even when he wasn't on a quest" (27-8). Despite his better intentions, however, he is turned into a frog and forced to search for a princess to break the curse. The princess he finds, like most from traditional versions of the tale, tries to break her promise to Sidney and is forced to fulfill it by her father. The real humor of this revision, as with many of Vande Velde's revisions, is in the end of the tale when, once the prince is restored to his human form, the princess is enthralled and wants to marry him. The prince, however, will have nothing to do with her, saying, "Are you out of your mind?" and detailing the very negative qualities she possesses before leaving her and "returning home, where he eventually married the goose girl" (35). The princess, who had worried about her father finding a strange man in her room, finds out that she "was right: her father didn't believe her story" (35) about the frog turning into a prince. This ending contains both a role reversal and a surprise.

Vande Velde's one-liner endings often add the final punch of humor to her quirky revisions. "The Granddaughter," for example, a revision of "Little Red Riding Hood" in which Granny and the wolf, reversing their traditional relationship, are good friends and Lucinda, the Little Red Riding Hood figure, is a spoilt brat who drives first Granny and then the wolf and woodcutter crazy, ends, "They [Granny, the wolf, and Bob the woodcutter] locked Little Red in the closet, then they went out in the backyard and had a picnic" (50), a fitting end to an unsympathetic character. And "Jack" (as in "Jack and the Beanstalk") is a revision in which Jack goes on a drinking binge after selling his cow to the tavern keeper for all he can eat and drink. After he has been expelled from the tavern, he mistakes a woman trying to help him for a giantess and her father's kiln, where she places him to hide and recover, for the giant's oven. He steals two of their possessions—a harp that sings discordantly and a hen that likes to eat gold and then lays golden eggs—and takes them home to his mother, who has previously threatened to cast him out if he can't find work. After he tells her his story and she observes the items he has stolen, she sends him outside to look for the "giant" and "While he was gone, his mother changed the locks" (70). Though not all of her tales end in such an irreverent tone after an already-humorous tale, most do. Even the darker, more serious "Hansel and Gretel" revision "Twins" ends on a one-liner as Isabella, the stepmother who has been terrorized by the evil Hansel and Gretel in a reversal of their traditional roles, runs away from the twins threatening her and "considered stopping for Sigfried" their father; however, she doesn't stop because "After all, he was the one who had gotten her into this" (106). Though the rest of the tale is dark-toned, this end acts as an immediate lightener of mood.

Vande Velde's revisions in *The Rumpelstiltskin Problem*, six revisions of "Rumpelstiltskin," are presented similarly. The first revision,

"A Fairy Tale in Bad Taste," is an excellent example. In this revision, Rumpelstiltskin is a troll who manipulates the players in the story so that he can get a baby to eat. He is defeated in the end by his bother and, as in the traditional tale, splits himself in half stomping through the floor. His brother ends up with Rumpelstiltskin's leg in his hand and notices the king and queen looking ill. The narrator indicates that Rumpelstiltskin's brother thinks the leg may be the problem and ends the story with the toss-off line that, from the brother's point of view, fixes the problem: "So he ate it" (16). This one-liner, combined with the clear cultural difference between the trolls and the humans, ends the story on a humorous, if rather sick, note.

The toss-off lines also extend to the poetic revisions in *Tales from the Brothers Grimm and the Sisters Weird*—"Excuses" ("The Pied Piper") and "Evidence" ("Cinderella"). "Excuses" appears serious in tone as the narrator wonders about the children of Hamelin and the piper's motivations but ends on a quirky note with the narrator now wondering how the piper explained all of the children and what he would say to his family. The last two lines are the speculated question the pied piper would ask: "Look what followed me home—can I keep them?" (52). Vande Velde once more subverts the tone of the revision with her final lines and the surprise they contain. "Evidence," though less serious than "Excuses," still has a serious tone; this time the narrator wonders how the glass slipper could survive the magic's reversal and decides that it is "Obviously a set-up" (107), then wonders who could have created the set-up, finally deciding on the stepmother who was

> tired of her [Cinderella's] unrelenting goodness,
> and beauty,
> and cheerfulness
> (not to mention all that singing) [108].

The parenthetical, the final line of the poem, once again subverts any possibility of a serious tone to the story.

Other authors employ humor in their tales to balance but not overtake the more serious tone of their revision. A good example of this type of revision is Gail Carson Levine's series The Princess Tales, six different revisions of folktales. Each of the tales is set during various unspecified times in the Kingdom of Biddle, and each retells a traditional folktale, usually in a decidedly humorous fashion with a more serious undertone. Each of these tales is significantly longer that the picture books and short story collections, though not novel-length.[4] Lengthier tales, no matter how humorous they are, require a balance between humor and drama to be successful. In *Cinderellis and the Glass Hill*, for example, a retelling of "The Princess on the Glass Hill," the humor lies to a great extent in Cinderellis' inventions and the king's quests. It is in fact Cinderellis' penchant for inventing that gets the *Cinder* attached to his given name, Ellis, for at age six, he invents "flying powder" and sends a cup up the chimney to test the effectiveness of the powder. Instead of flying straight up, the cup zigzags up the chimney and knocks cinders down on Ellis. When his brothers Burt and Ralph see him covered in cinders, they nickname him Cinderellis. Each time he invents something at the at the beginning of the story, it is in an attempt to impress his brothers so that they will pay more attention to him. They are farmers obsessed with their crops, so when they give Cinderellis a small, rocky piece of land to cultivate, not expecting success, Cinderellis vows to do an exceptional job. He clears the rocks from the land by mixing his perfected flying powder with popcorn and then produces perfect vegetables, all to no avail, for his brothers do not see them as perfect, claiming that the "tomatoes are too red" and the "carrots are too sweet" (9), though they still take the produce to market.

Several years later, when the hay starts to disappear before the brothers can harvest it, Cinderellis deduces that a horse has caused the damage when he discovers footprints, but his brothers are convinced it is goblins. They spend the next two years trying out songs to scare away the goblins without success. They mock Cinderellis when he demands to take a turn, but he is determined to show them that he is right and spends his time perfecting ideal horse treats: apple-shaped and made of "ground horse chestnuts, minced horse mackerel, and chopped horse nettles" (21). These he uses over the next three years, and each time he plans to give the horse he captures to his brothers if they will only recognize his success and include him in their closeness, something they never do. Most of the scenes of Cinderellis' life are presented humorously, though the underlying theme of loneliness is quite serious. Yet the drama of this theme is constantly undercut by various elements of the story, from Cinderellis' inventions, to his brothers' clear stupidity (shown best through their song to scare away the goblins) to the way in which he eventually interacts with the horses.

At the same time that Cinderellis is capturing the horses, Princess Marigold is growing up in the castle and longing for her father's attention the way that Cinderellis longs for his brothers' attention. King Humphrey III, however, is obsessed with going on quests, none of which turn out as expected. Each quest begins as a search for something from a different folktale and ends with an entirely unexpected item. Thus the search for "a dog tiny enough to live in a walnut shell" ends with the king bringing back "a normal-sized kitten and a flea big enough to fill a tea cup" (4), and the search for "the well of youth and happiness" begets "a flask of coconut milk" that "make[s] people's toenails grow, a foot an hour" (14). King Humphrey III's questing, however, is put on hiatus when he angers an imp from a candle (found instead of "the lamp that commands a genie" [38]). The imp curses the king to five years at home with no quests. In the passages about the king and his quests, it is clear that King Humphrey III, and his insatiable appetite for questing, is being mocked whereas the passages about Cinderellis's inventions, though humorous, are not meant to mock his character. Instead, the humor for the inventions lies in the types of inventions and the ingredients that Cinderellis uses in their creation, playing on words for the names of many.

The humor shifts away from the inventions and quests after the king is forbidden to go on a new quest. Because he cannot go on a quest of his own, the king decides to bring the quest to his kingdom by erecting a glass hill for the horrified Marigold to sit on while suitors try to climb it on horseback. The winner, to whom Marigold will give three golden apples, will marry her. Amid the preparations, including the revelation that the top of the hill is level (to the king's dismay) because "Marigold had flatly refused to sit on a point" (47), Marigold and Cinderellis make plans—Marigold to foil all who attempt to reach her and Cinderellis to succeed but not to marry her. Fortunately, Marigold doesn't need to use her secret weapon—oil that she pours on the hill—until the final "knight" appears. Cinderellis has had difficulty putting on the armor that came with his horse and, when he arrives just as the king is getting ready to call it a day, it looks as if he doesn't belong on the horse. The armor is pounded out of shape and he can barely stay on the horse because he cannot grip the reins or see out of the helmet unless it shifts into just the right position. It is only the horse's affection for Cinderellis, revealed when the point of view shifts into the horse's head, that keeps him mounted. Amid confusion and misdirection over the three days of the attempts to reach the princess, Cinderellis ends up with the apples from Marigold and wins the contest, but, not realizing that she is the same Royal Dairymaid he fell in love with before the contest, he has no wish to marry her, and Marigold does not realize that he is the young man she met when she was disguised because his armor makes it impossible for her to see him properly. As the confusion is cleared up,

Levine continues the humorous tone, for Cinderellis gets his head stuck in a helmet again and cannot see or hear Marigold agreeing to marry him. The humor, however, is undercut in the epilogue by the comment that Cinderellis "was never lonely again" (104), coming back to the underlying, more serious theme of loneliness.

The theme of loneliness is echoed to a smaller degree in another of Levine's Princess Tales, *Princess Sonora and the Long Sleep*. Once again Levine balances the serious and humorous in this revision of "Sleeping Beauty." Similar to the quirkiness of the main characters in *Cinderellis and the Glass Hill*, the characters of Princess Sonora and Prince Christopher are equally quirky. For Sonora, the quirkiness comes as a result of the "gifts" she is given by the fairies attending her naming ceremony. She is given the gifts of beauty, a loving heart, gracefulness, good health, intelligence, then brilliance — she is made "ten times as smart as any human in the world" (5). Levine describes the changes to Sonora in a humorous manner, starting with the painful transformation into a beautiful baby, a process that involves her entire body shifting shape, and adding a surprise to the idea of fairy gifts. The fairies also struggle to create better gifts for Sonora until the sixth one, at a loss, bestows brilliance on her. It is this gift, and not the subsequent curse of dying by pricking her finger, quickly altered by the seventh invited fairy to a hundred-year sleep, that causes much of the humor surrounding Sonora's character. Once she has the gift of brilliance, she is able to point out to the fairy altering the curse that if she sleeps for one hundred years her parents will be dead when she wakes, leading the fairy to broaden the sleep to much of the kingdom.

As Sonora is described growing up, her intelligence, which allows her to speak and read immediately, does not advance her body's development. Thus the Royal Nursemaids are put off by the baby because "It was so strange to change the diaper of a baby who was reading a book, especially a baby who blushed and said, 'I'm so sorry to bother you with my elimination'" (20). Even her parents are hard pressed to adapt to her intellect, which precludes her from doing things normal for an infant. Sonora is constantly striving to learn even more and regaling her parents with some of her ideas for improving the running of the kingdom, something no one in the kingdom wants to see implemented. Her desire to share her knowledge is such that she becomes the focus of a new proverb: "Princess Sonora knows, but don't ask her."

And because of the curse, Sonora is afraid to go to sleep, spending her first fifteen years of life avoiding sleep in every possible way. She decides early on to steal a spindle and hide it in her belongings so that she may prick her finger when she is ready to do so. This tactic does not work, of course, though she does come close to implementing it upon meeting Prince Melvin XX, who is courting her. His fairy gifts made him a Man of Action, but they did not provide him with an intellect. In fact, Levine mocks the concept of a Man of Action through this character, much as she did with the king in *Cinderellis and the Glass Hill*. Melvin speaks slowly, in short sentences, and shows that he takes the world at face value, as when he tells Sonora, "My father says you're smart.... And I believe him. He always tells the truth. If he were a liar, I wouldn't believe him" (*Sonora* 46-7). This comment and others gradually make Sonora long to prick her finger, but she refrains because he would also sleep since he is in the castle grounds and the problem would still exist after she woke. She decides to prick her finger after he leaves, but before that can occur, her mother discovers the hidden spindle and raises such a ruckus over the matter that Sonora runs to aid her and pricks herself by mistake, sending everyone within the castle grounds, including Prince Melvin XX into an enchanted sleep.

While they sleep, a great briar patch grows over the kingdom, noticed only by Elbert, a shepherd who passes the knowledge of the sleeping castle to his family. Prince Christopher is born long after Sonora's sleep begins and also after the convention of fairies coming to naming ceremonies is over. People have long forgotten about Sonora aside from the proverb about her. Like Sonora, however, Prince Christopher is something of an oddity, though his difference is not fairy-generated. He is insatiably curious and, much as Sonora drove people crazy with her information, Christopher drives people crazy with his questions, though they all answer him until they are "stumped," at which point they revert to the proverb "Princess Sonora knows, but don't ask her" (71). When a particularly bad problem crops up with the sheep in the kingdom, Christopher approaches all of the shepherds of Greater Kulornia—the kingdom his family rules and which had annexed Biddle, Sonora's kingdom, long ago. During these questions, he learns from Elbert's progeny that Sonora can't answer because she is asleep, and he vows to find her and get the answers to his questions.

Christopher finds and enters the castle easily but is horrified by the mess of one hundred years of slumber, a mess that includes so much dust that his feet make no sound when he walks through the castle. He searches for Sonora and finally discovers her in her room. When he reads the sign saying "*I am Princess Sonora. Kiss me, prince, and I shall be yours forever*" (91, emphasis in original), he is horrified for two reasons: "He didn't want her *forever*! And he certainly didn't want to *kiss* her" (91, emphasis in original) because she is covered with spider webs and dust. But his curiosity gets the best of him when Sonora talks in her sleep and shows that "Even in her sleep she knew things!" (93). He wakes her and they discover their compatibility, eventually becoming betrothed once they convince Prince Melvin XX that he would be better off as a Man of Action now that he is no longer the crown prince of Kulornia. The story ends on a humorous note after they are married and Sonora starts explaining to Christopher why dragons don't burn the roofs of their mouths. Like *Cinderellis and the Glass Hill*, *Princess Sonora and the Long Sleep* is largely humorous in tone thanks to its quirky characters, but it also contains the underlying theme of loneliness and isolation caused by the very quirkiness that makes the characters humorous. Though the loneliness is not as clearly shown as in *Cinderellis and the Glass Hill*, mostly because Sonora and Christopher's parents genuinely care about them even if they don't understand them, it is still an important element of the story that is resolved at the end with their marriage.

The Fairy's Mistake, by contrast, has a much more serious—and somewhat dissatisfying—tone throughout, despite the use of humor in the story. This retelling of "Toads and Diamonds," a story often rewritten to question the benefit of producing gems when speaking, places Rosella, the kind daughter, in the tenuous position of being betrothed to Prince Harold, who proposes when he realizes that she is producing the gems when she speaks. Myrtle, the mean daughter (and Rosella's identical twin), is "punished" by having to expel insects, reptiles and amphibians when she speaks. This punishment she turns to her advantage by promising not to speak if townsfolk give her what she wants. As the title of the story indicates, the focal point of the humor in the story is the fairy Ethelinda's reactions to the results of her reward and punishment, but the humor falls flat to some extent thanks to the misery of Rosella and the successful threats of Myrtle. The point at which the humor becomes effective only occurs at the end of the revision when Ethelinda attempts to make Rosella's life better. She has Myrtle pose as Rosella in front of Prince Harold and claim that her anger at Prince Harold's lack of consideration causes the vermin to escape her mouth.[5] This tactic scares Harold into treating Rosella better and not forcing her to speak unless she wants to. Though Harold nearly reverts to form, Rosella has learned to control him better and they strike a deal. The end of the story presents all of the characters as content but, much like the traditional tale on which it is based, the story is not completely satisfying despite the claim that Rosella and Harold "grew to love each other very much" (83) and that Ethelinda learns to be more careful with her rewards and punishments. The final line "And they all lived happily ever after" (84) rings hollow.

Levine's much longer, Newbery Honor novel and "Cinderella" retelling *Ella Enchanted*, published prior to the Princess Tales series, like *The Fairy's Mistake*, is more serious than *Cinderellis and the Glass Hill* and *Princess Sonora and the Long Sleep* as Ella attempts to escape the "curse" of obedience a fairy placed on her as a child. Humor in this novel is incidental rather than a primary element, though there are many incidents, from the ways in which Ella works around the curse and simultaneously humiliates her stepsisters to the fairy Lucinda's repentant appearance after she lives for several months in her two favorite curses— an obedient child and a squirrel. These humorous incidents act to underscore the more serious elements of the revision. Thus Ella can manipulate her stepsisters up to a point, but they still have the ability to order her around and make her miserable, and after Lucinda returns repentant she refuses to reverse Ella's curse because she has learned her lesson about doing "big magic." It is left to Ella to solve her own problems and to break the curse herself, which she does. As with The Princess Tales, *Ella Enchanted* ends happily with Ella married to her prince, but there is more solidity to this union, which happens only after she and Charmant have known each other for many years and have earned their happiness through a series of trials.

Most authors of novel-length revisions of folktales take a similar approach to Levine in *Ella Enchanted*, using humor to lighten briefly the mood of the story before the more serious threads overwhelm the humor. Though the shorter revisions of folktales— picture books as well as collections of short stories and poems—can contain a balance of humor and drama, their short length generally lends them to a single tone while longer revisions, though generally dramatic in nature, almost always contain some element of humor. Tracy Lynn's novel *Snow*, for example, a retelling of "Snow White and the Seven Dwarfs" set in Victorian Wales and England, is very serious in tone for most of the novel, from Jessica/Snow's childhood in Wales to her stepmother Anne's mistreatment of her, to Snow's flight from Wales to London, where she is taken in by the Lonely Ones, several part animal, part human creatures.

The humor of the novel does not appear until after Snow has been placed into a magical sleep by her stepmother, a scientist who also uses magic. As Mouser and Raven, two of the Lonely Ones, talk to a servant at Snow's former home in Wales, they learn her given name is Jessica and are not impressed, Mouser commenting, "It does seem a little plain" (206). Later when Alan, a musician brought to Anne's service upon her marriage to Snow's father and forced to obey Anne and keep her secrets, is freed from the magic keeping him silent, he goes on a rant about Anne. Lynn does not punctuate this section of dialog to emphasize the speed with which he speaks, as well as his freedom to do so, and this adds humor to the content that ends, "and I hate the bloody duchess [Anne] she is such a bloody *bitch!*" (22, emphasis in original). After Alan's extended circumspection, this passage's humor is even more noticeable, for it shows a reversal of his character. Later, new characters—the duke of Edington (the prince figure) and his man Henry — are brought in and provide further comic relief for the reader during this very dramatic section of the story in which the Lonely Ones and Alan are searching for a way to rouse Snow. Once Snow is wakened, healthy but without her memory, the serious tone returns to the story as she tries to work out how she will spend her life. Her expected marriage to the duke of Edington is not something she wants, but she cannot remember why until she meets up with Raven again at the ball thrown in her honor. At this ball, she regains her memory and decides that it is Raven with whom she belongs. The story ends on a serious but positive note, humor used only to lighten the mood at the height of the drama.

Jane B. Mason and Sarah Hines Stephens' The Princess School series also employs humor as a lightening device. The first novel in the series, *If the Shoe Fits*, a retelling of "Cinderella" that uses Rapunzel, Briar Rose (nicknamed Rose and Beauty), and Snow White as helper characters taking the place of Cinderella's fairy godmother, who is away at "*a fairy convention in Afaraway Land*" (25, emphasis in original) for the duration of the story. Though there are some humorous elements in the revision, such as when Rapunzel and Prince Valerian (known as Val) are interacting, particularly when he becomes, to Rapunzel's disgust, infatuated with Rose, the primary tone of the novel is serious as the girls adjust to the Princess School, including getting used to their new classes— Frog Identification, Stitchery, and Looking Glass Class, among others— as well as preparing for the Coronation Ball where one student will be crowned Princess of the Ball. Unlike most revisions of romantic folktales, this one does not end with a marriage or even a pairing off of Cinderella with someone. The closest to a pairing is Val and Rose, for Val clearly has a crush on Rose despite his relationship with Rapunzel, who sees Val as a playmate and not a romantic interest, and his denial of interest in Rose. At the ball, Rose, who has gotten sleepier and sleepier since pricking her finger on a needle, is kissed on the hand by Val "in a moment of chivalry" (135) and is woken from her stupor. Yet they do not end up romantically linked. The point of this novel is to establish the solidarity of the four princesses, and the end of the novel, after Cinderella has been crown Princess of the Ball, sets up the second book in the series with the arrival of Snow White's stepmother Malodora, headmistress of the Grimm School for witches.

The place in which this series shows the most humor is in the naming conventions, which resound with wordplay. While Show White and Briar Rose have their traditional names, Rapunzel is given the last name Arugula, playing with her background and how she received her first name, and Cinderella, the paragon of kindness, industry and beauty, is given the exceedingly normal last name of Brown. Further, the names of the classes they attend, particularly Frog Identification and Looking Glass Class, play with some of the traditional elements of folktales. This play is continued in the second book in the series *Who's the Fairest?* which is a revision of "Snow White and the Seven Dwarfs." In this novel, the Princess School and the Grimm School compete in the annual event known as the Maiden Games, in which the students from the two schools participate in events that reflect folktales. Of note are the Gingerbread Man Chase, in which Gretel is the favorite for the Princess School; Ball Fetch, in which the contestants must convince a frog to get their ball; Guess the Little Man's Name; Unicorn Shoes; Full Contact Maypole; and the Apple Bob, Snow White's main event. With these names, Mason and Stephens are clearly using word play to add an element of humor to a story that is otherwise quite serious in tone.

Donna Jo Napoli's folktale revisions, compared to most novel-length ones, do not possess much humor. Her revisions generally play with narrative conventions and explore the darker, dramatic elements of the tales without humor as a lightener. In fact, the narratives — almost always in present tense, and frequently in first person — make the revisions immediate and powerful and far from funny.[6] One exception to the dark revisions is her trilogy of novels based around "The Frog Prince": *The Prince of the Pond: Otherwise Known as De Fawg Pin*; *Jimmy, the Pickpocket of the Palace*; and *Gracie, the Pixie of the Puddle*. Each of these novels is told in first person, past tense by a different narrator, and each novel combines humor and drama, though none of them end in the happily ever after manner of most folktale revisions.

The first novel in the series *The Prince of the Pond: Otherwise Known as De Fawg Pin* contains the most humor, much of it revolving around the problems the newly made frog has adjusting to being a frog, though the narrator Jade, a female green frog, does not realize that he has not always been a frog, even at the end of the novel when he is transformed back into a human. Jade must teach Pin, the frog prince's mispronunciation of *prince*, to jump, swim, eat, and generally do everything else a frog does. The accompanying illustrations by Judith Byron Schachner add to the humor of Pin's learning to be a frog. Ultimately, he also teaches her some human traits, notably parenting when they mate, protect, and then raise some of their children, known as *fawgs*, once again thanks to Pin's problems with pronunciation. Jade is aghast at the unfroglike desire to protect and raise their young, but she comes to appreciate it at the end.

It is the problems that Pin has with language, due to his new tongue which he must learn to keep rolled in his mouth, that are truly funny. Napoli uses Pin's mispronunciations to color the identity of his and Jade's offspring, who think of themselves as fawgs, not frogs, and who stay together despite how frogs usually act. Yet despite the humor of Pin calling himself "De Fawg Pin" and other linguistic problems, ultimately this story is quite sad. After Jade and Pin mate and produce a brood of fifty fawgs, they return to the pond. Jimmy, the one fawg who remains with them after the return to the pond, is captured by the hag who had transformed Pin into a frog. Working as a family, Pin, Jade, and the other fawgs save Jimmy and appear ready to settle into a happy life, but Napoli returns to the traditional ending of the tale. Thus in the final chapter, Pin, attempting to save Jimmy from the woman Pin and Jade think is planning to bite him, is accidentally kissed by the woman and returns to human form, leaving Jade, Jimmy and the rest of the fawgs to wonder where he has disappeared to. The final illustration by Judith Byron Schachner emphasizes the despair of Pin's frog family, showing Jade hugging Jimmy, both of them crying.

The second novel in the series, *Jimmy, the Pickpocket of the Palace*, contains even less humor as it shows Jimmy, Pin and Jade's son and the narrator, trying to retrieve the hag's ring so that she won't dry up the pond. Along the way, he is transformed into a human boy and, much as Pin had to learn to be a frog, Jimmy must learn to be a human. His froglike behavior, while not funny to him as a narrator, is certainly amusing to the reader, though his language difficulties are not as amusing as Pin's had been. The new character Sally, sister of Princess Marissa whom the prince (Pin) plans to marry, also has some humorous scenes as she tries to catch and keep Gracie, Jimmy's frog friend. Yet this novel, despite the defeat of the hag, who is turned into a rock, and Jimmy's return to frog form, is more tragic than the first novel because Jimmy and the prince realize that they are father and son but that they cannot live with each other.

The final novel in the series, *Gracie, the Pixie of the Pond*, has a different kind of humor than the first two novels. The narrator is Gracie, a small green frog who has been "adopted" by Jade and who is good friends with Jimmy. Once again the hag, turned from a stone to a crocodile by Sally, who steals the ring from Pin, threatens the well-being of the pond, so Jimmy goes off to try to save them. Gracie ends up tracking him back to the pond where Jade met Pin and helping with the recovery of the ring and defeat of the hag. The humor of this novel revolves around the different males trying to "court" Gracie and her rejection of them. But as with the other novels in the series, this novel ultimately takes a serious turn with Gracie realizing it is Jimmy she wants as a partner. Jimmy, who turns human again, must choose between remaining human and living with his father or returning to life as a frog, which he does. The end is much happier that the first two novels because Jimmy and Gracie end up together (and the narrator is content), but there is a lingering feeling of discontent because the prince cannot truly be a part of their lives and all of them realize the separation is permanent.

This trilogy is very different from most of Napoli's novels, however, partly because it is written for a younger audience than most of her other revisions. Other revisions, such as *The Magic Circle*, *Zel*, and *Spinners* (written with Richard Tchen), all focus on the angst of the stories, which Napoli expands to fill in the back story, the motivation of the characters both good and bad in traditional versions. Humor is rare in these revisions, and the overarching tone, particularly when the traditional antagonist's point of view is shown, is oppressive, for Napoli is utterly faithful to the basic plot structure of the traditional tale once her characters enter that path. She develops the tales by adding tremendous amounts of back story showing how her characters arrive at their place in the traditional plot. Thus the reader sees the development of the witch in *The Magic Circle*, a revision of "Hansel and Gretel," from a respected midwife to a sorceress to the "Ugly Witch," who must fight against the devils who want her to eat children. Though she does not possess the strength to send Hansel and Gretel away from her house, eventually she manipulates Gretel into pushing her into the oven. The readers, who are getting the story in first person present tense from the witch's point of view, are witness to her death, for she narrates as she dies. There is no humor in this short novel, and the same is true for many of Napoli's other novels for older children and young adults. Napoli's focus is on the dramatic events of the folktales and she wants no humor to cut the tension of that drama.

Naopli's humorless novels are unusual, for most authors of novel-length revisions employ some kind of humor, most often through word play, though role reversal can come up in these novels as well. The use of word play is a natural choice in these texts because not only is it enjoyed by children, but it also enhances the intertextual nature of the folktale revisions since for many of the tales the word play is at the expense of the folktale tradition. This is particularly true of the names given to people and events, for they generally poke fun at the very tradition from which they spring. It is also natural that in shorter folktales revisions, a single tone is usually present. For the revisions that are humorous, the focus lies solely on the humor while revisions that present the drama of the traditional tale are always serious. And in fact there are numerous short folktale revisions that do not rely on humor — many of the tales in the collections by Ellen Datlow and Terri Windling, for example. When it comes to the longer revisions, however, the tone is almost always a combination of the serious and the humorous. The reason for the balance, and the tendency to return to the serious, is that most of the folktales that are revised by contemporary authors are inherently serious in tone. Tales such as "Cinderella" and "Snow White and the Seven Dwarfs" are not humorous in nature, and most of the authors who expand on the tales are exploring possible motivations for flat characters, rounding them in their own way. This rounding of the characters, and development of the folktale's plot, is naturally dramatic in nature, and it would be difficult to sustain a humorous tone throughout the length of a novel. The result is that these contemporary authors employ bits of humor, again usually a type of word play, to ease the tension before raising that tension all over again. Julie Anne Peters' eight devices of humor, while they all exist in folktale revisions, are largely limited to word and language play and role reversal in these revisions.

3

Cultural and Regional Folktale Revisions in Picture Books

Culture is an inherent aspect of folktales, for folktales reveal cultural norms and ideologies, as well as question those cultural norms and ideologies. Steven Swann Jones, in his book *The Fairy Tale: The Magic Mirror of the Imagination*, claims that "the fairy tale functions to instruct the young about who they are, how they relate to others, and what they should know about the world" (18). And Jack Zipes, in *When Dreams Came True: Classical Fairy Tales and Their Tradition*, comments that while "one could say that the literary appropriation of the oral wonder tales served the hegemonic interests of males in the upper classes of particular communities and societies," it is equally true that "[t]he more the literary fairy tale was cultivated and developed, the more it became individualized and varied by intellectuals and artists, who often sympathized with the marginalized in society or were marginalized themselves. The literary fairy tale allowed for new possibilities of subversion in the written word and in print" (7). Zipes continues, arguing that "whereas many oral wonder tales had been concerned with the humanization of natural forces, the literary fairy tale ... shifted the emphasis more toward the civilization of the protagonist who must learn to respect particular codes and laws to become accepted in society and/or united to reproduce and continue the progress of the world toward perfect happiness" (8).

Folktales establish a worldview that promotes the triumph of good over evil. Yet while folktales inherently present these cultural norms or challenges to the norms to their audiences, they often do so without naming specific times or places that reflect the culture. Zipes argues that "the timelessness of the [wonder] tale and lack of geographical specificity endow it with utopian connotations—utopia in its original meaning designated 'no place,' a place that no one had ever envisaged" (4). Settings that are "once upon a time in a land far away" do not necessarily point to a specific place in this world, though of course the most popular ones in the culture of the United States seem to have a vaguely European setting. The utopian nature of these settings broadens the appeal of the tales, at least theoretically, as does the rather generic, unspecific description of characters—often a "girl" or a "boy" without much more information than a first name, though even those tend to be common names (e.g. Jack) if they aren't merely descriptive as in the case of Little Red Riding Hood, named for her favorite piece of clothing, and Rapunzel, named for the plant her mother craves during pregnancy.

In children's literature,[1] the picture book has caused this "lack of geographical specificity" to disappear. Though not all picture book renditions of folktales are geographically specific, those that are generally present geographic culture in one of two ways. First, authors (or editors or translators) and illustrators find tales from different cultures that resemble traditional European tales (the myriad versions of "Cinderella," for example) or they find traditional tales from other cultures unfamiliar to their audience (for example, some of the African tales that Verna Aardema has published), and these authors and illustrators bring the tales to their audience through the use of illustrations that enhance what may be unfamiliar motifs and/or other cultural elements in the tales. They also have a tendency to incorporate specific cultural items, from flora and fauna indigenous to the region represented to traditional customs not specified in the original versions. These additions enhance the reading experience for the readers while altering the traditional presentation of folktales.

The second way in which picture book authors and illustrators can present geographic specificity in folktales is through revisions of traditional tales to reflect a particular region. The authors of these cultural revisions take well-known tales from the European fairy tale corpus and reshape them to fit a new venue. These stories possess consciously placed cultural elements, from the dialect characters (and sometimes the narrator) speak, to the places they live, to the alteration of well-known artifacts from the stories, to the recasting of characters to make them fit culturally. These tales can also be reflexive—presenting references to the tradition from which they come — and it is in this last manner that they differ most from the other type of cultural versions of folktales.

Of all familiar folktales in the United States, "Cinderella" arguably possesses the most variants from other lands that can still be categorized as a Cinderella tale, and the picture book industry has in the past twenty-five years published over twenty different versions from other cultures across the globe. While each of these versions has recognizable elements from the Perrault version of "Cinderella," the fascination for the reader lies in the difference. Several authors in particular — Shirley Climo, Jewell Reinhart Coburn, and Robert D. San Souci — have adapted many versions of these tales. Despite all of the versions' emphasis on the different culture represented, almost all of them rely on the name Cinderella in the title to attract readers. The name may appear as the primary title, as in Climo's *The Egyptian Cinderella* or *The Persian Cinderella*, or it may be part of the subtitle as in Coburn's *Angkat: The Cambodian Cinderella* or *Domitila: A Cinderella Tale from the Mexican Tradition*. Only in few cases, such as Rafe Martin's *The Rough-Face Girl* and John Steptoe's *Mufaro's Beautiful Daughters*, is the name Cinderella missing from the title, and it is only Steptoe's text that does not mention Cinderella at all in the book (it is referenced in the Author's Note in Martin's book).[2]

As authors adapt these traditional versions of Cinderella tales from other cultures for the picture book format, there are numerous ways in which they incorporate the differences of this culture for an audience unfamiliar with it. The first way in which cultural difference is brought about often appears in the opening lines of the story. Rather than the generic "once upon a time in a land far away," many of the versions present a more specific location if not time. Myrna de la Paz's *Abadeha: The Philippine Cinderella*, for example, begins, "Once upon a time in the islands of the Philippines, where sea stars bloom in a shimmering emerald sea, there lived a fisherman named Abak, his wife Abadesa, and their beautiful daughter Abadeha." Though the actual place in the Philippines is not specific, just the mention of a country name is more geographically specific than Perrault's version, which begins, "There was once upon a time, a gentleman who married for his second wife the proudest and most haughty woman that was ever known" (Opie 123). The Grimms' version is no more specific: "The wife of a rich man fell ill, and when she felt her end approaching, she called her only daughter to her bedside..." (Zipes, *Great* 468). Nor do most tales from other lands contain specific geographical information in them. William Bascom, in his essay "Cinderella in Africa" presents an African version of Cinderella that begins "There was once a man had two wives, and they each had a daughter" (151). A Haitian version of Cinderella, "The Magic Orange Tree," in Joanna Cole's collection *Best-Loved Folktales of the World* begins, "There was once a girl whose mother died when she was born" (727). The authors of the cultural variants, however, almost universally include additional information to make the tales more geographically specific for their readers.

Shirley Climo's *The Egyptian Cinderella*, like de la Paz's Filipino story, opens very specifically: "Long ago, in the land of Egypt, where the green Nile River widens to meet the blue sea, there lived a maiden called Rhodopis." Not only does this version's opening give a country's name, but, though no town is named, the locale of the story is a specific area of Egypt. Later in the story, the city Memphis is mentioned as the place the servant girls are going to see the Pharaoh, furthering the geographical specificity of this version. Similarly, Nina Jaffe's *The Way Meat Loves Salt: A Cinderella Tale from the Jewish Tradition* opens in a specific location: "Once upon a time in Poland, in a small town near the city of Lublin, there lived a rabbi who had a wife and three young daughters." Each of these openings, along with most of the other cultural versions of "Cinderella," makes a point of situating the reader in a particular location immediately in the tale, thus setting up the initial difference between the better-known Perrault version and the different version being presented.

A second manner in which these cultural differences are presented in "Cinderella" variants is through the character names. In the Perrault and Grimm versions, the character of Cinderella is named only once she starts sitting in the ashes after her father's remarriage. The only other named character in either tale is one of the stepsisters in the Perrault version — Charlotte or Jayotte (depending on the translation). The names of the characters are irrelevant to the story since they are types of characters rather than individuals. Lack of given names is a common trait among most folktales, yet in the cultural variations of "Cinderella" for picture books, many of the characters are named, not just the Cinderella character. In most cases the Cinderella character is given a name to reflect a characteristic, as happens in the Perrault and Grimm version, though she will also sometimes have another given name. For example, in de la Paz's Filipino version, the main character is named Abadeha but is mocked as being a "Kitchen Princess" by her stepmother. In Robert D. San Souci's *Sootface: An Ojibwa Cinderella Story*, she is called Sootface by her sisters because they rub soot on her face (she is also scarred by the fire), but when she is transformed at the end of the story, she receives a new name — Dawn-Light — to reflect her transformation. In San Souci's *Little Gold Star: A Spanish American Cinderella Tale*, the main character is named Teresa, but she is later nicknamed "Little Gold Star" by her stepmother and stepsisters after the Virgin Mary, the helper character in this version, marks her forehead with a gold star to bless her.

Naming (and nicknaming) the protagonist of the versions is natural since it is this quality that often distinguishes her. However, the naming of other characters is not common in traditional tales, yet many of the cultural versions of "Cinderella" name her father and stepfamily, as well as other characters in the story. For example, in *Little Gold Star*, Teresa's father is Tomás, her stepsisters Inez and Isabel, and the prince figure is Don Miguel. As seen above in the Filipino version, de la Paz names the father, mother, and main character in the opening sentence. She later also names the prince's father — Datu — though the prince himself is never named. Meredith Brucker, in *Anklet for a Princess: A Cinderella Story from India*, names her protagonist, Cinduri, as well as her stepsister, Lata, and, though the Prince is not given a first name, Brucker does say that he is the Prince of Suyanagar, not just a prince. This additional naming of characters, though it might seem a small detail, actually enhances the cultural specificity by presenting names bound to the culture. While the name Cinderella has become representative of the tale type — at least in the United States— these other names do not have that same meaning and instead offer another aspect of the "exotic" with unfamiliar, foreign-sounding names.

Readers of these picture book versions of "Cinderella" also see cultural specificity through new vocabulary in the tales that are different from their own culture. Most often, these artifacts are flora and fauna as well as clothing and food items, and in some cases these items are presented with the specific vocabulary of the culture represented, followed by an explanation in plain English to explain the concepts, something that would naturally be unnecessary in the original version. Shirley Climo's *The Korean Cinderella*, for example, mentions the main character Pear Blossom calling her new stepmother "*Omoni*, or Mother," and later in the story when Pear Blossom meets her helper character, the text reads, "'A *tokgabi*!' Pear Blossom gasped. 'A goblin!'" In both of these cases, the second, unitalicized words are the English explanation for the Korean words. Other texts, such as Jewell Reinhart Coburn's *Domitila: A Cinderella Tale from the Mexican Tradition*, present a glossary of terms in the book to aid the readers' understanding of the new terms. Words in Coburn's glossary include *abuelo*, *casa*, *malvina*, *nopales* and *pueblo*, and these terms are all used in the story frequently. Not all of the new items are defined in the stories, but the very nature of these details make the tales more geographically specific for the readers who are unfamiliar with the locations of the stories.

Along the same lines as the new vocabulary for cultural items are specific festivals and authority figures in these different versions of "Cinderella." In the versions of the story that contain the festival or gathering the Cinderella figure wants to attend, quite frequently the festival is one that is an integral part of the culture. Similarly, the prince figure takes the form a high authority and/or wealthy figure in the society. For example, in Climo's *The Persian Cinderella*, though the authority figure is still the prince (Prince Mehrdad), the gathering is to celebrate "*No Ruz*, the New Year." The fact that Climo presents both the name in its original language (if not orthography) and then translates it in the same sentence, in Settareh's father's dialog, shows her awareness of the cultural differences and also her desire to define the unfamiliar celebration within the text itself. In *The Turkey Girl: A Zuni Cinderella Story* by Penny Pollock, the Turkey Girl longs to attend the Dance of the Sacred Bird in Hawikuh, but there is no prince figure in this version of the tale. In *The Golden Sandal: A Middle Eastern Cinderella* by Rebecca Hickox, Maha manages to attend the henna painting of the master merchant's daughter, and it is his son, Tariq, who finds her sandal and wants to marry her. Both *Rough-Face Girl* and *Sootface: An Ojibwa Cinderella Story*, though they have no festival, both have the Cinderella figure seeking out the Invisible Being (or Invisible Hunter), a great hunter in the community. While the type of authority figure that is mentioned in each of the stories fits into the story as a matter of course, often the specifying of the festival (and even a geographic location for it sometimes) adds once more to the cultural specificity of the versions.

Finally, in these different cultural versions of Cinderella, the textual additions mentioned above are all supplemented by the illustrations presented. In many of the books, the illustrators include patterns and other small details that add to the cultural nature of the text. Ruth Heller, for example, in her illustrations for *The Korean Cinderella*, includes examples of Korean pendants for women's dresses in several locations as well as various patterns based on temple patterns that "are symbols of good luck, protection, and the cycle of reincarnation." Connie McLennan's illustrations for *Domitila: A Cinderella Tale from the Mexican Tradition* not only portray the scenery and architecture of Mexico, but she also uses text border designs that show aspects of the culture, whether the cactus that the *nopales* are made from or the adobe or needlework mentioned in the text. The illustrations are the primary place that readers unfamiliar with the culture can experience it, and the fact that the authors take the time to place names for these items in the text makes these picture book versions of "Cinderella" geographically specific in a way that they are not in their more traditional form.

The explanation for this specificity may lie with the fact that the books are written with children in mind, and these children will be able to use these versions of a familiar tale to explore other cultures within the realm of a story that they know well. The hook is the inclusion of the name Cinderella in the title; the fascination is with the places of difference in each tale, and the authors and illustrators emphasize that difference through specific geographical and cultural elements. Yet these specific elements do not necessarily take away from the "utopian connotations" Zipes mentions because, though there is specific geography and culture presented, it is still foreign to many of the readers who approach the work. Egypt (or the Spice Islands or even Mexico) for many is unknown. Part of the difference is in the unspecified time frame presented, but an equal part is in the unfamiliar nature, even with the added information, of this other culture. It adds a new mystique to the familiar tale.

The second method of incorporating geography and culture into folktales is through the revision of popular tales in the Western folktale tradition to reflect a different, more specific culture. This type of cultural revision has been made to "Cinderella," of course, but also to "The Three Little Pigs," "Snow White and the Seven Dwarfs," "Goldilocks and the Three Bears," and many other of the popular Grimm and Perrault tales. Certain authors have made it a point to revise many tales to reflect the region from which they come, including Sheila Hébert Collins (Louisiana), Susan Lowell (the Southwest), and Donivee Martin Laird (Hawaii). The tale that seems to have garnered the most revisions of this type is "Little Red Riding Hood."

"Little Red Riding Hood," one of Charles Perrault's most well-known tales, is a popular tale for cultural revisions. There are different versions from other cultures, including the Grimm brothers' "Little Red Cap" (which is often conflated with Perrault's, as in the case of Trina Schart Hyman's Caldecott Honor version called *Little Red Riding Hood*) and the Chinese version "Lon Po Po," which has been translated and illustrated into a Caldecott-winning picture book by Ed Young. Cultural revisions of "Little Red Riding Hood" include a Wild West version by Susan Lowell, who has rewritten numerous tales to reflect a Wild West theme, called *Little Red Cowboy Hat*; Lisa Campbell Ernst's *Little Red Riding Hood: A Newfangled Prairie Tale*; Donivee Martin Laird's Hawaiian revision *'Ula Li'i and the Magic Shark*; and three Cajun revisions.

In *Little Red Cowboy Hat*, Lowell immediately situates the reader by saying, "Once upon a ranch, far away in the wilds of the West, there lived a little girl with red, red hair." Though there is never a specific town or state named here, something that allows for the retention at one level of Zipes' "utopian connotations," the location is specific enough to allow the author and illustrator to adapt the story to a more specific landscape and culture than the traditional versions of "Little Red Riding Hood." Some of the initial cultural alterations include the replacing of the hood with a red cowboy hat and the mother's warning to be careful because "It's rattlesnake season." The story also includes Buck the buckskin pony, which Little Red, as the main character is nicknamed (short for Little Red Cowboy Hat), rides to her grandmother's house, and which helps protect her from the wolf on the way to her grandmother's. That protection is needed because she stops to pick not just the generic flowers of the traditional version, but "gold poppies and blue lupines" on the grass of the "wide mesa."

As with many of Lowell's folktale revisions[3], there is a decidedly feminist perspective in *Little Red Cowboy Hat*, for Little Red quickly figures out that it is not her grandmother in the bed. She decides to "string the wolf along until she found out" where her grandmother is. And it is the grandmother who saves Little Red from the wolf after he grabs her — first by brandishing an ax and then her shotgun. At the end of the story when the grandmother asks if Little Red has learned her lesson, Little Red replies, "Yep. A girl's gotta stick up for herself," thereby emphasizing the feminist message of this revision.

In addition to the cultural elements presented in the alteration of the story's artifacts and events (and reflected in Randy Cecil's illustrations), Lowell uses dialect, particularly the grandmother's dialect as she is chasing the wolf and later as she's talking about him with Little Red, to enhance the cultural specificity of the tale. The grandmother's final description of the wolf is "That yellow-bellied, snake-blooded, skunk-eyed, rancid son of a parallelogram!" and these words are clearly supposed to emulate the creative invectives (with editing for children's reading) of that dialect. Even the narrator makes use of this comparison-heavy dialect when commenting that the wolf wore "a cowboy hat three shades blacker than a locomotive." All of Lowell's alterations in this tale point to its geographical specificity, even while it still has a small element of the utopian in it and even though it still attempts to enculturate the main character through an adventurous lesson, as do most folktales.

A second cultural revision of "Little Red Riding Hood" is Lisa Campbell Ernst's *Little Red Riding Hood: A Newfangled Prairie Tale.* Like Lowell's revision, Ernst's starts out with a much more specific location than the more traditional "land far away." She writes, "Once upon a time there was a little girl who lived at the edge of a great prairie." This Little Red Riding Hood gets her nickname because "she always wore a jacket with a red hood when she rode her bike." The journey to her grandmother's is not made because of the grandmother's illness; rather, it's because it's a hot day and the lemonade and muffins she brings will make her grandmother less "crabby." However, unlike Lowell's, the time setting for Ernst's revision is clearly the twentieth century, for some of the artifacts she mentions, such as Little Red Riding Hood's bike and the places she rides by — especially the gas station — are very modern. So Ernst is not only taking away the "utopian connotations" through geography, but she's also removing the more traditional timeless feel of the tale.

Ernst enhances the geographical feel through some of her descriptions of Little Red Riding Hood's ride to her grandmother's. Not only does she ride on the prairie, but she "zigzagged between the crops, taking the shortcut to Grandma's house. Blackbirds startled and sunflowers swayed as she whizzed by." These descriptions are much more specific than the general flora and fauna descriptions of most traditional versions and tie the reader to this specific region, much as Lowell does in her revision.

Ernst also seems to want to change stereotypes of people who live on the prairie, and she does this by allowing the wolf to voice the stereotypes before his eventual defeat. The wolf represents the city-folk in this version of the tale, for Ernst draws him dressed in city clothes and makes reference to his "fancy suspenders" later in the book. She also makes him not interested in eating Little Red Riding Hood and her grandmother but rather in getting the grandmother's secret wheat berry muffin recipe (as well as the muffins Little Red Riding Hood is bringing to her grandmother). There is a sense that this wolf could be the corporate wolf looking to take advantage of the country folk. As he's traveling to grandmother's house after meeting with Little Red Riding Hood in the field, he thinks of her and her grandmother as "country bumpkins," and later when he tries to sneak up on the grandmother (believing she's a farmer), he says, " I love surprising these dim-witted hicks." The fact that he is swiftly defeated by these "bumpkins" and "hicks" acts as a clear refutation of the stereotypes of prairie farmers.

In addition to refuting the stereotypical notions of the prairie farmer, Ernst, like Lowell, presents a feminist revision. Once again the wolf gives voice to the stereotypes of the grandmother character, calling her "a dear, sweet woman" (which she may well be), a "feeble old granny," "off her rocker," an "ancient granny," and finally, when the farmer has him by his "fancy suspenders," a "frail, loony, muffin-baking granny," not realizing that the farmer is the grandmother. Not only does the grandmother stop the wolf from causing trouble with her or her granddaughter, but she frightens him so severely that the wolf is relegated to the traditional role of the granddaughter, stammering out exclamations about the grandmother's big eyes, ears, and hands. And it is only Little Red Riding Hood's appearance that saves the wolf from being crushed "like a bug" by the grandmother. Though Little Red Riding Hood saves the wolf from being crushed, she cannot save him from the grandmother's lecture: "Didn't you think if there was a Little Red Riding Hood there might be a *Big* Red Riding Hood? I thought I'd got rid of bullies like you when I moved away from that forest!" The stereotype of a frail, helpless grandmother is turned upside down in this revision of the tale.

The lecture that the grandmother gives the wolf also adds another element to this cultural revision of "Little Red Riding Hood." Not only is the tale modernized to the twentieth century, but it also appears that the grandmother could have been the Little Red Riding Hood of the more traditional version. Certainly her comments lead the readers back to the traditional version set near the forest and remind them that wolves, in varying guises, with varying agendas, exist everywhere. They can also be reformed, or at least held in check, according to this revision, for the grandmother not only foils the wolf's plans, but she then puts him to work at her new muffin shop as the "chief baker, salesclerk, and dishwasher," which keeps him "much too busy to cause trouble for anyone." She is, of course, too savvy to trust him with the complete recipe, however.

Ernst's "newfangled prairie tale," like Lowell's Wild West revision, presents a much more concrete geography than the traditional version while also retaining the enculturating nature of traditional tales. In

Ernst's version, there are two types of enculturation going on: Little Red Riding Hood learns not to talk to strangers again, but the wolf is also taught a valuable lesson about the people who live on the prairie and about the strength of grandmothers and women.

Donivee Martin Laird's 'Ula Li'i and the Magic Shark is the only "Little Red Riding Hood" cultural revision that ties back to a previous text by the author. The same Magic Shark who is the antagonist in Laird's The Three Little Hawaiian Pigs and the Magic Shark is brought back from the dump, literally, and becomes the antagonist in this story.[4] In fact, her story starts with characters unrelated to the story finding the rolled up shark and, thinking he's a "perfectly good beach mat," taking him to the beach where a wave crashes over him and allows him to regain his old form and his freedom. He cannot be content with his regained freedom, however, and soon he is looking for something to eat on land again. This is where the "Little Red Riding Hood" revision truly begins.

Unlike Lowell and Ernst's revisions, Laird's does not take time with a ritual set-up of the story — there is no "once upon" anything. The audience recognizes the Hawaiian setting from the opening, which reads more like the middle of the story: "The Magic Shark had been in the dump, where the Three Little Hawaiian Pigs had thrown him, for several weeks." 'Ula Li'i does not appear until page eleven of the book, when the Magic Shark comes upon her being sent to her grandmother's with the very food he likes best — "poke, kūlolo, and a nice piece of kālua pig." Though the text does not explain what these food items are, there is a glossary at the back of the book that defines them for the reader,[5] and a pronunciation guide at the beginning to help with unfamiliar Hawaiian words, something necessary since Laird intersperses Hawaiian terms with the English throughout the book, from types of food, to names for people, to common words and phrases. Even the name 'Ula Li'i, while it might seem very specific to the reader, is actually a combination of the Hawaiian words for "little" (Li'i) and "red" ('Ula). There is no explanation about why she is called 'Ula Li'i as in other versions of "Little Red Riding Hood," but the name is still descriptive while also being more culturally bound.

There is further cultural specificity in Laird's revision when the Magic Shark attempts to get the basket of goodies from 'Ula Li'i. First he poses as a malasada (a type of pastry) cook and then as a shave ice vendor. Both times he almost convinces 'Ula Li'i to give him the basket, but at the last minute she remembers her mother's warning about talking to strangers and about bringing the basket to her grandmother and escapes. The Magis Shark must then resort to going to grandmother's himself. Here is where there is another split from the traditional versions of "Little Red Riding Hood," for the shark tricks the grandmother into leaving her house by telling her about a sale on her favorite fish. He has no interest in eating either her or ʻUla Liʻi; rather, he's only interested in the food in the basket. Disguised as the grandmother, he nearly gets the basket, but at the last moment, ʻUla Liʻi screams and the hanawai man (irrigation ditch cleaner) next door comes to her rescue, captures the Magic Shark, and folds him in a bundle that he ties up and takes to the dump at the end of the story.

Though Laird's revision of the story is not feminist in nature, it is much milder than the traditional versions in terms of the violence. There is violence in the story, but it is only against the shark, and even then it is a comic violence since the shark has already escaped once from a similar predicament and can be expected to do so again. Culturally, Laird's revision is quite specific, presenting as it does a new type of antagonist indigenous to Hawaii, as well as native terminology for familiar concepts — grandmother, grandchild. There is also the presentation of new cultural items such as different plants (hibiscus and papaya) and food items. There is no mistaking the geography of this revision of the story, even though it is clearly still "Little Red Riding Hood." ʻUla Liʻi, however, seems to be more obedient than other Little Red Riding Hoods since, though she does talk to the shark, she always comes back to her mother's warning about talking to strangers and taking shortcuts and leaves before the shark can take advantage of her. The main message of this revision seems to be for the shark, who, as he is lying once again in the dump, vows "Next time I will just invite myself to supper and forget all the fancy tricks." Like the wolf in Ernst's revision, the Magic Shark in this revision is the true lesson learner and possibly a reformed character.

The three Cajun revisions of "Little Red Riding Hood," like Lowell, Ernst, and Laird's revisions, present this traditional tale with distinctive geographical traits — most notably the use of an alligator instead of a wolf as the antagonist — yet each of these revisions is different from the others. In Mike Artell's *Petite Rouge: A Cajun Red Riding Hood*, the story is presented in rhymed quatrains in a heavy dialect. The story begins:

> Back in de swamp
> where dat Spanish moss grow,
> I heard me a story
> from long time ago.

Though "swamp" is not necessarily more specific than "forest," the addition of the Spanish moss and later details clearly does situate this story in Louisiana. From there the narrator explains that all the people there called her Petite Rouge Riding Hood.[6]

Like Artell, Berthe Amoss begins her story *A Cajun Little Red Riding Hood* with the location, but unlike Artell, she is very specific about her main character's given name. Her story begins, "Once upon a bayou, there lived a little girl whose name was Marie Berthe Aspasie Philomene" but because the name is "too long and too hard to pronounce," she's nicknamed Katrine, and it is this name she keeps throughout the story. She is the only main character in the revisions who does not possess the Little Red Riding Hood nickname, though she does wear a red riding hood like the traditional character.

Sheila Hébert Collins, like Amoss, is very specific about naming her character as well as the geographical setting in her book *Petite Rouge: A Cajun Twist to an Old Tale*. She writes, "Once upon a time there was a family named Mouton. They lived on Bayou Tigre near the town of Delcambre in Southern Louisiana." A short time later she names all three of the family members more specifically—the parents are Clodis and Ophelia, the daughter Clotilde, though she is nicknamed Petite Rouge. Of all of the cultural revisions of "Little Red Riding Hood," Hébert Collins is the most specifically situated — none of the others breaks Zipes' "utopian connotations" to the extent of naming specific towns the way that Hébert Collins does. Though they are all more specific geographically, they still retain some utopian qualities except this one. The only setting convention that Hébert Collins does continue is the use of an unspecified time.

All three of the Cajun revisions, like the Laird revision, also alter the conventional food offerings (generally bread or some other kind of baked good) brought to the grandmother. Artell sends Petite Rouge out with gumbo and boudin; Amoss with a basket of pecans to make pralines; and Hébert Collins with a shrimp etouffée. These alterations also indicate the cultural nature of the revisions, and in fact the Amoss and Hébert Collins versions both supply a recipe to the readers to enhance their experience with Cajun culture.

In addition to the alterations in setting and food, all three of these revisions offer Cajun terms in the texts, with glossaries, to expand the readers' knowledge and help them better understand that the culture is more than just food and location. Artell and Amoss both have separate pages with the glossaries, but Hébert Collins presents each new term's definition on the same page on which it appears. Each term in her book is also italicized for the readers' benefit. All three explain the food they use as well as basic terms such as *cher* and *mère* (or *grand-mère*). Hébert Collins goes further to explain some of the proper names and places she specifies as well, furthering the geographical specificity of her revision.

Another aspect of language that all three have in common is their use of dialect. Each one presents characters who speak in some form of dialect. Amoss' use of Cajun dialect is mildest, consisting mostly of a few word substitutions, such as *mère* and *cher*. Hébert Collins uses a more pronounced dialect in her revision, showing how inhabitants of the area pronounce words in conversation as well as using different words like Amoss does. Thus the gator in her story says, when learning that Peitite Rouge is going to her grandmother's, "You take dat way, I'll take dis way and we'll see who gets dere first. *Dépeche-toi!*" The use of *d* instead of *th* in the story is consistent with all the characters, as is the use of French words mixed with English.

While Hébert Collins uses dialect only for her dialog, Artell presents the whole tale in dialect — narrative and dialog. The dialect in his story is much more exaggerated and, at times, seems almost offensively stereotypical. Not only does he use *d* instead of *th*, but he also presents other sound changes and various other grammatical differences that make the story fairly difficult to read. For example, when Artell is describing the gator creeping up on the grandmother, he says,

> He open de door and
> den stick in his head.
> An' den he see Grand-mère
> asleep in de bed.
>
> He try to tiptoe
> so she don' hear no sound,
> but his tail bomp de shelf
> an' two cup fall down.

He seems to be trying to show an authentic Cajun storyteller's voice, but his success is questionable because in the presentation of this voice he's over exaggerating and presenting, with some of the grammatical problems (even if they're authentic), a questionable authority. All three of the authors present Cajun culture through dialect; they just do so to various degrees and with varying success.

One major way in which the Cajun tales do differ is in their endings. In Artell's revision, Claude the gator scares the grandmother into hiding in a closet then impersonates her in traditional fashion. Before he gets the chance to gobble Petite Rouge up, however, her helper character—a cat named TeJean and one of Artell's major alterations to the traditional tale—finds the bottle of hot sauce and throws it at Petite Rouge, who catches it and applies it to the piece of boudin TeJean also throws her. When Claude eats it, he ends up dancing around with his tail in a knot "'cause dat boudin so hot." He runs away a reformed character and leaves Petite Rouge and her grandmother to enjoy the rest of the boudin and gumbo. That Petite Rouge and her cat defeat Claude themselves (after scaring him away once on the way to the grandmother's) presents a feminist message to the reader, though not as strongly feminist as the Lowell and Ernst versions.

Amoss' version is also feminist in nature. The alligator scares the grandmother out of the house, "so fast, she dropped her robe and night cap." Katrine, when she arrives at her grandmother's house, is not fooled by the alligator's disguise and saves herself by throwing "the whole basket full of pecans, shells and all, into his mouth," scaring him away. Amoss emphasizes the feminist sentiment with the grandmother's praise for her granddaughter: "You have saved us both with your quick thinking and bravery!" This story is also reflexive. Katrine and her grandmother have essentially relived a version of Katrine's favorite fairy tale—"Little Red Riding Hood"—and the story ends with them reading the story together.

Hébert Collins' revision, while it is not a feminist retelling (and in fact remains in many ways the closest to the traditional version in terms of plot), is also a reflexive story. After the gator has eaten Petite Rouge, the narrator says, "That's the way some say the story ends, but people down in Bayou Tigre swear the shrimpers heard Petite Rouge screaming and came running to help her." Hébert Collins is clearly making reference here to Perrault's traditional version and then moving on to the Grimms' version with her ending, in which the shrimpers find the gator and cut him open to rescue Petite Rouge and her grandmother. Though the story is reflexive in a different manner than Amoss,' there is a clear play on the story's tradition being made. This reflexiveness is an element in many folktale revisions in children's literature.

All three Cajun revisions, as with the three previous different ones, work to enculturate their audiences—the feminist nature of Artell and Amoss' versions show that it is important for little girls to protect themselves (and also to avoid evil strangers), while Hébert Collins' reemphasizes the traditional admonitions to young girls about trusting the wolves (or in this case gators) of the world. It also reemphasizes the patriarchal nature of this society since it is the shrimpers—all male—who ultimately save Petite Rouge and her grandmother, just as it is the huntsman who saves Little Red Cap and her grandmother in the Grimms' version.

In all six of the cultural revisions, there is an attempt made by the author to bring the unspecified geographical region of the traditional version into a clear cultural region, be it the Wild West, the prairie, Hawaii, or Louisiana. Most of the authors, even while making this change, keep some element of what Jack Zipes calls "utopian connotations" in their tales. The only one who does not do so in the "Little Red Riding Hood" revisions is Sheila Hébert Collins, yet her tale is in many ways the most like the traditional versions of "Little Red Riding Hood." By being so geographically specific, she seems to need to keep the tie to the tale in another manner than the less geographically specific tales do, thereby keeping the connection to the original folktale in tact.

Though the stories are revisions of the tales, the changes do not remove them from the fairy tale tradition. If anything, these alterations show ways in which the tradition continues to prosper in children's literature, for all of the tales continue to follow the rules that Steven Swann Jones and Jack Zipes discuss in their texts by, as Jones says, "instruct[ing] the young about who they are, how they relate to others, and what they should know about the world" (18). With "Little Red Riding Hood" in particular, the tales come back to the training of little girls in their dealings with strange men (or beasts). The "particular codes and laws" that the characters "must learn to respect," to use Zipes' terms, may vary from region to region—though since all of the revisions ultimately descend from European cultures, the codes and laws are remarkably similar—but the ultimate goal of reinforcing cultural norms remains. Geographical specificity (and modern writers' sensibilities) may color the details of the tales, but the ultimate goals in the folktales remain the same.

4

Breaking the Picture Book Rules

Picture books, like folktales, have certain conventions attached to their form. In the chapter "Picturebook Paratexts" from their book *How Picturebooks Work*, Maria Nikolajeva and Carole Scott discuss how the covers, endpapers, title page, and back cover are presented in picture books, saying that

> These elements are ... more important in picturebooks than in novels. If the cover of a children's novel serves as a decoration and at best can contribute to the general first impact, the cover of a picturebook is often an integral part of the narrative, especially when the cover picture does not repeat any of the pictures inside the book. The narrative can indeed start on the cover, and it can go beyond the last page into the back cover. Endpapers can convey essential information, and pictures on title pages can both complement and contradict the narrative [241].

Though these elements can contribute to the narrative in some picture books, this is not always the case, but even when they do contribute, they generally follow the same order in the book.

Typically picture books will contain a title page and copyright page before the story itself begins. There may be a separate dedication page or the dedication may appear on the copyright page. Once the main content — often a story — begins, the pictures and text (except in the cases of all-picture books) present that story in a very clear chronology. If the copyright page is not at the beginning of the book, it will appear after the story ends. In some cases, however, when authors and illustrators are revising folktales for picture books, they also revise these picture book conventions at the same time. For the majority of picture books, the story or content itself is separate from the concept of storytelling or bookmaking, but in some folktale revisions, it is not merely a new story being told but a rethinking of the concept of storytelling and of picture books as a whole. The result can be presented in the physical setup of the picture book, the manner in which the story is told, or a combination of the two.

The most basic way in which picture book conventions are revised alongside folktales can be seen in the Steck-Vaughn Point of View series by Alvin Granowsky as well as in a more recent Disney Press publication by Daphne Skinner called *My Side of the Story Cinderella/Lady Tremaine*. Granowsky's series presents a revision of a folktale in one half of each book, and on the flip side of the book, the traditional version of the same tale. While the actual stories on each side are presented following the traditional picture book format, that the reader must flip the book to read everything represents a revision of the picture book form, however small. It is also interesting that, while Granowsky does present the traditional version on the flipside, his focus is clearly on the revision, for the revision is the primary side of the book (the traditional version's cover is the one with the ISBN number on it, indicating that it is seen as the back cover, and thus the second story). Each of Granowsky's revisions is told in first person by one of the characters of the traditional story, usually the antagonist. For example, in *The Unfairest of Them All/Snow White* the narrator of *The Unfairest of Them All* is Snow White's stepmother; in *Friends at the End!*, it is the hare that narrates the revision. The flipside of this book is *The Tortoise and the Hare*. The traditional version of the story, however, is in the standard third person narration of most folktales. Each side is illustrated by a different artist as well, further challenging the tradition of picture books, which generally use only one illustrator for the entire book.

Skinner's *My Side of the Story Cinderella/Lady Tremaine* is also two-sided like Granowsky's versions and also otherwise a conventional picture book. Her book differs, however, in that she presents two separate first-person narratives, one from Cinderella's point of view and the other from Cinderella's stepmother Lady Tremaine's point of view. And like Granosky's versions, Skinner's are illustrated by two different artists. Though neither Granowsky's nor Skinner's revisions are particularly interesting in other ways, they have challenged the traditions of both picture books and folktales in their writing.

Gail Carson Levine's *Betsy Who Cried Wolf* also alters the picture book form in small measure by the use of illustrations on the endpapers. These illustrations show the sheep talking with each other. On the inside front cover endpaper, the conversation is about the new shepherd who will arrive shortly — Betsy. The story itself is a modern telling of "The Boy Who Cried Wolf," and makes no challenges to the picture book form until the very end when there is another conversation among the sheep. This conversation starts on the final page of the book with one sheep commenting, "You know, there's a moral in this somewhere" and another saying "Someone should write a book about these two [Betsy and the wolf]." The next page is back endpaper, and the sheep are once again talking to each other, this time offering different morals for the story. That the sheep are discussing the content of the story — and in a location not traditionally used in the picture book story[1] — indicates a revision not just of the traditional tale but also of the picture book format.

Colin and Jacqui Hawkins likewise offer a minimal revision of the picture book form with their book *Fairytale News*. The story itself is a fairly conventional revision — Jack from "Jack and the Beanstalk" gets a job delivering the local newspaper and weaves in and out of several other folktales before reentering his own story's main plot again. The revision of this form comes not in the actual story presented but in the enclosed copy of the newspaper Jack delivers. This newspaper presents numerous more revisions of folktales in a very different technique, one that certainly challenges the conventions of picture books by the very fact that it is an artifact mentioned in the picture book as well as a separate document.

Other picture book folktale revisions are more noteworthy, both in terms of the quality of the revision and in the manner in which they challenge notions of picture books. David Ellwand and Christine Tagg's *Cinderlily: A Floral Fairy Tale in Three Acts*, for example, sets up the entire text as a ballet performance of "Cinderella," from the opening of the cover, where the words "Silence, please...." start the text to the final word on the back endpaper: "Applause!" Even the copyright material at the end of the book is set up like a program from a performance, placed beneath the "Principle Cast," a listing of the flowers that are "portraying" the characters of Cinderella (Lilium Oriental), The Sultan (Iris Xiphium), and The Fairy Godmother (Lilium Stargazer). Though the story and its pictures, photographs manipulated in Adobe Photoshop, form a fairly standard narrative, that narrative is presented as if it were not a picture book but a performance and thus alters the conventions of traditional picture books.

Bruce Whatley's book *Wait! No Paint!* makes more significant changes to picture book conventions than any of the previously mentioned books. The book contains the conventional title page, copyright and dedication page setup, and even the story itself appears to be a mild revision of "The Three Little Pigs" for a few pages. It is on the eighth page of the book that the picture book rules start to crumble. At this point in the story, the first little pig is settling into his straw house when "he heard a splash" followed by "a Voice from nowhere in particular" saying it has spilt its juice (8). The accompanying illustration is a tipped over glass with what appears to be orange juice spilling from it onto the straw house, making it "soggy and sticky" (8). Though the pig is unaware of the source of the Voice or the juice, he and his story are nonetheless impacted by the mysterious Voice. Before the wolf, who comes along just after the juice spill, can blow down the house, it "collapsed with a wet *plop*" (9).

The Voice's influence continues as the first little pig relates the story to his brother. In fact, the Voice returns to the story after the wolf smashes his nose on the door of the second house. It interrupts the wolf's second huff and puff statement — which is somewhat muffled because of the injured nose — with "Wait. I've got to redo the nose" (12), and the accompanying picture is of an unfinished wolf, paintbrush, pencil and eraser. It is also the nose fixing that allows the two pigs to escape the wolf this time and reach the third little pig's house. As the smartest of the pigs, this pig naturally figures out that the Voice is actually the Illustrator. Here is where the picture book rules crumble, for the Illustrator, like the author, is not supposed to be a participant in the story. The reader is led to believe that the Illustrator's presence is scary, for the third pig is described as turning pale as he announces the identity of the Voice.

The Illustrator explains this paleness in the next page: "I'm sorry to tell you, but I just ran out of red paint" (16), and in fact the new illustration shows three white pigs. Once again the Illustrator's efforts affect the pigs, for "The first pig felt so faint he had to sit down" (16). A correlation between the Illustrator's artwork and how characters feel is being made explicit in this section, once again bridging the gap between Illustrator and character. The interaction goes both ways. The third pig demands some sort of color, at which point the text reads, "Suddenly the three little pigs felt queasy" (18). The Illustrator has painted them green, with one of the associated results of being that color. The fight between Illustrator and pigs continues until the Illustrator warns the pigs that the wolf is coming. The wolf demands entrance as usual for the traditional story, but the pigs' "chinny chin chins" response is enhanced with their use of green to describe their hair and chins.

Again the wolf's actions are interrupted by the Illustrator, who demands, "How's this?" (21). The next illustration shows the third little pig colored the same pattern as his chair, a fact that he does not appreciate, though it send the wolf into gales of laughter. He declares that he feels like a clown, at which point the Illustrator mistakes his comment for a request and draws him as a clown on the next page. This error is soon remedied and the Illustrator returns the pigs to their pale selves. The unconventional interaction of creator and creation has continued in this story to comic effect—for reader and other characters.

Despite these divergences from the traditional story, all of the story's characters try to follow the storyline to the best of their ability. As a result, while the pigs are fighting with the Illustrator over their coloring, the wolf climbs the roof and plans to go down the chimney. The pigs' plan to build a "red hot" fire is naturally unsuccessful since the Illustrator is out of red paint (28), and the problem leads the third little pig to demand the Illustrator do something to fix the problem. He ends bellowing, "WE DON'T WANT TO BE IN THIS STORY ANYMORE!" (29). The result is the final page of the book: the three little pigs dressed as three bears and the wolf dressed as Goldilocks, with the text on the page being the introduction to "Goldilocks and the Three Bears."

The actual structure of *Wait! No Paint!* can fit within the realm of a traditional picture book since the Illustrator can be read as just another character in the story, much as the Looney Tunes cartoon "Duck Amuck" uses Bugs Bunny as the Illustrator tormenting Daffy Duck. However, the book can also be read as a challenge to the picture book form in that it removes the line between illustrator/author and character by making them interact with each other and by showing how what happens to the illustrator can (and does in this case) affect how the story plays out. Further, Whatley's story happens on two levels. The first level is the traditional story of "The Three Little Pigs," a story that is always in progress in this book. The second level is that of the "actors" in the story, for the three pigs and the wolf all move in and out of character much as actors do, and all of them are clearly aware that they are players in a story. This fact is clearest at the end, of course, when the third little pig declares that they no longer want to be in the story. Their recasting as the three bears and Goldilocks merely emphasizes this second level of the story, in which the Illustrator acts almost as a director, however inept he may seem to his actors. *Wait! No Paint!* is a metatextual look at picture book creation.

Another book that challenges the traditional form of the picture books is David Wiesner's Caldecott Medal winner *The Three Pigs.* Like Whatley's book, Wiesner's begins in a conventional manner: the story does not begin until after the standard opening materials, and once it does begin, it looks like the traditional story. Wiesner draws the story in a series of panels, usually two to a page, with the text at the top of each panel. It's when the wolf blows down the first pig's house that the picture book conventions are also blown away, for the picture shows the panel with the wolf blowing the house to bits and the pig coming out of the panel. Above the pig's head is a cartoon bubble that reads, "Hey! He blew me right out of the story!" To emphasize the separateness of character and actor, Wiesner has drawn the pig in a different texture where he is out of the story while his feet, which are still in the panel, match the artwork of the actual story. The next panel, in which the wolf is supposed to have eaten the first pig, shows a confused wolf searching for the pig. Its caption remains part of the story being told, but the artwork has changed to reflect the missing character.

The story continues in this manner with the text reflecting the traditional story but the illustrations revealing the changed action as the second pig escapes the story with his brother. As with Whatley's revision, the characters in Wiesner's story are aware that they're in it, and of the story's conventions. As the third pig leaves the story, he asks the others, "Wow! Why didn't you two get eaten up?" From that point the story shifts from "The Three Little Pigs" to these characters' adventures outside the story. One of the pigs, in jumping around outside the panels, bumps several of them out of place. The pigs then decide to explore this new territory, and they do so on an airplane formed from one of the panels of their story. The resulting flight takes them through several pages blank except for them on the plane. It is a creative use of white space, and one that is not used often, for picture books rarely fail to fill every page with pictures and text. Even those pages that are primarily text are often enhanced with designs or colors to alleviate the starkness of white space.

In the page after the pigs crash land comes the only occurrence of the pigs' awareness of a world outside the page. A large picture of one of the pigs looking out along with the statement, "I think someone's out there" reveals that the pigs are aware that someone, though that someone is never named, is witnessing their unconventional adventure. As with Whatley's book, there is an "outside world" for these characters, though Wiesner's characters cannot interact with this world as Whatley's pigs do. While Wiesner's pigs have escaped their story (and their storybook fates), they have not escaped the storybook world, and it is this world that they're exploring after the paper airplane crashes. Their appearances are also transformed as they cross through the different stories, first into a Mother Goose rhyme and then into a dragon-slaying story. As they enter the Mother Goose rhyme "Hey Diddle Diddle" they become cartoonish in appearance, while in the dragon story, they are black and white drawings.

The pigs also cause alterations in these new texts they enter, for the cat with the fiddle follows them out of the Mother Goose rhyme, and they rescue the dragon from the prince about to slay him. As with the pigs' own story, the illustrations for the dragon slaying story match the confusion of the prince unable to find the dragon while the text of that story follows along the path it is supposed to take. All five of the characters then explore the outside world of storybooks, walking through and examining a variety of picture book panels before they rediscover their story and decide to go home again. This time, however, they have control of their own story, and they send the dragon out to confront the wolf at the brick house. The dragon causes the text of the story to scramble, so the pigs collect the letters and rewrite the end of their story literally as one of the pigs creates the caption "And they all lived happily ever after" with the collected letters.

Like Whatley, Wiesner presents two levels of story, the traditional story level of "The Three Little Pigs" and the "actors" level. The actors in this case, however, are not at the mercy of the Illustrator as they are in Whatley's version and can explore the world outside their story to their heart's content. A third level of the story also exists, if briefly. This level is the world outside the book, where "someone" is. The pigs cannot reach this someone, and so their interest moves back to the world they can wander around in. The metatextual aspect of this story, and the fact that the story is consciously manipulated by the characters in it, challenge the conventions of the picture book as well as the story "The Three Little Pigs."

Unlike Whatley and Wiesner's books, Lauren Child's two books *Beware of the Storybook Wolves* and *Who's Afraid of the Big Bad Book?* allow physical interaction between the characters in the folktales and their readers. In this case, Herb, the little boy who owns the books, is able to change the stories in his books when the characters emerge into his room or he climbs into the stories. The first of the books *Beware of the Storybook Wolves* sets up this ability, when the wolves from his storybook (one from in the story and the other from the back cover) emerge one night when his mother does not take the book out of his room. As

Herb tries to save himself from the wolves, he uses his book, finally shaking the fairy godmother from "Cinderella" out of the book and convincing her to help him. She is not pleased with being removed from her story — and her removal results in Cinderella missing the ball (and one of the wolves going in Cinderella's place) — but she eventually saves Herb from the other wolf by turning him into a caterpillar and putting him back in his book, where he remains in that form to confront Little Red Riding Hood in future readings. She also decides to take a break from being in the book and disappears.

Though the actual setup of this book does not break the conventions of picture books since it is a story of a boy's struggle with storybooks, it does have a similar metatextual element to Whatley and Wiesner's books because of the interaction between Herb and the characters from his books. He is not the author or the illustrator, but he does represent that second level of story that both the other authors have in their picture books. *Beware of the Storybook Wolves* also sets the stage for the second book in the series — *Who's Afraid of the Big Bad Book?* The first noticeable challenge to the picture book form in this book is the cover, which shows Herb holding a copy of the book the reader has. This connection is furthered on the inside the book on the dedication page, which declares, "This book belongs to Herb" in a child-like handwriting. As the story unfolds, the reader learns that Herb has a tendency to eat while he reads, which leads to rather messy books. And since this book is supposed to be Herb's, the reader is allowed to see the squished peas and other alterations that Herb has made to his book (as well as see him read the same book).

The folktale revision begins in the story when Herb falls asleep on a book of fairy tales and wakes up inside the book to the sound of Goldilocks' shrieking. As in the Whatley and Wiesner books, his new presence in the story alters the course of events, and it does so in a metatextual manner, for Goldilocks declares, "I AM THE STAR AND I SAY YOU ARE NOT ALLOWED IN THIS STORY!" The characters are aware that they are characters. What's more, they cling to the traditional form of their story in Child's book in a way that they do not in Wiesner's story. It is Herb who, like the Illustrator in *Wait! No Paint!*, forces the alterations on these characters. As Herb struggles to leave Goldilocks behind, he runs into the three bears, who are as kind as Goldilocks is shrill. With Goldilocks following him, he runs through other tales — "Hansel and Gretel," "Rapunzel," and "Puss in Boots" — before arriving at a door. This door, according to the text, is hard to open because "the illustrator had drawn the handle much too high up." Here is the same kind of comment that occurs in *Wait! No Paint!* in which the way the book is constructed by the author/illustrator is mentioned, and it enhances the unconventional nature of this picture book.

The reader opens the door with Herb to two fold out pages of Cinderella's ball — minus Cinderella and the prince. Most of the women in this section of the story sport mustaches, and as soon as Herb introduces himself as the book owner, the queen says, "so you're the doodler who ruined my looks." Again Herb's editing of his books has led to changes in the happenings— the queen is also missing her throne, and there are phones in all of the rooms in the book. None of the characters is pleased with the alterations, so once he is recognized, he becomes a wanted man and several of the characters chase him. He is fortunate to find his pencil case which he'd misplaced and is able to use some of the contents to try to rectify his destructiveness, much as the Illustrator of Whatley's book does. When that doesn't work, he cuts a hole in the palace floor and moves into the next scene. This hole exists in the actual book as well, furthering the notion that this is Herb's book.

Here appears the next alteration in picture book form, for Herb finds himself in a page that is upside down because he'd torn it out and replaced it wrong. What's interesting about this exchange, between Herb and Cinderella's wicked stepmother and sisters, is that his text appears right side up (for the reader) while the others' text is written upside down to reflect their position in the story now. To escape the women, he acts as illustrator again and draws himself a door, which takes him to Cinderella's kitchen. This is where he remembers "where Prince Charming was: Herb had cut him out to make a birthday card for his mother." As a result, Cinderella is in her kitchen without having met the prince before the Fairy's magic ended. To help Herb get out of the book to find Prince Charming, Cinderella uses her recently installed telephone to call her fairy godmother. Once again, the fairy godmother is not pleased at being called to Herb's rescue. As she is rebuking Herb for asking for help, she makes reference not only to her role in the story — claiming she only helps girls— but also to Herb's rudeness for tampering with his book and for "jumping into other people's stories."

Before the fairy godmother can finally help Herb, the characters chasing him arrive, and he is instructed to climb the text to escape. Once again there is a play on the picture book conventions with the use of aspects of the picture book itself to aid a character. Herb cannot escape on the text however, but Goldilocks' unpleasant voice saves the day, for she yells at him so loudly "that the whole book shook and slipped off the bed, sending Herb falling headlong through the air." The next thing he knows he's back in his own room, where his sleepover guest Ezzie wakes up. They spend their night fixing the book, including the return of Prince Charming to the story and the righting of the torn pages. He does, however, alter the Goldilocks story, "drawing a padlock on the three bears' front door." The boys also put a wig on Goldilocks, leaving "a very cross little girl with mousy brown hair" at the bears' cottage.

Child's alteration of picture book conventions is very creative and is a step further than either Whatley or Wiesner's revisions, for not only is there is an outside force that changes the way picture books and their stories progress, but that force can enter and exit the stories at any time and make permanent changes that the characters may or may not like. The characters here are generally portrayed in traditional manner, and they seem to long for a return to the traditional stories that Herb has disturbed. Only the fairy godmother, who is not the kindly benevolent figure of old, seems to want the change. Thus the two levels visible in Whatley and Wiesner — the story level and the actor level — are both visible in Child's stories as well. But because there are books within these books, the third level visible briefly in Wiesner, when the pig thinks "someone's out there," actually exists in Child's stories, and that someone has the ability to bring characters outside the book or to climb inside the book himself. The separation between book and audience, in other words, is eliminated, and they have a direct impact on each other. This literal interaction can be seen metaphorically as well, for books and stories *do* have an impact on people, and that impact can and does lead to the alteration of the stories, something clearly reflected in the proliferation of folktale revisions both in children's and adult literature.

The fact that the book the reader holds is supposed to be Herb's adds another level to the alteration, for if the book is supposed to be Herb's, then perhaps the reader too is supposed to be Herb and to be part of the story. Child has created a metatextual revision not only of the folktales referenced in the story, but of the picture book tradition and the way that children read and interact with their books. Whether the story is supposed to be a warning against defacing picture books is unclear, though it seems less likely that Herb will deface his books as dramatically ever again. He is not a completely reformed character, however, as his manipulation of Goldilocks indicates, but he does change his attitude toward many of the characters he runs across when he sees the repercussions of his actions.

Jon Scieszka takes the revision of picture books to its most extreme form in his Caldecott Honor book *The Stinky Cheese Man and Other Fairly Stupid Tales*. In this book, Scieszka presents the multiple levels of story that the other picture books discussed have, but he goes a step further, allowing the narrator, Jack, who is also a character in one of the stories, to take responsibility for constructing the book as a whole. He is hindered in the process by several different characters, most notably Little Red Hen, who appears on the endpaper, before the title page, speaking lines from her story. When Jack interrupts her in an attempt to move her to a later position in the story, she is less than pleased, demanding, "But who will help me tell my story? Who will help me draw a picture of my wheat? Who will help me spell 'the wheat'?" These questions echo her earlier questions, except that they are about the story rather than part of the story. Right away Scieszka's book is presenting the second level of the story, showing that the characters are also actors and aware of their role in the story.

After the end paper with the Little Red Hen comes the title page, which appears to be in progress, for it is set up more as an outline showing where the title page should be rather than the actual title page. Following the title page is the dedication page, which is upside down, as Jack is quick to point out. Once more Jack shows that he is in charge of the creation of the book by discussing its setup. The book appears to be stabilizing into a more traditional picture book after the problem with the dedication page; there is an introduction by Jack, along with a Surgeon General's Warning about the stories, and then the first of the stories, "Chicken Licken," appears, only to be interrupted by Jack calling a halt because he forgot to include the Table of Contents. The characters, after commenting that he doesn't belong in the story, ignore him and continue the narrative, a retelling of "Chicken Little." It is at this point that the construction of the book interferes with the story, for the Table of Contents falls on the cast and "squashed everybody."

The book once again seems to be following a smooth, traditional picture book order — text and picture together, however odd the stories being told — until the story "Little Red Riding Shorts." The image that accompanies the text to the story features two white spaces where the figures of the wolf and Little Red Riding Shorts should be. On the page with the text, the two are seen stalking away from Jack because he's spent time summarizing the story and "We're not going to tell it again." Jack is left wondering what to do when they turn the page since their story was supposed to include that page. The result of them leaving the picture book is a blank page. The characters have essentially done to Jack in this book what the Illustrator in *Wait! No Paint!* does to the three little pigs, leaving him to cope with the repercussions of missing characters in this case rather than missing color. This time, however, it is the director left in the lurch by the actors. The actors' ability to leave the story completely also shows the third level of the outside world that Wiesner and Child's books contain since these characters depart the text entirely and force an end to their story.

The blank page leads to the return of Little Red Hen, who demands to know where the lazy people — from the characters in her story to Jack, to the author and illustrator — are. Ignoring her, Jack begins his own story, only to be interrupted once again, this time by the Giant, who doesn't like Jack's story and decides to tell his own, a cobbling together of fairy tale motifs beginning with "The End" and ending with "Once Upon a Time." At Jack's mocking of the story, the Giant demands Jack tell a better story, and so Jack proceeds to tell a looped story of the Giant demanding a story until the Giant falls asleep. Here again the tradition of picture books is challenged, this time by the type face which gets smaller and smaller with each repetition of the tale and which trails off the page without a margin.

With the giant asleep, Jack's book gets back on track with three more stories. Following "The Stinky Cheese Man" is the endpaper again, but this time the endpaper is appropriately blank, and comes before the end of the book. Jack claims to have put it there to trick the Giant into thinking the story is over. Naturally the Little Red Hen returns at this point to finish her story. As she asks who will eat the bread she made, she wakes the Giant and meets her expected fate between two slices of her own bread, and the book ends. The copyright page follows "The End" page, and is the most conventional of the pages until the reader notices that one of the last lines reads, "Anyone caught telling these fairly stupid tales will be visited, in person, by the Stinky Cheese Man." The Little Red Hen also makes an appearance on a very unconventional back cover, commenting about the ISBN number and wondering "Who will buy this book anyway?"

While the "fairly stupid tales" that Scieszka writes are parodies of the traditional versions, they still act as the first level of the picture books. The second level, in which the characters show themselves as actors, is also visible here, as is the third level, as shown with the "Little Red Riding Shorts" section. But this level is also the construction level on which Jack the Narrator exists. He and the other actors are assumed to be part of that world. That is why the wolf and Red Riding Shorts can leave and why Little Red Hen moves in and out of the book as she does. Since Jack is shown to be responsible for the creation of the book, he must be from the outside world like the reader, for the inside can only affect the story content, not the structure of the book.

Without doubt Scieszka's collection of folktale revisions strays the furthest from the traditional concept of a picture book. He not only presents a metatextual story in which the characters shape their own tales, as do Whatley and Wiesner, but he also lets the characters shape the form of the book itself. Lauren Child does a similar thing in her books, but whereas her character Herb is reshaping a book that some-one else has written, Jack is creating the actual book being read. Scieszka has taken the revision of the form one step further than Child has in her books.

The revision of the concept of picture books as well as the folktales adds another layer to the creative ways in which modern storytellers alter their stories. While the picture book form can be altered in slight ways, such as in the flip books, it is the more dramatic revisions of the form that are most interesting. What Bruce Whatley, David Wiesner, Lauren Child, and Jon Scieszka do with their picture books is offer mul-tiple levels on which the story participants can be read. Stock characters suddenly have depth because they are aware of their roles in the stories in which they appear, and they are not afraid to comment about these roles. They are also able to resist the stock nature of their characters by moving in and out of their stories and interacting in some cases with the very people responsible for their existence, at least in their present form. Part of their resistance is against the very type of book in which they reside. Picture books, as a major contributor to the spread of folk-tales in the United States, make a logical target for storytellers to work with. Challenging the form of the picture book is also a challenge to the tales themselves, for the readers of picture books, whether of folktales or not, have certain expectations. Even the basic flip books force the reader to turn the tale's tradition on its head, in this case literally since to read one side means to put the other version upside down. When it comes to the more elaborate revisions of form, the challenge is more direct. Characters demand to understand their role in the story and, if dissatisfied with that role, to have a better role. The result is the reshap-ing not just of the folktale but of the concept of the picture book and a chance for readers to join characters in contemplating the makeup of these staples of children's literature.

5

Feminist Folktale Revisions

Alison Lurie, in the essay "Folktale Liberation" from her book *Don't Tell the Grown-Ups: The Subversive Power of Children's Literature*, discusses the role of women in folktales, commenting that in contrast to *Dick and Jane* and other children's literature of her childhood,

> Fairy tales ... portrayed a society in which women were as competent and active as men, at every age and in every class. Gretel, not Hansel, defeated the witch; and for every clever youngest son there was a youngest daughter equally resourceful. The contrast continued in maturity, when women were often more powerful than men. Real help for the hero or heroine came most often from a fairy godmother or wise woman, and real trouble from a witch or wicked stepmother [18].

The literature she was often given showed women and men unable to have the same jobs, and the men were always the ones with the power; however, folktales did not show this same disparity of power. Women could be and in fact were as powerful as men.

Lurie's interpretation of folktales differs from many others who see folktales as inherently sexist. She comments that

> some contemporary feminists have joined the chorus of critics and attacked fairy tales as a male chauvinist form of literature: they believe that giving children stories like "Cinderella" and "Snow White" is a sort of brainwashing, intended to convince them that all little girls must be gentle, obedient, passive, and domestic while they wait patiently for their prince to come [18].

This commonly held position is due in large part to the particular stories that have come to represent the canon of folktales in the United

States. Folktales such as "Cinderella," "Snow White and the Seven Dwarfs," and "Rapunzel" present passive main characters who rely on others to save them from the bad things that happen in their life, to give them the "happily ever after" they long for. Catherine Orenstein in *Little Red Riding Hood Uncloaked* emphasizes this idea when she says, "Complete submission to these trials is the heroine's ticket to happily-ever-after — for if the heroine is loved for her beauty, she is *rewarded* for her passivity" (142, emphasis in original). It is this passivity that most irks critics of folktales.

Yet these canonical folktales, Lurie points out, are not typical of folktales; rather, they are the tales that those in power, generally males, chose to publish (20). Orenstein supports this idea, saying, "The stories of the fairy tale canon little resemble oral tales ... and the heroine triumphant has all but disappeared" (84). Often the compilers of folktales left out the tales with strong female characters and presented tales with female characters who had qualities that fit the ideal of womanhood of the time. As they were published and republished, they presented more and more passive heroines until they became the tales that are familiar today. Jack Zipes comments in *When Dreams Came True: Classical Fairy Tales and Their Tradition* that "one could say that the literary appropriation of the oral wonder tales served the hegemonic interests of males within the upper classes of particular communities and societies.... However, such a crude statement must be qualified, for the writing down of the tales also preserved a great deal of the value system of those deprived of power" (7). So while women were often ignored in the tales, the tales were at least validating a value system different from the majority. And despite this bowdlerization, the tales can still be seen as possessing strong female characters, even if they are not the main characters. In "Snow White and the Seven Dwarfs" and "Rapunzel," the most powerful characters are women, even if they are evil women and eventually defeated.[1] In Charles Perrault's "Cinderella" the fairy godmother is the most powerful character in the story, and she helps Cinderella because Cinderella has earned the help through her hard work and goodness.

Regardless of how these canonical tales can be interpreted, however, the fact remains that many people regard the tales as sexist, and this regard has influenced the way folktales are rewritten today. Zipes, in the title essay from his collection *The Trials and Tribulations of Little Red Riding Hood*, explains that revisions of "Little Red Riding Hood" that show stronger depictions of the title character "can be attributed to the gradual rise of civil rights and women's movements, along with progressive developments in child rearing and sexual education" (58). Though Zipes is referring specifically to "Little Red Riding Hood," his comments can be expanded to include other canonical folktales. The changes made to "Cinderella," "Snow White and the Seven Dwarfs," and "Rapunzel," among other folktales, reflect the changes in society in the twentieth century, and the changes in the role of women in folktales are not limited to alterations of the familiar texts.

There are four ways in which authors have tried to combat the sexism they see in folktales. The first way in which sexism is fought is through the reclaiming and publication of some of the less popular traditional folktales that have strong female characters. This is the reason Jane Yolen published her collection *Not One Damsel in Distress: World Folktales for Strong Girls*. In "An Open Letter to My Daughter and Granddaughters," Yolen says, "This book is for you because for the longest time I didn't know that girls could be heroes, too. Not heroines. Not sheroes (a term Maya Angelou made up). Because *heroines* and *sheroes* sound like lesser or minor heroes..." (ix). She is responding to the sexist folktales she learned as a child, and the result is this collection of traditional folktales, including "Fitcher's Bird" from the Grimms, "Molly Whuppie," and "The Samurai Maiden."[2] Ed Young's book *Lon Po Po: A Red-Riding Hood Story from China* also fits within this category, for it is a traditional version of "Little Red Riding Hood" from China in which the oldest daughter is able to outwit the wolf.

A second manner in which authors challenge sexism in folktales is in the creation of original tales containing folktale elements. These new tales often feature girls in positions of strength, whether physical or mental strength (or a combination). Robert Munsch, for example, in his story *The Paper Bag Princess* creates a story in which the main character, Princess Elizabeth, defeats the dragon through her cunning and then rejects the prince because he's "a bum." Robin McKinley's novel *The Hero and the Crown*, a Newbery Award winner, also contains many folktale elements throughout the adventures of Aerin, princess and dragon slayer. This novel is, in fact, a bildungsroman tracing Aerin's development from an uncomfortable princess to a powerful and popular queen. This type of feminist approach to folktales is also seen in some of the stories in collections by Jack Zipes (*The Outspoken Princess and the Gentle Knight*) and Bruce Lansky (the Girls to the Rescue series).[3] While these stories are not revisions of specific tales, they do challenge the sexist notions often seen in the form and thus fit within the scope of feminist revisions.[4]

The third manner in which authors take on the sexism in folktales is through switching the genders of characters in some tales. Mary Pope Osborne has written two stories of this type: *Kate and the Beanstalk* and *The Brave Little Seamstress*. Both of these picture books take the traditional versions of the tale — "Jack and the Beanstalk" and "The Brave Little Tailor," respectively — and present them with a female protagonist instead of a male one. There is no attention focused on the changed protagonist; the stories are presented as if the characters were always female. In *Kate and the Beanstalk*, which Osborne bases on the version in Andrew Lang's *The Red Fairy Book*, other alterations to the story, such as delaying the revelation that it was Kate's family the giant stole from, are not a result of the gender switch but of making the story more suspenseful.

The Brave Little Seamstress, on the other hand, has more significant changes in it. Instead of winning the king's daughter (or son) and half the kingdom, the seamstress is offered only half the kingdom if she can defeat the giants, the wild unicorn, and the wild boar. The storyline lasts a shorter amount of time as a result of this change, for the same night that she defeats the boar, the seamstress is overheard talking in her sleep by a maid (rather than a spouse), and it is one of the king's knights (rather than a trusted servant) who warns the seamstress about the king's plan to have her sent away from the kingdom by force. She is able to scare away the king and his men in the same manner as the tailor does in the original version, but the end of the story once again differs from the original. Once the king and his knights have run away "never to return," the seamstress asks the knight who'd warned her of the king's plan to marry her because "she'd grown quite fond of him." She also becomes the ruler of the kingdom.

This feminist revision of "The Brave Little Tailor" is interesting, yet the end result — the seamstress instantly proposing to the knight — makes the feminist statement of the tale seem less clear. Why change the reward for completing the king's tests so that it no longer includes marriage if the end result will only be marriage for the seamstress? Even though it is she who proposes to the knight, something that often happens in the feminist revisions, the fact that Osborne has her propose so quickly makes it seem as if she must marry in order to be a success. The final page of the story emphasizes this idea: "And so the brave little seamstress married the kind knight, took over the throne, and ruled the land for the rest of her life." Before she is able to take over the throne and rule, this statement implies, she must marry the kind knight. The knight is, in fact, receiving the reward usually reserved for the hero of the story, yet he is not the hero. Even the gender switch for this story does not remove the sexism inherent in the tale since the seamstress (and primary female figure) remains the reward bestowed on a male character.

Like Osborne's books, Gail Carson Levine's book *Betsy Who Cried Wolf* presents a traditional tale, this time the fable "The Boy Who Cried Wolf," with a female main character instead of a male one. Unlike Osborne's books, however, Levine's makes significant other changes to the story. In fact, *Betsy Who Cried Wolf* is more of a sequel to the traditional tale than a revision of it, for reference is made in the book to the other shepherd: "Long ago, Bray Valley had lost its sheep because of a mischievous shepherd." Betsy is an excellent shepherd who genuinely sees a wolf in this version of the story; unfortunately, the wolf is clever and hides before the townsfolk can see him. Betsy nearly loses her job as a result of his trickery and is forced to save the flock herself when, the third time she cries wolf, the townspeople do not respond. Rather than having Betsy kill the wolf (or lead him to his death), Levine has her character tame the wolf by feeding him some of her mother's famous pies. In return for her generosity, the wolf helps save the sheep when several nearly fall off a cliff. They become an incomparable herding team after this, and Betsy takes the wolf home to live with her family. While Levine's story is not overtly feminist, the fact that it presents a female character to replace a traditionally male one challenges the sexist traditions of folklore, as does the fact that Betsy is an honest shepherd unlike her male counterpart. She is everything that the original boy who cried wolf should have been and female to boot.

This third manner of feminizing folktales shows authors claiming the popular tales that contain male protagonists for females and showing that women can do the same jobs and have the same adventures as men.[5] The fourth manner of challenging the perceived sexism in folktales (and the most popular one) is through the use of the canonical tales that contain female protagonists perceived as weak. In these revisions, authors alter the traditional folktales and characters in a variety of ways. Some of these revisions present the characters as strong to begin with, while others use the revision to devise ways of explaining the characters' "weakness." Examples of this type of revision include Frances Minters' *Princess Fishtail*, Mary Jane Auch's *The Princess and the Pizza*, Diane Stanley's *Rumpelstiltskin's Daughter*, Jane Yolen's *Sleeping Ugly*, Ellen Jackson's *Cinder Edna*, and Gail Carson Levine's *Ella Enchanted*.

Minters' *Princess Fishtail*, a loose revision of Hans Christian Andersen's "The Little Mermaid," contains a very modern Mer-Princess whose prince is a "handsome surfer" named Burt. She receives her legs from the troll, though she does not lose her voice, and goes to live with Burt in southern California (G. Brian Karas' illustrations depict Hollywood). Though she loves Burt and enjoys her life on land, she misses the sea and her father. When she tries to get her tail back from the troll, however, he demands that she trade her voice for it, and it appears that she will end up unhappy much as Andersen's Little Mermaid did. But the Mer-Princess is too smart to take up that bargain and decides to take matters into her own hands. Unfortunately, she cannot swim now because she doesn't know how to swim without her tail, and two fish help her return to shore. It is then that Burt arrives again, complete with scuba suits for both of them so that the Mer-Princess can have the best of both worlds. He has even "hired a fishwife / To teach you how to swim." This same fishwife also teaches the Mer-Princess how to sew, and she then makes her own fishtail.

Though the Mer-Princess needs help to realize she can have the best of both worlds and that helps comes from Burt, which would seem to emphasize the sexism of the tale, there are several ways in which this revision is still feminist in nature. She will not be tricked by the troll when he asks for her voice, and she is brave enough to try returning to the sea without her tail before Burt brings the scuba gear to her. Further, it is the fishwife, not Burt, who teaches her to swim and to sew, and it is the Mer-Princess who chooses to make a new tail for herself. Thus in many ways the Mer-Princess is more successful than the Little Mermaid for she is creates her own happiness and is able to balance who she is on land with who she was in the sea.

Mary Jane Auch's *The Princess and the Pizza* is also a loose retelling of a tale, this time "The Princess and the Pea." As with many revisions, Auch provides back story for Princess Paulina to explain how she came to be as she is. In this case, Paulina's father decided to renounce his throne to become a wood carver, and though she loves her father and supports his decision, Paulina misses being a princess. When Queen Zelda announces that she's searching for a "true princess" to be her son's wife, Paulina jumps at the chance to return to the position she loves. She and eleven other princesses arrive at the castle to undergo the tests Queen Zelda has for them to ensure they are true princesses. This setup would seem to indicate a validation of the sexism in folktales because Paulina wants to be that ideal, yet already the sexism in folktales is questioned, for Paulina is pivotal in getting the position she wants as she makes her own plans to go to the castle and take her position. The first test irritates Paulina, who says, "Oh, for Pete's sake. The old princess-and-the-pea trick. That's so once-upon-a-time." This is the first instance of intertextuality in the story, but it is not the last. And though Paulina is aware of the "trick," she is still part of the very story that disgusts her, for she doesn't sleep well because of the pea's presence. So once again the stereotypical nature of a "princess" is both questioned and validated by the tale.

The pea test is not the only she must endure, however. The next day Paulina and the remaining four princesses are required to write an essay called "Why I Want to Have the Gracious and Exquisitely Beautiful Queen Zelda for My Mother-In-Law" and then perform a second test — trying on a glass slipper, the second major instance of intertextuality. Paulina is once again disgusted by the test and demands, "For Pete's sake, you never heard of sneakers?" yet she passes this test as she had the first one. She and the remaining two princesses — described as if they are Snow White and Rapunzel though never named — must then perform a third test, cooking a feast. Paulina once again objects to the test and incurs the ire of the queen, who dislikes Paulina because she has "a big mouth." Because the other two princesses beat her to most of the good ingredients to make their feast, Paulina is left with only a small amount to create her feast and no bowls or other equipment for making it. She does her best with the few ingredients she does have — "some flour, yeast, water, three overripe tomatoes, and a hunk of stale cheese" — but finally decides being a princess is not worth the trouble. When the queen threatens to behead the losers, Paulina is left scrambling to make something edible from the mess and ends up sprinkling some garlic and herbs (which she'd brought with her for good luck) over the concoction she created before placing it in the fireplace.

The result — a pizza, so named because of Paulina's penchant for saying "For Pete's sake" and her problems coming up with a name for the concoction — pleases the queen and prince so much that they declare Paulina the winner. It is at this point that the queen tells Paulina she was only kidding about beheading her, to which Paulina replies, "Then I was only kidding about wanting to marry Prince Drupert. Who needs him? I have other plans." She leaves the castle and opens a pizza house, which the queen and Prince Drupert frequent on the cook's night off. This revision of "The Princes and the Pea" features a very strong female protagonist (as well as antagonist in the form of Queen Zelda) and is clearly a feminist tale since it emphasizes not only the resourcefulness of Paulina in her victory but also her spirit. She is not afraid to speak her mind, even when she annoys the queen, and she is aware of the stereotypes of princesses even as she still fits some of those stereotypes— most noticeably in the pea test and the slipper test. That she rejects marriage to the prince at the end and becomes self-sufficient as a business owner further showcases her strength as a character. Unlike the traditional princess from "The Princess and the Pea," Paulina knows what she wants and works toward that goal, yet shows that she is not afraid to change her mind when the original goal loses its appeal. She is a much stronger female character than the one in the traditional "The Princess and the Pea."

Like *Princess Fishtail* and *The Princess and the Pizza*, *Rumpelstiltskin's Daughter* by Diane Stanley is a loose revision of a tale — "Rumpelstiltskin." Stanley presents a fairly traditional version of this folktale until the place where the original story should end. On the third night that the miller's daughter Meredith is supposed to spin a room full of straw for the king, Rumpelstiltskin returns and demands her first child as payment, explaining that he will take good care of the child. Meredith tells him "I'd rather marry *you* than that jerk!" Here, as in the Auch revision, the traditionally passive heroine takes control of her own life, choosing marriage to Rumpelstiltskin rather than the greedy king. The remainder of the story, most of the picture book, is about their daughter, Hope. Hope is happy with her life with her parents, who have all they need to be happy. Most of the things they need they can produce for themselves, but any time they need something from town, Rumpelstiltskin spins gold to pay for the items. When the king finds out about the gold being exchanged, he orders his men to go get Hope, who is the one exchanging it in town, and bring her to his castle.

On the way there, Hope notices how poor the people are and witnesses how much they dislike the king. When he demands she spin straw into gold, which is not one of her talents, she instead tricks him into thinking her late grandfather taught her to make it in an attempt to protect her father. His greed makes him willing to do anything she asks to get more gold, so she is able to convince him first to pay his subjects gold to plant crops (telling him that she thinks her grandfather grew the gold). The gold does not, of course, grow, but the subjects are no longer starving at the end of the summer and are grateful to the king for giving them the means to produce their own food. Because the planting of gold does not produce more gold, however, the king is displeased, so once again Hope pretends to remember how her grandfather made gold, this time by knitting it. She convinces the king to distribute gold-colored yarn and knitting needles to all the people of his kingdom in an attempt to produce the most gold that can be made. Again the plan is a ruse, but at the end of it, the king's subjects love him because now they not only have food for winter but also warm clothes as well. The king is still disappointed that Hope does not remember the way her grandfather created gold, but she has done so many other good things that "as a reward I have decided to make you my queen." Hope has other ideas, though, and requests instead to be made prime minister. In that post, she makes sure that the king continues to take care of his people.

Clearly, Stanley's story is feminist in nature. Not only does Meredith choose to marry someone besides the greedy king, but her daughter chooses not to marry him as well. Further, while Meredith can still be seen as a prize, Rumpelstiltskin's this time rather than the king's, Hope is no one's prize. Instead, she is smart enough to outwit the king, to protect her father from the king's greed, and to reverse the fortunes of the entire kingdom. Further, she is able to name her own reward for her actions, and this reward allows her to be self-sufficient and to continue taking care of the kingdom by overseeing the king's actions. Hope is what her name indicates—hope for the kingdom—and this is perhaps why Stanley chooses to withhold her name until the very end of the story. Stanley has rewritten "Rumpelstiltskin" to validate the traditional villain, and to vilify (and then redeem) the paternalistic figure of the original while at the same time showing the strength of the female characters.

Jane Yolen's *Sleeping Ugly* and Ellen Jackson's *Cinder Edna* approach their feminist revisions in a different manner than Minters, Auch, and Stanley do. Instead of creating stronger main characters alone, both Yolen and Jackson parallel the lives of two very different characters. In Yolen's case the parallel is between Princess Misrella, "the meanest, wickedest, and most worthless princess around" (8) despite her outer beauty, and Plain Jane who is not a beauty by any standards, though "she loved animals, and she was always kind to strange old ladies" (10). Already Yolen is challenging the traditions of folktales by making the beautiful character unpleasant and the unattractive one good. They meet up when Misrella gets lost in the woods (and stranded by her horse) and stumbles upon an old woman, a fairy in disguise. When she demands that this woman help her get home, the woman leads her to Plain Jane's house, hoping she will be able to get them home. Because Jane is kind to both the fairy and to Misrella, the fairy offers her three wishes. Misrella continues to be rude and stamps her foot until the fairy turns it to stone. Jane uses her first wish to change the foot back, and then her second wish to undo another of the fairy's punishments to Misrella — having toads come from her mouth. Another altercation occurs between the fairy and Misrella, but just as the fairy is about to send the princess into a sleep, she hits her wand against the wall, causing both the wall and the wand to break, and sending all three women into an enchanted one hundred year sleep.

It is Jojo the prince who arrives to wake them. As the "youngest son of a youngest son with no gold or jewels or property to speak of, he had never kissed anyone before" (50), so he decides to practice on the fairy godmother and Jane before kissing Misrella. When he bends down to kiss Princess Misrella, Jane inadvertently makes her final wish: "I wish he loved me" (56), which the fairy grants with her broken wand. Instead of kissing Misrella, Jojo compares her to several of his cousins who are "[u]gly within" (59) and turns back to Jane, professing his love for her. He never wakes Misrella, who becomes a coat rack and conversation piece in their house. Yolen ends the story with the following moral: "Let sleeping princesses lie or lying princesses sleep, whichever seems wisest" (64). Though the story ends with Jane being granted her wish for love by someone else and not her own hand, she has earned that love through her actions, and Jojo's reflections on the shallowness of the beautiful princesses he knows make the love seem more genuine than it would have if he had just turned around and declared his love for Jane. The story is certainly feminist in its rejection of the parallel between beauty and goodness that is a staple of most folktales.[6] Jane as a self-sufficient, kind person has earned the love she receives, and though Misrella never wakes up to address this issue, it seems likely she would have rejected Jojo because he was a poor prince and thus beneath her notice. Yolen has, essentially, turned several standards of fairy tales on their head in *Sleeping Ugly* to present this feminist revision.

Ellen Jackson's *Cinder Edna*, like Yolen's *Sleeping Ugly*, presents parallels between two characters. The characters in this picture book, however, lead more closely related lives. Jackson starts with the opening for Cinderella, who is presented in a fairly traditional manner despite the modern pictures by Kevin O'Malley. The contrasting story begins on the next page and introduces Edna to the reader. Edna appears to be a more practical and cheerful girl who "had tried sitting in the cinders a few times. But it seemed a silly way to spend time. Besides, it just made her clothes all black and sooty." Rather than sitting in the cinders, Edna works to earn money. Jackson next contrasts the girls' looks, calling Cinderella beautiful despite the dirty clothes, while Edna is "strong and spunky" if not "much to look at."

When the ball is announced, Cinderella's story follows its usual path, with the fairy godmother providing her with everything she needs to get to the ball. Edna, on the other hand, wears a dress she bought on layaway using her own money. Instead of a glass slipper, she wears loafers, which "will be perfect for dancing." With no coach to take her to the ball, Enda takes the bus instead. At the ball, Edna is bored by Prince Randolph (who takes a break from Cinderella to greet her), but charmed by Prince Rupert who "lives in a cottage in the back and runs the recycling plant and a home for orphaned kittens." As Edna and Rupert dance together, they discover they have many things in common. Their conversation is cut short by the chiming of midnight, however, and both Cinderella and Edna rush out, Cinderella because of the spell and Edna to catch the last bus. Both girls lose a shoe on the way, and both are eventually found by their prince. Jackson gives a description of their life after their weddings, commenting that Cinderella lives in a palace and "went to endless ceremonies and listened to dozens of speeches" while Edna lives in a small cottage and "studied waste disposal engineering and cared for orphaned kittens."

Jackson's comparison of the two heroines clearly validates Edna, with her more positive outlook and practical nature. Because Edna can take care of herself, the story implies, she will be happier with her choices in life. The story even ends with the statement "Guess who lived happily ever after" and a picture of Edna, Rupert and one of their kittens laughing over a joke book. Cinderella's weakness is even noticed by the fairy godmother, who "was surprised that her goddaughter couldn't seem to figure anything out for herself." The stronger character Edna is the role model for young girls in this story, not Cinderella, and presents a feminist version of the traditional folktale.

Like Jackson, Gail Carson Levine rewrites "Cinderella" in her Newbery Honor novel *Ella Enchanted*. Levine, however, presents a clear reason for Ella's obedient nature — a fairy's curse (or gift, depending on the point of view) given at birth. Because the novel is written in first person from Ella's point of view, the reader is left in no doubt that Ella is not a docile child even though she is obedient. Ella explains her obedience in the novel's opening: "That fool of a fairy Lucinda did not intend to lay a curse on me. She meant to bestow a gift. When I cried inconsolably through my first hour of life, my tears were her inspiration" (3). Lucinda then bestows the gift of obedience on Ella, forcing her to follow all orders no matter what they are or from whom they come. Reflecting on the curse's impact, Ella later comments, "Instead of making me docile, Lucinda's curse made a rebel of me. Or maybe I was that way naturally" (5). Ella cannot escape the curse, for if she tries to ignore an order she becomes physically ill, but she learns ways to follow orders and frustrate those giving the orders simultaneously, whether it's to inch forward when told to move closer or to add a sprig of bogweed (which makes the person who smells it tell the truth and allows her to question that person) to a bouquet of flowers she's ordered to pick for her future stepsister. This Cinderella is clearly not the Cinderella of Perrault's tale, yet her story still parallels that of the traditional Cinderella, from the death of her mother to the acquiring of a wicked stepmother and stepsisters, to a fairy helping her get to the ball, to the loss of one of the glass slippers and the eventual return of the slipper.

The difference in this revision is that its length allows Levine to create additional events that show how strong a character Ella is despite her enforced obedience. Her skill with languages is one of her greatest strengths, and it serves her well throughout the novel, first when she helps a lost gnome child find his family and later when she is captured by ogres and uses their own skill with words to stop them from eating her. Her skill is compared with Prince Char's, and he is found wanting compared to her, for he does not have her innate capacity to learn languages. Ella's bravery and clear-headedness in dangerous situations also shows her strength of character in this novel. Rather than reject a valued friend from school at her future stepsister Hattie's order, she sets off on a quest to find Lucinda. Along the way, she must get directions to the giants' land, a trek that takes her through the land of the elves and into the hands of the ogres. When Char eventually asks her to marry him after they have been corresponding for several months, she sacrifices her happiness and refuses, afraid of what the curse will mean for Char and the kingdom since her obedience could pose any number of dangers if the wrong people learned of it.

Ella is also the only one who can break the curse, for Mandy cannot change it, and Lucinda, once she is forced to understand that it is indeed a curse and not a gift, refuses to lift it because it is "big magic" and she has renounced big magic. Though Ella despairs of ever breaking the curse, she learns that she truly does have the power to break it when she has the right reason. In this case that reason is the protection of both Char and the kingdom. After he comes to her with the glass slipper, he orders her to marry him, though it is not an order in his mind but a fervent request. However, his phrasing of that request — "Marry me, Ella.... Say you'll marry me" (224) — is presented as an order. She struggles with herself, for this is an order she dearly wants to obey, but she fears the consequences of saying yes now, just as she did when Char wrote his request six months earlier. It is this fear — for Char's safety and the safety of the kingdom — that allows her to break the curse, and she does so with a shout. Once the curse is broken, of course, she is free to marry him, but she had to be willing to sacrifice her happiness to achieve that freedom.

Levine's novel is strongly feminist. Despite her forced obedience, Ella is a smart, courageous hero who has the strength of will to protect herself and the people she cares most about. Though she is clumsy and small at the start of the novel, by the end she has grown into a graceful woman who can fit into her mother's clothes (literally). She has also grown intellectually, so much so that when she realizes the curse has been lifted, she can ask Prince Char to marry her rather than wait for him to ask again. Her love for Char is also not an instant thing; it has grown over a year of correspondence and thus seems more solid than in the traditional version in which it is love at first sight.[7] After their marriage, she also refuses the title of princess, instead choosing to be "Court Linguist and Cook's Helper" (231). Ella has shown herself to be a strong individual whose individuality is presented through her choice of titles that describe her abilities rather than her relationship to her husband. Levine's Ella is one of the strongest representations of Cinderella in folktale revisions.

Along with the presentation of a strong lead character where a weak one traditionally exists, Levine makes small digs at male characters. The portrayal of Ella's father, for example, shows him to be a rather unscrupulous man who will do anything to earn more money, including lie about the origins of some of his materials. In the end this trait loses him his fortune and forces him into his marriage with Dame Olga (a marriage that Lucinda also curses/gifts with eternal love). This negative portrayal is to be expected in some ways, though, for Cinderella's father is traditionally an absent and/or useless husband. The interesting depiction of men really comes in the character of Prince Char. Though he is a likeable character and worthy of Ella, he is clearly less capable (and intelligent) than his future wife. At the beginning of the novel, when Ella is saying goodbye to the royal menagerie at the palace before she leaves for finishing school, she meets Char while she is looking at the centaurs. They have a discussion about centaurs in which the reader learns that "They're not smart enough to talk. See how blank their eyes are" (41). To make Char laugh, Ella pretends to be a centaur asking for an apple, and Char later declares that he will capture a centaur and give it to her. This he does while she is at finishing school. When she returns home after her adventure with the giants, the centaur, named Apple, is there. What is interesting about this section of the book is the descriptions of Apple. He becomes Ella's confidante, and she says, "His wide-eyed attention was an invitation, and his trick of cocking his head to one side while I spoke made me feel that every word was a revelation, although he understood none of it" (145). A short time later, after Ella has talked to him about her concerns about her future stepmother and stepsisters, she observes, "Apple watched my face, his sweet empty eyes staring into mine, his lips curled into a smile" (145). Later when Ella meets up with Char at her father's wedding, she comments that Char "was smiling so happily that he reminded me of Apple" (150). This comparison of the Prince Charming character with a mindless half man, half horse creature puts the main male character in a position traditionally held by female characters and makes an interesting twist to this feminist revision of "Cinderella." The fact that Levine shows a shift from Ella comparing herself to a centaur to comparing Char to the same creature underscores what she is doing with the shift in power from men to women in this novel. Ella is not a mindless character, and by the end of the novel she has come to see that for herself.

The feminist revisions discussed above are just a small sample of many revisions that alter the role of the main female characters in familiar folktales. Despite Lurie's defense of folktales and the women in them, a large portion of readers of traditional versions of tales such as "Cinderella" and "Snow White and the Seven Dwarfs" see these tales as inherently sexist and by proxy the folktale tradition. It is only natural that modern authors of children's literature should revise the role that women play to reflect some of the changing views of women in the world. The passivity that Catherine Orenstein talks about being rewarded in traditional tales is no longer rewarded in the revisions. These female characters are a long way from their passive relations. Strong female character can be seen far more in folktales today than in the past, whether it is in "rediscovered" tales, new tales in a folktale form, or revisions of popular tales that change the gender of the main character or develop the traditional female characters. Since folktales are a reflection of the world in which the tellers live (or see as an ideal), it should be no surprise that women's roles were limited early in the publication of the tales or that they are now, with the greater power women have in society, expanding to reflect that greater power. As authors continue to revise folktales, the feminist revisions will only continue to be written in an attempt to reverse the sexism, real or perceived, in traditional folktales.

6

Postmodern Folktale Revisions

In the explosion of folktale revisions in children's literature during the past thirty years, female characters have not been the only ones altered by authors. In addition to the proliferation of feminist revisions, there has also been an increase in the number of revisions that explore the role other characters play, whether those characters are helpers, antagonists, or other characters. These explorations challenge the standardized nature of folktale characters and force readers to reexamine the lens through which traditional folktales are presented. Many folktale revisions decenter the world traditional folktales validate through the use of these different perspectives.

Cristina Bacchilega, in her book *Postmodern Fairy Tales: Gender and Narrative Strategies*, analyzes several adult postmodern folktales revisions. She believes that

> postmodern fairy tales reactivate the wonder tale's "magic" or mythopoeic qualities by providing new readings of it, thereby generating unexploited or forgotten possibilities from its repetition.... Semiotically speaking, the anti-tale is implicit in the tale, since this well-made artifice produces the receiver's desire to repeat the tale anew: repetition functions as reassurance within the tale, but this very same compulsion to repeat the tale explodes its coherence as well-made artifice. Finally, and perhaps most simply, the postmodern fairy tale's dissemination of multiple versions is strangely powerful — all re-tellings, re-interpretations, and re-visions may appear to be equally authorized as well as unauthorized [22-3].

In children's literature, as in adult literature, the validity of the traditional folktales comes into question with each revision while the tradition still acts as the touchstone for the story. While a revision may have some coherence as an individual text, it is through the intertextual play that it is most successful. Folktales rely on the audience's understanding of the tradition, and postmodern folktales, as an extension of the folktale tradition, are equally reliant on the tradition, even as they struggle against it.

Almost any folktale revision can be seen as postmodern since all revisions are intertextual in nature, but those revisions that pull a character other than the traditional protagonist to the forefront of the story are particularly fruitful to analyze. While it is more common to see the traditional antagonist become the protagonist in these revisions, other characters also occasionally come to the forefront. This is the case in the revisions *Cinderella's Dress* by Nancy Willard, *Cinderella's Rat* by Susan Meddaugh, and *The Youngest Fairy Godmother Ever* by Stephen Krensky.

Willard's *Cinderella's Dress* presents a revision of "Cinderella" from the perspective of two magpies nesting near "a wealthy merchant's home." The first several pages set up the character of these magpies, who collect a variety of castoffs from the merchant's household, most notably a "gold ring that shone so bright / the magpies kept it out of sight." The point of view of this revision comes almost entirely from the magpies, and it is not until several pages into the picture book that Cinderella is mentioned by name as the magpies discuss her and decide to adopt her because they feel bad that she is being abused by her sisters. When they overhear the ball being announced, they're excited about it, wishing they could go themselves but also wondering about Cinderella and what she will wear. This leads them to create a dress from the items they've been collecting. The resulting dress is a pastiche of materials that includes "rose-petal tissue, silver thread," "amethysts," "golden leaves," and

> An emerald fan to cool her wrist,
> a topaz cat to hold her hair,
> a ruby purse with silver handles,
> and strapless, backless silver sandals

though the magpie mamma is unwilling to give up the gold ring. When Cinderella dons the dress to attend the ball, her stepsisters recognize some of the materials in it and tear the dress to shreds.

In tears, Cinderella struggles to fix the ruined dress and, as she does so, laments the loss of her mother's gold ring, given to her with the words, "Hammered from fairy gold, / this simple band can change your fate." The mamma magpie, when she hears these words, regrets clinging to the ring and returns it to Cinderella without showing herself. The ring calls the fairy godmother to her, and the story returns to the traditional "Cinderella" with the simulated jewels being turned into real ones, though "my small magic will not last." As Cinderella rides to the ball within the transformed coach, the magpies perch on top and go along. The result of their attendance is that "Now every magpie knows the tale, / although it happened long ago." The rest of the Cinderella tale, however, is not told. Rather, after the lines telling how all magpies know the story, a first person narrator appears, describing how the magpies build a nest outside her room and explaining how they tell their children "a favorite fairy tale." The book ends with the narrator commenting, "I heard the story just last week. / I got it from the magpie's beak." What had at first appeared to be a standard third person narration reveals itself to be first person and also reveals the nature of storytelling — passing stories from group to group — without telling the "happily ever after" end of the traditional "Cinderella." The marriage and happy ending for Cinderella is less important for the magpies than that they helped her arrive at the ball, and the final illustration shows the magpies watching Cinderella and the prince climbing the stairs to the castle.

Aside from the recasting of the main character from Cinderella to a pair of magpies, this revision exhibits another element of the postmodern, for not only is the dress a pastiche of materials, but so is this story. In a note on the copyright page, the author comments that "The black magpie is very rare and only seen by those who share the power to make a wish come true." Willard is thus taking lore about magpies and combining this lore with the folktale "Cinderella" to create a new version that is a pastiche of the two, a fact echoed by the pastiche dress created by the magpie.

Like *Cinderella's Dress, Cinderella's Rat* by Susan Meddaugh revises "Cinderella" from a different perspective, this time the rat that becomes the coachman (or coachboy in this case). This revision, presented in first person by the unnamed rat, only peripherally connects to "Cinderella." Instead, the rat relates his autobiography, which begins with the problems of being a rat, most notably hunger and cats. When he and his sister Ruth become caught in a trap, they fear the end, but they are released. As they try to run away, however, the narrator is transformed into a coachboy. He is unaware why he has been changed, but he follows the old woman's directions to "Take this girl to the castle" (10). This is a clear reference to Cinderella, though the rat is unaware that she is anyone but a girl. At the castle, they separate, and the rat in boy form goes to the kitchen where, as he is eating some bread with another boy, his sister, still in rat form, is discovered. Confusion ensues when the other boy believes that the sister was transformed into a rat, and most of the remaining story centers on their attempt to turn her human. Though eventually she becomes human in form, she is unable to speak (though she barks) by the time the wizard they consult declares himself too tired to keep working that night. By then it is midnight and the narrator finds himself undergoing a change this time, only this change returns him to his rat form. His sister, however, does not return to her form since she was transformed with a different spell. Life is good for them, however, since his sister as a human comes to own a cottage and takes care of all her relatives. She is also able to scare away the dangerous cats with her barking.

Though *Ciderella's Rat* presents only marginal connections to the "Cinderella" story, without that intertextual connection, the story would lose some of its impact. Several of the illustrations are based on "Cinderella," most notably the scenes in which Cinderella's dress is transformed and in which she leaves the ball at midnight. Further, the title of the story makes the indelible connection between the rat and Cinderella even though the rat who narrates the story does not even know who she is, let alone that she is the lynchpin for the changes in his life. Her story impacts him only from the audience's perspective, for the audience as consumers of "Cinderella" cannot help but make the connections. Even had the story not mentioned Cinderella in the title, the connection would be clear through the events depicted by the rat and the illustrations. Yet at the same time the story adds a new voice to the Cinderella tale corpus. Cinderella is no longer the focal point as she is in most revisions of the tale, yet the reader of this revision still knows exactly what to expect from her story even while reading the rat's narrative. At his mention of midnight, there is no surprise at the reversal of the spell that made him a coachboy. Even his version of "happily ever after," with the safety and end of hunger, parallels the "happily ever after" of Cinderella, and both are the result of the same story, since without the fairy godmother's interference, neither of them would have gotten a happy ending.

The Youngest Fairy Godmother Ever by Stephen Krensky, unlike either Willard or Meddaugh's revisions of "Cinderella," is a modernized, subtle retelling that tells the story from the point of view of Mavis Trumble. On career day, Mavis decides she want to be a fairy godmother because "I want to make wishes come true." Mention is also made of the

new girl Cindy who "felt like she had too many jobs already." While reference to Cindy triggers the possibility of a Cinderella story, as does the
mention of fairy godmothers, the story does not dwell on Cindy. Instead,
Krensky presents Mavis' efforts to become a fairy godmother, from
telling her parents, who use her desire to try to get her to take out the
trash and clean her room, to her practicing what she perceives fairy godmothers doing. She is shown popping out of store displays, making a
magic wand, and trying to help her friend Laura become a circus star,
a bid that fails though luckily without injury. She also spends time in
the library reading books about fairy godmothers and related topics.
When she finally decides she's ready to work her magic, she starts with
trying to turn Hector the classroom mouse into a coachman. The fail-
ure of this leads to her staying to clean up the mess, which allows her to
talk with Cindy, who offers to help because "I do a lot of cleaning up at
home."

This is the point where Mavis' story and "Cinderella" really merge.
While her practicing to be a fairy godmother and the tricks she tries are
often clearly references to Cinderella's fairy godmother, it isn't until she
learns that Cindy cannot go to the Halloween party because "I don't
have anything to wear" even though her stepsisters do, that the Cinderella story is explicit. Mavis as a budding fairy godmother "still had a
long way to go" before she could work magic on Cindy, but the text
shows several attempts and ends with a picture of her sewing a costume
for Cindy. Though readers don't see Cindy getting to the Halloween
party, there is an indication that Mavis will not fail in her first true test
as a fairy godmother. Once again the point of view of the character affects
where and how the story ends. The traditional end of "Cinderella" is
unimportant for these new, postmodern voices because the voices proj-
ect a reshaped version of the tradition that does not need to follow the
Cinderella character through to her conclusion. The audience already
knows Cinderella's end; it is the end of these new protagonists' stories
that is more important in these revisions that focus on secondary characters.

In revisions in which the antagonist becomes the protagonist, however, the end of the traditional story will often play some kind of part
in the revision, whether the revision is a whole retelling of the traditional
tale from the antagonist's point of view, as in Jon Scieszka's *The True
Story of the 3 Little Pigs*, or an original story that takes off where the traditional one ends, as in the case of Margie Palatini's *Bad Boys* and Simon
Puttock's *Big Bad Wolf Is Good*. Other revisions, such as Eugene Triv-

izas's *The Three Little Wolves and the Big Bad Pig* and Bob Hartman's *The Wolf Who Cried Boy*, present a complete reversal of the traditional stories.

Scieszka's well-known retelling of "The Three Little Pigs" is one revision that presents that story in first person from Alexander T. Wolf's perspective. The story, presented "as told to Jon Scieszka," originates from Al's jail cell. Because he knows that he is seen as an antagonist, he is attempting to clear his good name by telling the story from his perspective, insisting that "The real story is about a sneeze and a cup of sugar" (4). From there he proceeds to tell the "real story," which begins when he is trying to make a cake for his grandmother even though he had "a terrible sneezing cold." When he runs out of sugar, he goes to his neighbor's house to borrow a cup, but a sneezing fit comes on him and he "huffs and snuffs" until he sneezes the house down. Amidst the straw rubble is the first pig "dead as a doornail," so, not wanting to waste "a perfectly good ham dinner," Al eats the pig. The second pig fares no better in Al's quest for a cup of sugar, but it is at the third pig's house that the trouble really begins. Not liking the way this pig responds to his request for sugar — "And your old granny can sit on a pin!" — Al does try to break down the third pig's door to no avail and ends up in jail, where "The rest, as they say, is history."

Scieszka presents this humorous revision of "The Three Little Pigs" so that most of the events of the traditional version — including the death of the first two little pigs — appear. The different voice allows the wolf to be seen as a protagonist and the three little pigs, particularly the third one, the antagonists. Yet despite Al's logical plea, he is still seen as the villain of the events within the story, even if the reader of the book begins to see him as a possible victim. As in the case of many postmodern writings, however, the wolf sets himself up both as the protagonist and the antagonist, even for those willing to see him as innocent. Though he is logical in the presentation of his case, the altercation with the third pig reveals that Al has a temper and is perhaps not as reliable as he seems to be. The first time Al presents the third pig's response to him, he says, "And do you know what that rude little porker answered?" Though Al does not try to break the door down at this point, his unpleasant description of the third little pig weakens his position as victim. And the fact that he does shortly try to break down the door only increases his questionable innocence and his claim that "I was framed." As the traditional version of the story validates the pigs, this version validates the wolf, but only up to a point, and with the combining of voices that the intertextual nature of folktale revisions contains, the reader is able to see both versions as "equally authorized as well as unauthorized" as Bacchilega claims (23).[1]

Unlike Scieszka's book, which is a complete retelling of a single tale, Margie Palatini's picture book *Bad Boys* tells a new story that follows on the heels of both "Little Red Riding Hood" and "The Three Little Pigs." No explicit textual reference is made to either of those traditional tales at the opening of the story, but Henry Cole's first illustration clearly indicates that the "trouble" the wolves are in is a result of the bad endings of those stories, for Red Riding Hood and the three pigs are chasing the wolves, one dressed in a nightgown and cap, the other carrying a basket of goodies, into a corn field. Once in the field, Willy Wolf "stepped out of his granny skirt" and Wally Wolf, comments that they have had a close call —"As close ... as a hair on my chinny-chin-chin," the first textual references to other tales. As a result of the problems they had in their previous adventures, Willy and Wally decide to lay low and stay out of trouble, and they think they've found the perfect place when they discover a flock of sheep where they can both hide and not have to worry about food. Disguising themselves as ewes, they join the flock and introduce themselves as the "Peep Sheep." This third intertextual play introduces the nursery rhyme "Little Bo Peep" to this story, and Palatini plays up the intertextuality by having the wolves declare they've come home "Wagging our tails behind us."

The intertextual play returns to "Little Red Riding Hood" when two of the ewes they've run into— Trudie Ewe and Meryl Sheep — notice "what big eyes you have" and "What big ears you have." Then the matriarch, Betty Mutton, comments on their "lousy-looking coats" with a return to "Little Bo Peep" and declares "There isn't three bags full from either one of you." Desperate to keep their cover, they claim the problem is the humidity, something Betty tells them she can help them with. By the time Willy and Wally realize what the buzzing noise at the end of the line they're in is, it is too late for them to avoid being sheared. Only Betty exhibits no surprise when they are revealed to be wolves. She tells the other two ewes, "They're those two nasty, naughty —*naked* big baa-aad wolves." Once the wolves run away from the sheep, the narrator commenting "And the big, bad wolves thought they had trouble with pigs," they end up together waiting for their hair to grow back. Cole's illustration shows both wolves knitting clothing in the meantime. The book ends with the declaration, "Oh yeah, they were bad. Bad. Really, *really* bad."

Palatini's humorous intertextual play in this picture book, something enhanced by Cole's colorful illustrations, is clearly postmodern, but so is the way in which her main characters Willy and Wally are portrayed. Both wolves relish their "big bad" role, yet they are so inept that the term "bad" comes to define them differently than in the traditional version when *bad* means *evil*. For Willy and Wally, *bad* means *inept*, though they are incapable of seeing that meaning since they are caught up in their own publicity. They strive to be evil, of course, but the reader of this book can see them as nothing but amusing thanks to the word play Palatini uses and the illustrations Cole supplies. Both enhance the absurdity of these characters and thus question how audiences must approach the traditional tales from which the wolves come, for if they are laughable after the stories, they must surely also be laughable within those stories. Palatini and Cole have reinterpreted these fearsome characters until they no longer have the power they once had to scare the audience.

Like *The True Story of the 3 Little Pigs* and *Bad Boys*, Simon Puttock's book *Big Bad Wolf Is Good* presents a protagonist struggling with his "big bad" reputation. In this case, Big Bad Wolf is lonely and decides that it's because he's so big and scary and bad. In an attempt to gain friends, he decides that he will be good. When he tries to make friends with Mrs. Goose and her goslings so that they will play with him, however, they run away and refuse to come out. He decides to be good and helpful after that and offers to babysit Mrs. Chicken's chicks when her babysitter does not show up on time. The result is predictable — they run inside as did the geese. After rethinking how he can be seen as good, Big Bid Wolf decides, "I will be useful and good, and I will do a noble deed. Then someone will surely be my friend." He finds Mrs. Duck looking for Number Five of her ducklings and offers to help her find him, but Mrs. Duck fears he's already eaten Number Five and hides herself and her remaining ducklings from him. Frustrated at this third rejection, Big Bad Wolf decides, "I'll show them! I won't be good, I'll be BAD, BAD, BAD!"

At this point he naturally runs into Number Five, who, like everyone else, expects Big Bad Wolf to devour him, which Big Bad Wolf threatens to do if Number Five doesn't "stop being silly *this* minute." When Number Five cries that he wants his mommy, Big Bad Wolf tucks him in his pocket and takes him home where Mrs. Duck snatches him inside and closes the door. Dejected, Big Bad Wolf leaves, only to be called back by Mrs. Duck, who invites him in to tea, where he makes friends with her and all the ducklings. His final request to Mrs. Duck is that she call him "Big Good Wolf," to which she replies, "Don't be silly.... You will always be Big Bad Wolf. But you are *good*, too!" This final comment shows just how ingrained the label big bad wolf is in this culture. Wolves will always retain their title of big and bad no matter what they do to earn a "good" label, and it seems likely that Big Bad Wolf will still petrify everyone except the Duck family because of this enculturation of his character. Of note in this picture book is that at no point is there an explicit reference to any other folktales, yet the reader know so much about who Big Bad Wolf is from these unmentioned tales that it is impossible to separate this character from his storied relatives. There is nothing in this story to indicate that Big Bad Wolf was ever bad except that he assumes he must be lonely because of his name. Only the inherent intertextuality in that name makes this story work as it does, so while Puttock's text is not a revision of a particular traditional tale, it does act as a revision of a traditional character from several tales.

Unlike Scieszka, Palatini, and Puttock, who keep the wolf in the traditional position in stories even while showing how the story may not be accurate, Eugene Trivizas in *The Three Little Wolves and the Big Bad Pig* creates a complete role reversal of characters that plays off the tradition. In Trivizas' revision, the three little wolves "with soft fur and fluffy tails" leave home and promise their mother that they will "beware of the big bad pig." Instead of separating, however, they build a brick house together. These initial events signal a major alteration in the traditional version, in which the main characters are not only pigs, but also in which the most secure house is brick. In this revision, the brick house is the least strong. Though the big bad pig cannot blow it down when he tries— after an exchange in which the wolves refuse to open the door in the traditional manner, "not by the hair on our chinny-chin-chins"— he is able to knock the house down with a sledgehammer. The wolves escape and build successively more secure houses, first of concrete, then of "barbed wire, iron bars, armor plates, and heavy metal padlocks" as well as "Plexiglas and some reinforced steel chains." Despite the security of both of these new houses, the big bad pig is able to destroy them with a pneumatic drill for the second house and some dynamite for the third.

After their third escape, they decide that "Something must be wrong with our building materials" and, when they see a flamingo coming their way with a wheelbarrow of flowers, they ask for some to build their fourth house. The big bad pig returns to destroy their house, but as he takes a deep breath of the flowers, the "scent was so lovely, the pig took another breath and then another. Instead of huffing and puffing, he began to sniff." The scent so attracts him that "he decided to become a big *good* pig." Once the wolves get over their suspicion of his new behavior, they make friends with him, playing games and having tea and "ask[ing] him to stay with them as long as he wanted." The happy ending for all characters is a rare type of revision for "The Three Little Pigs" since most continue to punish the antagonist in some manner, not convert him to goodness.

The story itself seems a reflection of the "flower power" movement despite its 1993 publication date and sends a message that the beauty of nature will make peace possible when building more secure, separate homes/fortresses will not. There is no true security for the wolves until they change the type of building materials they use. This postmodern revision not only switches the protagonists and antagonists of the traditional story, but it seems also to reverse the message of the original which presents the straw house as being least secure and the brick as the safest. Nature alone in Trivizas' revision can save the wolves from the pig. This message seems also to be emphasized by Helen Oxenbury's illustrations, which depict all of the animals mentioned in the story without clothing. The majority of picture book versions of "The Three Little Pigs" portray the animals with clothing, but their lack in this version underscores the power of the natural in the text.

Bob Hartman's *The Wolf Who Cried Boy*, unlike Trivizas' revision, does not parallel the traditional story as closely. The title of the story invokes the Aesop fable instantly; however, the story is much more developed that the fable and centers around Little Wolf's dislike of what his mother prepares for dinner each night. He complains about the "Lamburgers," "Sloppy Does," and "Chocolate Moose" that is put before him and wishes to have Boy for dinner. Unfortunately, "boys are hard to come by these days," his father tells him. When pressed, his father assures him that if Little Wolf finds a boy, he will catch and cook him. The parallels to the fable begin after this, for as he arrives home, Little Wolf smells the "Three-Pig Salad" his mother has made and, to avoid eating it, screams that he's seen a boy. His parents come running and by the time they give up searching for the boy, dinner is ruined so they "make do with snack food tonight." He plays the same trick the next night to avoid the "Granny Smith Pie" his mother has made.

Little Wolf's parents discover that he's played a trick on them and, as in the fable, decide to ignore his cries the next day. That is, of course, when Little Wolf sees not just a boy, but a whole troop of boys. His parents ignore his cries when he calls to them and continue to ignore him even when one of the mischievous boys enters their cave and sits on their couch. Father Wolf finally looks up after the boy has gone and, when Little Wolf tries to get them to follow the boy out of the cave, refuses, saying, "From now on, you will eat your dinner without complaining." His mother demands that he stop fibbing. Little Wolf gives into their demands and "never, ever cried 'Boy!' again." The story ends with the line "And that's why the boys, at least, lived happily ever after," signaling that though Little Wolf obeys his parents, he is not fully content with the end of his story. Though Hartman's revision of the fable is more focused on the humor of Little Wolf's efforts at avoiding dinner, the parallels to the fable are strong, including the fact that this wolf who cries boy ruins his chance at a boy feast, much as the boy who cries wolf ruins his chance to save the flock he's guarding. Neither of the versions ends happily for the main character because of that character's own actions. Hartman's postmodern revision alters the traditional focal characters, but it also plays with modern American consumer culture, adapting it to the wolf world, most notably through the humorous food names, named using a pastiche of folktales including "Little Red Riding Hood" (Granny Smith Pie) and "The Three Little Pigs" (Three-Pig Salad), and typical food for wolves combined with popular modern food (Chipmunks and Dip, Sloppy Does, etc.).

All of the picture books discussed above present single postmodern revisions of traditional folktales and folktale characters. These revisions add to the multitude of voices that have come before them and told the tale in different ways, the difference for these being the conscious alteration of some of the traditional characters, whether secondary or antagonistic. They still, however, present a single reinterpretation, a single revision. Vivian Vande Velde, in her book *The Rumpelstiltskin Problem*, however, takes the next step in postmodern revisions of tales and reworks "Rumpelstiltskin" not once but six times, offering a variety of ways to comprehend this odd folktale.[2] Likening folktales and their development to the child's game of Gossip, Vande Velde claims that she wrote this book because she feels that "Rumpelstiltskin" "makes no sense" (viii). Her Author's Note contains many different problems that she has with the story and its setting in the "kingdom of the mentally challenged" (xi), from people's gullibility to Rumpelstiltskin's inept bargaining skills to the miller's daughter's weakness. The six different versions she has written, then, are her attempt to address the problems she has with the traditional tale.

Each version has one particular character as its focal point, and the point of view is usually limited to that character, though there are occasional moves into other characters' heads. Each of her tales starts out with the classic "once upon a time" and then moves into a "before" phrase that ties the traditional to the modern, a fact that makes her attempt to recreate the "original" motivation of characters a clear fabrication. The first version "A Fairy Tale in Bad Taste," for example, begins "Once upon a time, before pizzerias and Taco Bells, there was a troll named Rumpelstiltskin who began to wonder what a human baby would taste like" (1). Other versions mention Social Security and supermarkets and so combine the traditional and the present in a type of pastiche, however brief. The other thing that most of Vande Velde's opening sentences do is present the character from whose point of view the story will be told. In the case of "A Fairy Tale in Very Bad Taste," the point of view is the troll who longs for the taste of baby and goes out of his way to get that flesh. Another version, "Ms. Rumpelstiltskin," also presents the Rumpelstiltskin character's point of view, only this time the character is a witch who goes from being a plain girl to a homely woman to an ugly old woman who wants a baby of her own. And the story "The Domovoi" presents the story from the Rumpelstiltskin character as well. In this version the setting is Russia, and Rumpelstiltskin is the domovoi, a household spirit who lives in the king's castle and makes sure everyone is kept happy. The other three stories are presented from other points of view. "Straw into Gold" is from the miller's daughter Della's point of view; "Papa Rumpelstiltskin" is mainly from Otto the miller's point of view; and "As Good As Gold" comes from King Gregory's point of view. All of these different points of view allow Vande Velde to address her concerns about the tale in different ways.

Some of her first questions revolve around why the miller tells the king that his daughter can spin straw into gold and why the king believes him. Her resolution to why the miller tells the king usually involves the father being something of a braggart. This is certainly the case with "Papa Rumpelstiltskin," and after the miller and his daughter Christina escape the castle, Christina makes sure her father has learned not to be a braggart by threatening to tell of *his* extraordinary exploits fooling a king. In other cases the father tells the king this information out of desperation, as in "As Good As Gold" when they are desperate to survive after their mill burns down. In "A Fairy Tale in Bad Taste," the troll tricks them into telling the king Siobhan can spin straw to gold. The king's gullibility is explained similarly in this version, for the troll convinces the king that the miller is crazy and that he should give the daughter a break by playing along and taking her to the castle to rest. In most of the stories, in fact, the king does not believe that the miller's daughter can spin straw into gold until gold appears before him, and in the case of King Gregory in "As Good As Gold," he never believes her because he can see the straw sticking out of various places in the bedroom he has offered the miller's daughter Carleen after she arrives more or less uninvited at his castle. He plays along with her, however, until he can devise a way to get her to leave the castle of her own accord.

Another question that Vande Velde struggles with in her revisions is why Rumpelstiltskin makes the bargains that he does. Why does he take a small ring of gold and a necklace for a roomful of gold, and why does the miller's daughter agree in the end to give her firstborn to him? Further, Vande Velde wonders why Rumpelstiltskin then gives her a chance to get out of the bargain. Once again, the way she addresses this issue in the stories varies widely. In "A Fairy Tale in Bad Taste," the troll Rumpelstiltskin uses the tokens as a way to get to his ultimate goal — a very young child to eat — and he does not agree to give them another chance until they offer him "double or nothing" on the deal (14). In "Straw into Gold," the elf Rumpelstiltskin agrees to take the paltry payment apparently from fondness for the miller's daughter Della, and in fact he does not demand her first child but helps her the last night "for nothing" (33). He reappears later and pretends, with Della's help, to want the baby in an attempt to get the king to love his new daughter, but when their efforts fail, Della asks to be taken with him rather than stay with the king. In "The Domovoi," Rumpelstiltskin never makes demands of Katya, but she assumes he must want something for his help and makes the payments herself, including offering her child to him. He accepts the bargains only because nothing else will make her happy and he cannot leave anyone in his household unhappy. When he finally leaves at the end of the story, he decides that "Some people ... just aren't happy unless they aren't happy" (59). In "Papa Rumpelstiltskin" and "As Good As Gold," the deals with the "little man" are both made up by the characters, in Christina's case in an attempt to escape the king, but in Carleen's case to try to ensnare him.

The sheer variety of ways in which Vande Velde deals with her questions about this well-known folktale is fascinating. She presents a new collection of tales, most of which are a pastiche not just of traditional storytelling with a modern tie in at the beginning (and, in "As Good As Gold," with Carleen's favorite saying "duh"), but with other folklore. She incorporates characters and creatures from other areas of folklore, whether it's trolls, elves, or domoviye, or even the witch from "Rapunzel" who begins her quest for a child in "Ms. Rumpelstiltskin" and tries again later with "a couple with an unwholesome appetite for the greens she grew in her garden" (96). All of Vande Velde's revisions of "Rumpelstiltskin" present new solutions to questions about the story and, as Bacchilega comments about postmodern re-visions, "appear to be equally authorized as well as unauthorized" (23). The revisions expand the possibilities of "Rumpelstiltskin" without ever losing the initial thread of the story. In fact, Vande Velde's Author's Note can be seen as a retelling of its own, for she goes through the entire plot of the traditional version, however sarcastically it is presented, and makes sure that her audience knows the traditional tale as she sees it before she dismantles it and then reconstructs it in her new revisions. Her varied creations of "Rumpelstiltskin" epitomize postmodern revisions, for they establish clearly the importance of disparate voices over a single authoritative voice. There is no authoritative voice in Vande Velde, only an exploration of possibilities without a conclusion to tie them all together.

However folktale revisions are approached by authors and audiences, there can be no doubt that they are inherently postmodern in their de-emphasis of an authoritative voice. This is particularly the case with authors who remove the traditional main character from that position and replace that character with one from either a secondary position or even the antagonist's position. The new perspectives on the story from these other characters force audiences to evaluate what they think they know about the characters and story and force them also to consider that all versions may be equally valid despite the tradition. It is even possible to see folklore as a tradition, from its very roots, to be postmodern since it is a tradition that relies on the shifts and changes in authority and the de-centering and re-centering of the story for its existence, much like the game of Gossip Vande Velde refers to in her Author's Note. Whereas folklore originally relied on the oral for passage and the ways in which the stories were reshaped cannot be known, the revision of folktales in contemporary children's literature can be traced, and the disparate elements informing the revisions uncovered to reveal the depth of this postmodern form of writing. As Bacchilega comments, these postmodern revisions "appear to be both authorized and unauthorized" (23). They challenge the folktale tradition while simultaneously taking a place within that same tradition. They question the values of folktale convention, attempt to reshape it, yet never lose touch with that tradition.

7

Narrative in Folktale Revisions

One of the most common critiques of folktales once they are written down is that they lose their vibrancy as stories because they have been taken out of an interactive sphere. Oral, performed renditions of tales contain elements that written tales cannot possess. Alan Dundes argues in "Fairy Tales from a Folkloristic Perspective" that "A vast chasm separates an oral tale with its subtle nuances entailing significant body movements, eye expression, pregnant pauses, and the like from the inevitably flat and fixed written record of what was once a live and often compelling storytelling event" (259). Rudolf Schenda echoes Dundes' comments in his essay "Telling Tales—Spreading Tales: Change in the Communicative Form of a Popular Genre," claiming, "Fairy tale communication in the age of the book is thus nearly completely depersonalized and objectified. Even at public fairy tale readings the fairy tale texts are reduced to and cast into standard literary forms. The fairy tale has become a museum piece, like most of the daily activities of the traditional folk culture from bread baking to singing songs" (85). For both Dundes and Schenda, it is the performative nature of folk and fairy tales that make them unique and that define them as a genre. Writing down tales removes them from their natural sphere and indelibly changes them.

While it is certainly true that there is something lost from oral to written versions of traditional tales, children's literature has in many ways counteracted this loss through the use of various illustrators' conceptions of the tales in their picture books, though the loss is still there in the anthologies of traditional tales that do not contain illustrations. In illustrated books of folktales, however, the artists can reveal some of

94

the same drama that the oral tellers could, presenting the mystery and terror of tales as well as the pageantry in some of them.[1] In these cases then, traditional forms of folktales can contain some of the variety expected in oral versions even though the basic text remains similar.[2]

Folktale revisions take the next step from different illustrated versions in reclaiming a sense of the oral tradition. While there is still none of the interaction Dundes and Schenda desire, the revisions do offer new shapes to the folktales that, though they can be identified as related to a particular folktale tradition, differ significantly from the traditional versions, much as storytellers would likely have adapted their texts to their audiences. With this complete textual alteration, there is also no need for the pictures that make the traditional tales vary in a world that values books over orality. Though many revisions of folktales in children's literature are published as picture books, there is a growing corpus of revisions in the form of short story collections— such as Francesca Lia Block's *The Rose and the Beast: Fairy Tales Retold*, Vivian Vande Velde's *The Rumpelstiltskin Problem* and *Tales from the Brothers Grimm and the Sisters Weird*, Priscilla Galloway's *Truly Grim Tales*, and Ellen Datlow and Terri Windling's collections *A Wolf at the Door and Other Retold Fairy Tales* and *Swan Sister: Fairy Tales Retold*— as well as novels. One of the main ways in which these new, unillustrated texts alter the traditional version is through different narrative techniques that bring the stories to their audiences from new perspectives.

In written versions of traditional folktales, the narrative structure appears as formulaic as the content of the tales. In addition to the use of standard openings and closings— usually "once upon a time" and "they lived happily ever after"— the stories tend to be told in third person with very little, if any, intrusion into the mind of the characters. If the first person is used in these traditional tales, it is often only a brief comment made by a narrator who is outside the story being told. The main characters of traditional folktales are never the narrator in traditional versions. Further, the point of view, while omniscient, is not intrusive. Characters are described in brief, unspecific terms and their emotions limited to basic descriptions from "scared" to "happy" without additional information to help the reader sympathize more with the characters. The very shortness of the tales makes fuller descriptions impossible.

Picture book revisions often retain this type of narrative, though there are some exceptions. Jon Scieszka's *The True Story of the 3 Little Pigs*, for example, is narrated in first person by the wolf, and Alma Flor Ada's series of books *Dear Peter Rabbit*; *Yours Truly, Goldilocks*; and *With*

Love, Little Red Hen weaves numerous folktales (as well as Beatrix Potter's *The Tale of Peter Rabbit*) in a series of letters that the characters,
from Goldilocks to Little Red Riding Hood to Baby Bear send to each
other. Authors who use the third person for their tales, such as Lisa
Campbell Ernst in *The Three Spinning Fairies: A Tale from the Brothers
Grimm* and *Goldilocks Returns*, usually follow a very similar style of narrative as the traditional forms since the length of the story makes a more
elaborate point of view somewhat difficult. There are moments, however, when the characters' psyches are revealed in more depth than in a
traditional folktale, such as when Ernst presents Goldilocks' thoughts
to the reader in dialog as Goldilocks "makes amends" for what she did
to the bears when she was a child. It is the use of first person in picture
book revisions that really offers a different narrative technique than in
traditional versions.

For the unillustrated short story and novel revisions, however, the
narrative shift is usually a necessity to make the revision work. The
longer forms require a tighter connection with at least one character's
psyche to be effective. Narratives that are presented in third person like
their traditional counterparts often have a point of view narrower than
the traditional version, whether the point of view lies with the protagonist, the antagonist, or some combination of the two. The point of view
may also fall to one or more of the secondary characters instead of (or
in addition to) a traditional main character. In addition to the third person, authors of folktale revisions may use first person narrators to tell
the story, and in fact this narrative technique is very popular in longer
revisions. These narrators, unlike the occasional first person narrators
of traditional versions, play a role in the story, usually either the traditional protagonist or the antagonist. The use of the first person ensures
that the depth of information increases for the reader compared to the
traditional versions, though as with the longer third person revisions,
the information is limited by the point of view.

Though none of the written revisions can counteract the social
interaction lost when tales are no longer presented as oral interactions,
they can and do increase the reader's emotional connection to the characters in the stories, something storytellers do through the "nuances" in
their performances that Dundes mentions. The expanded stories also
take a different tactic in addressing audience concerns about tales that
storytellers could deal with in an interactive setting, but they are no less
effective. Often these revisions, especially novel-length ones, incorporate storytelling events within the text and make reference to how sto-

rytelling occurs and how a live audience can and does react to a storytelling event. The revisions thus acknowledge their predecessors — oral tales — while continuing the folktale tradition in a written manner. The altered narratives of longer revisions of the tales bring the audiences closer to characters that already fascinate them from their more traditional written versions, and while the narrative alterations are visible in both short story and novel forms, the novel forms act as the most dramatic example of how authors can increase the emotional connection between traditional characters and their modern audiences.

The third person narrative used in revisions, while closest to the traditional narrative forms in some ways, offers authors a chance to explore characters in depth and expand the emotional impact of the story when used in a novelized revision. Robin McKinley's revision of "Beauty and the Beast" called *Rose Daughter* is a telling example of how the third person can be used to increase the emotional impact of a story.[3] McKinley's narrative in *Rose Daughter* focuses primarily on the point of view of Beauty, though in parts of the novel, the father's and one sister's points of view are revealed. *Rose Daughter* differs from many folktales revisions in that, while it does elaborate on the details of the characters' lives, it retains the naming conventions of folktales. The majority of folktale revisions that are novels name characters in a modern manner, giving a first name that is not descriptive, but McKinley extends the descriptive naming tradition in this novel. Beauty is still named Beauty, and her sisters are named Lionheart and Jeweltongue. Not surprisingly, Lionheart, the eldest sister, is a brave character who has something of a temper and is frequently referred to as roaring when upset and later becomes adept with horses. Jeweltongue, on the other hand, has a way with words and before tragedy befalls the family is known for her salons in the city where participants take turns being vicious with their language; later she becomes a well-respected seamstress who trains her tongue to deal with the people she makes clothes for. Beauty, the youngest, is the least defined of the characters, for though she does possess beauty, she is a shy girl who would rather spend time in the garden working with the plants or tending to animals. And late in the novel she reflects that "She was beautiful, but that would fade, unlike Jeweltongue's skill with her needle and Lionheart's horse sense. She'd always been the least of the sisters, called Beauty because she had no other, better characteristic to name her as herself" (249). Lack of a more definitive name bothers her, though she is practical enough not to let it show most of the time.

The naming conventions continue when the family moves from the city after their father's finances collapse. Discovering that they have been willed a house named Rose Cottage near a town called Longchance — roses being a flower very rare and something none of them have ever seen — they decide to take possession of it, far away from the place where they have been disgraced. Once they start going into the town, they naturally meet up with the occupants, including Mrs. Bestcloth, the draper; Mrs. Oldhouse, from the family who has lived in Longchance longest (and nicknamed Mrs. Words-Without-End when she reads her poetry); Mr. Whitehand, the baker; the Truewords, the local Squire's family; and Mr. Horsewise, the stable master at the Truewords' house. The beast, too, is known as Beast. By keeping this naming convention throughout the novel, McKinley retains the feel of a folktale even as she expands on the "Beauty and the Beast" story.[4]

Despite the naming convention, *Rose Daughter* presents a much more elaborate story than traditional versions of "Beauty and the Beast," and this difference is mainly due to the narrative. The novel begins with the mention of Beauty's earliest memory of a dream she is haunted by throughout the story — walking down a long corridor where a beast awaits her — followed by a description of her mother and an analysis of the mother's character. Though her mother is never named, she is described as being beautiful, fearless, and articulate, traits she passes on to each of her daughters in part. Beauty is five when her mother dies, and her life is irrevocably changed after that, even though she has little memory of her mother. Though the narrative is fairly sparse to begin with, as Beauty grows older, the depth of the narrative grows as well. With the discovery of Rose Cottage comes the first entrance into Beauty's thoughts in a direct manner: "Rose Cottage, she thought. What a romantic name. I wonder what the woman who had it was like. I supposed it's like a lot of other house names — a timid family naming theirs Dragon Villa or city folk longing for the country calling theirs Broadmeadow. Perhaps — she almost didn't dare finish the thought — perhaps for us, just now, perhaps the name is a good omen" (15). The cottage has a strong effect on her, one that is reflected in the narrative that reveals the nature of her thoughts in her voice for the first time. The commentary she makes on naming is also interesting here, for though her sisters are well-named, Beauty is uncomfortable with her own name (and its lack of a character reflection) and this discomfort comes across in her suspicion that Rose Cottage is named out of longing rather than reality, even though she has hopes that just the name will be a good omen. It is, after all, named after the scent her mother always wore and possibly represents a longing for what has been lost.

The next time the narrative intrudes on Beauty's direct thoughts is when the family arrives at Rose Cottage. As they are inspecting the cottage, which has lain empty for many years, the narrative moves in on Beauty:

> Beauty was standing in the middle of the floor, slowly turning in her place, half watching Jeweltongue touching the walls, half looking round herself, thinking. It does not smell of mice, nor of damp, but it does smell of something — I don't know — but it's a friendly smell — not like a years-closed-up house. Well, there may be horrors tomorrow — birds'-nests in the chimneys, snakes in the cellar — but... And her heart lifted for the second time since the Duke and Baron had written those final lines [breaking their engagements to Lionheart and Jeweltongue], and she remembered that the first time had been when she discovered the papers saying that they still possessed a little house called Rose Cottage [23].

Once again the cottage, Beauty's "good omen," brings her pleasure despite the hardships she has been enduring, and her inner thought are revealed to emphasize this pleasure. As the family settles into the cottage and a new life, the narrative remains close to Beauty and reveals her growing pleasure and confidence in this place where she is able to be herself, gardening and tending the animals to her heart's content. Of particular interest to her are the rose bushes that cover the walls of the cottage as well as form a large part of their garden, though she is unaware that they are rose bushes until they finally bloom for her. Her love of the roses, in fact, leads her to ask her father to bring her one from his trip to the city three years after they move, for the spring that year is so rainy and cold that none of her roses bloom. Her request is more to salve his pride, for neither Lionheart nor Jeweltongue will ask him for anything, and Beauty wants him to have a small quest for her, though she has no expectation of receiving the rose since they are hard to grow and the weather has been so miserable.

The narrative point of view shifts for a short time when news arrives of the father's returned ship, and, when he travels to the city to take care of it, the reader goes with him. This trip follows a similar path to the traditional versions of the tale, with the father learning that there is nothing for him from the ship before he heads back for home, though as with Beauty's sections, the point of view adds information about the happenings, from the specifics about his former clerk to his internalized response to the ship's captain's comment "you could die of [the winter's cold on the trip back], and then where would your daughters be?": "My daughters would do very well without me, thought the old man" (64). But, like his daughters, he has come to view Rose Cottage as home and longs to return there. As in traditional versions, however, he is caught in a blizzard and driven to seek shelter at an enchanted castle. The theft of the rose for Beauty differs from most versions; instead of plucking it from the garden, the father takes the rose from the vase on his tray, assuming there are many more roses around for his host. But the theft has the same result: the Beast demands that Beauty return to live with him within a month. The father's point of view ends shortly after his arrival back at Rose Cottage.

The return to Beauty's point of view comes once again with her dream, which has become more detailed each time she has had it. This time it is influenced by the scent of the rose her father has brought her, and when she wakes from the dream in which the corridor she walks down is lined with roses that cut her, she discovers that she has bit her lip and that "three drops [of blood] had fallen on the pillow slip, making a shape like a three-petalled flower or a rose-bud just unfurling" (79). This shape is an echo of the one made by the Beast's blood when he pricks his hand on the thorns of the rose her father brings, though Beauty is unaware of this fact. The connection between the Beast and Beauty, which has existed since her dreams began, is now even clearer. Her decision to go to the Beast, despite her father forbidding it, she labels fate: "But it was equally clear to her that this was her fate, that she had called its name and it had come to her, and she could do nothing now but own it" (81). With this label in mind, she departs Rose Cottage and walks to the enchanted palace, where the majority of the story takes place.

The narrative remains with Beauty during her stay at the palace, but an additional feature enters it as Beauty in her isolation — except for the evenings she spends with Beast — begins to talk to herself as well as to the animals that start to appear and to the palace's "magic" when she needs anything. This is also the section of the novel when storytelling begins to play a larger role. Earlier in the novel, Beauty learns of a curse that is attached to Rose Cottage if three daughters should ever live there, but no one explains the full curse to her because they think it irrelevant as Lionheart has disguised herself as a boy to work with the Squire's horses. Once she has to leave home to join the Beast, Beauty and her family assume it has something to do with the curse, though they do not learn the content of the curse until much later. While she is at the palace,

Beauty begins to dream different dreams in which she sees her family in snippets of discussion, first worrying about her and later progressing in their lives. She also tends the Beast's roses, which are dying, and socializes with him in the evenings at dinner. One evening, they climb to the roof and start discussing constellations, a conversation which leads to them relating the stories of the various constellations. This is also the evening that Beauty discovers the Beast is an artist and that he has depicted the stories of the constellations on the roof. At the end of the evening, Beauty, who has always sympathized with the Beast, does not refuse the Beast's marriage proposal but instead wishes him "good night" as she leaves him. Though not an acceptance, it is no longer an outright rejection either. The sharing of stories — as well as seeing the Beast's artistry — has tightened the connection between these characters.

The next night when Beauty is collecting fertilizer for the roses, she ponders her role at the palace: "This is a story like any nursery tale of magic? Where any maiden will do, any — any — monster, any hero, so long as they meet the right mysterious old women and discover the right enchanted doors during the right haunted midnights..." (192). Beauty has difficulty seeing herself as special, and her concerns about her role — and whether any maiden could substitute for her — reflect her self-doubt. She is, however, a practical person, and a short time later shakes off her concerns, saying, "Well, I cannot know that, can I? I can only do what I can do — what I can guess to try — because I am the one who is here. *I* am the one who is here. Perhaps it will make a good nursery tale some-day" (192). She has shifted herself from being a pawn in a nursery tale to the originator of her own nursery tale in just a few moments, and these words strengthen her, though she still feels as if she needs the "small comfort" — warmth she can call by cupping her hands — given to her by a retired sorcerer's familiar, a need for which she is rebuked.

The most significant use of storytelling appears the next day. When Beauty climbs a ladder to examine the weathervane on the glasshouse that holds the Beast's roses, she becomes caught up in a storm so violent she loses consciousness while clinging to the weathervane and "dreams" that she is at a literary night at Mrs. Oldhouse's home where her father, Jeweltongue, and others are sharing their works. Mrs. Old-house's cat Becky stares at the chair in which Beauty sits, and Mrs. Old-house attributes the attention to their ghost, a comment that leads to her telling the story of the ghost, a story that ties into the reason magic, so abundant in most places in this novel, does not live in Longchance, as well as how Rose Cottage is connected to the story. This storytelling event is highly interactive and in fact resembles Dundes' list of "nuances" of a storytelling event. The story also has the traditional narrative form that *Rose Daughter* itself lacks, for Mrs. Oldhouse reveals the details without delving into characters' psyches.

Following Mrs. Oldhouse's story, Jack Trueword, one of the few characters with a non-descriptive given name, enters the room and gives his own version of the same story, but his story is told from the point of view of the character portrayed as the villain in Mrs. Oldhouse's story, and so the interpretation of the events, whether true or not, varies greatly between the stories. This story variation within the novel shows the malice that Jack feels for Jeweltongue — who had refused his advances earlier in the novel — and her family, and his disregard of anyone's feelings. His story is also less interactive, for he tells it as if it were truth, whereas Mrs. Oldhouse had told hers with the warning that it was what she had heard but that no one knows if it is a true story. The use of storytelling here also emphasizes how stories alter with their teller and over time, since Jack Trueword can be seen as a more modern teller of the story than the elder Mrs. Oldhouse. McKinley is essentially recreating the way storytelling was performed before writing took precedence over orality, and she is doing so within the new tradition of rewriting (as opposed to retelling) tales. Just as what Jack Trueword tells holds a basic connection to Mrs. Oldhouse's story, so too does McKinley's *Rose Daughter* (and *Beauty* before it) hold the basic connection to "Beauty and the Beast."

The offsetting versions of the stories here lead to the revelation of the curse on Rose Cottage: "Three in a bower / And a rose in flower / Until that hour / Stand wall and tower" (227). Mrs. Oldhouse deconstructs the curse, which the children of Longchance skip rope to, to tie it to Rose Cottage, but as with the other story, she cannot definitely explain the story. She can only offer speculation, and before much discussion of the curse can be had, Beauty is seen briefly by Jeweltongue before she is brought back to herself clinging to the weathervane. After being helped down the ladder by Beast, Beauty enters the glasshouse and discovers that her roses have grown and bloomed for her. Feeling that she has done what she came to accomplish, she begs the Beast to let her go see her family, which he does with the admonition that if all of the petals drop from the rose he gives her, he will die, a warning that chills her and nearly makes her change her mind about leaving. Before she can change her mind, however, the Beast places a rose petal in her mouth and she is returned to Rose Cottage.

It is at this point that the narrative point of view shifts again, this time to Jeweltongue, who is still at Mrs. Oldhouse's home. This shift serves to reveal how Beauty's family has explained away her absence, as well as how the townspeople react to the truth being revealed, not just about Beauty but about Lionheart's disguise. Not surprisingly, they are supportive of the whole family. The narrative shift also allows readers to see how Jeweltongue comes to find Beauty, for the cat Becky who had seen Beauty and triggered the tale telling, commands everyone's attention and convinces Jeweltongue to follow her, leading her to Rose Cottage, where she arrives just as Lionheart does. During the reunion that follows, the point of view shifts back to Beauty, who is shocked to learn that the seven days she thought she was away were seven months to her family; she is also worried about Beast and concerned that she cannot remember his final admonitions to her. When she finally does remember his warning about the rose, it is too late, for the petals have fallen during the short time she has spoken with her sisters. Desperate, she searches for the two cuttings of the original rose that she planted before leaving for the Beast's castle and finds a single unfurling bud. At this moment, though she loves her sisters dearly, Beauty makes the final transition to individuality and understands that her life is on a different path than her sisters'. She is continuing to form her own "nursery story."

With a promise to return when she can, she plucks a petal from the new rose, places it into her mouth, and finds herself in a corridor of the palace that replicates her recurring dream. At first, she is caught up in the dream and struggles, deprived of some of her senses, to walk the path in the direction she always walks in her dream. When following this path proves exhausting and unfruitful, she changes her fate — and the Beast's — by turning around and walking in the opposite direction, defying both the dream and the palace, which tries to punish her for breaking the rules of the dream. The remainder of her search for the Beast reveals her continued defiance of the palace's attempt to keep them separate. Eventually, after she is misled down several corridors in the palace, she escapes the confines of it by climbing out a window and finds the Beast, nearly dead, in the wild woods near the palace. Her declaration of love and promise to marry the Beast follows her discovery, but this is where McKinley's revision makes it greatest departure from "Beauty and the Beast." As the magic responds to her declaration —"There was a noise like a thunderclap, and the ground shook, as if the lightning bolt it heralded had struck within the glen where they lay" (273)— Beauty tries not to be afraid, thinking, "This is the baying of wicked magic, but we

have won. I know we have won. It can do nothing to us now but howl....
It will be over soon, and I will tell the Beast again that I wish to marry
him, for I am not sure that he heard" (274). Whereas traditional versions of "Beauty and the Beast" use this moment as the point that the
Beast is returned to his human form, McKinley uses this moment to
present a third version of the story told by Mrs. Oldhouse and Jack Trueword.

The old woman who has been supplying cheese and milk to the
palace, where no animals were willing to live — except Fourpaws the
cat — before Beauty's arrival, tells her that Beauty has a choice to make:
she can choose to keep the Beast in his Beast form and return with him
to Longchance, or she can "return your Beast to what he was before"
(274), a choice that brings with it wealth and influence as well as a handsome mate. Before Beauty makes her choice, however, she comments,
"I think you are not telling me all of this story" (275). It is at this point
that the old woman tells the third version of the story Beauty overheard
at Mrs. Oldhouse's home, this time from the point of view of a participant in the story, for the old woman, Beauty learns, was the greenwitch
who had known the Beast as a human and who had raised Beauty's
mother and bequeathed Rose Cottage to Beauty's family. When the
philosopher/sorcerer who is now the Beast comes too close to learning
"the first and last secrets of the universe" (276) merely because he desires
knowledge, the Guardians of this secret try to keep him away without
killing him and inadvertently turn him into a beast, so he secludes himself. The magic leaves Longchance only after another sorcerer, wanting
to know the Beast's secrets, seeks revenge when the Beast will not tell
those secrets simply because the secrets had been denied the Beast by
the Guardians. The result is the lack of magic at Longchance and the
Beast's complete isolation.

Though the old woman narrating the story is a participant in it, the
focus of her narrative is the Beast and most of the narrative is presented
in the familiar tradition of storytelling — without much closeness to the
main characters' psyches, though her feelings are presented clearly as
with most first person narratives. The old woman's story shows the roots
of storytelling — the source of the original story — and Mrs. Oldhouse and
Jack Trueword's versions reveal how a story can evolve over time and
speculation, including the addition of a curse that does not truly exist,
for the old woman says, "It is no curse! It has never been a curse! Children are more sensible than adults about many things; can you suppose
that generations of children would have used it as a skipping-rhyme if

it were a curse?" (280). While validating one story, then, the old woman dismantles another then forces Beauty to make her choice between keeping Beast as he is and transforming him back to his human form. Once Beauty learns that "Your names will be spoken of in fear and in dread" despite the promised wisdom and power they can have, she chooses "Longchance, and the little goodness among the people we know" (281).

Her choice would seem once again to call for the end of the story, but again the thunderclap comes and she and Beast, who is barely able to move with Beauty's help, must seek shelter in the glasshouse from the hordes of evil magicks and creatures that are trying to attack them while the good magicks and creatures face off with the evil, including "two other Beasts, looking much like her own Beast, huge and shaggy and kind, but as much bigger than her Beast as her Beast was bigger than she" (283). Yet the evil hordes continue to come at them until Beauty finally grows angry, thinking, "We have come through so much.... Is it all for nothing?" (284) and she charges after them, clutching "the rag of the [Beast's] shirt in one hand and her embroidered heart [given to her by her sisters] in the other," both so important to her, and orders the hordes away with the final words, "*There is nothing for you here!*" (284). Her words act as a battle cry for all of the creatures that she had brought to the palace with her — insects and reptiles and small mammals — and also brings the final creatures that had been missing from the place — birds. These earth-bound creatures, who respond to Beauty's needs, drive the hordes away as Beauty loses consciousness. She wakes back at Rose Cottage with her sisters and the Beast, who remains a Beast, around her, and McKinley resolves the story with the Beast, who has been accepted unreservedly by her family, declaring that "everything is exactly as it should be" (287) as they plan their life together at Rose Cottage.

McKinley's use of the third person, with a very limited point of view, works well in her revision of "Beauty and the Beast," allowing her not only to show through the use of storytelling within the novel itself how this revision is part of the storytelling chain, but also to show how the country life that all of the character choose is preferable to their city life. This she does not only through the characters' comments about the peacefulness and happiness they find in the country, but also in how much more Beauty's interior is shown once Rose Cottage is brought into the novel. It is only the mention of this cottage that reveals her inner thoughts to begin with; it brings her and the narrative alive, just as she, who is in many ways Mother Nature personified, brings life to the enchanted palace and Beast's world. And while not all third person revisions work to this extent with storytelling, many use stories and story-telling within the revision as a way of keeping the connection to the "nuances" of storytelling that Dundes says are lost with the writing down of tales. The authors, then, are able to balance the tradition that they are following with the convention of longer fiction that requires a closer connection to characters than traditional folktales.

Like third person narratives, first person narratives, a popular technique employed by those creating long revisions of folktales, also allow authors to explore deeper emotional depths of the traditional characters in a more limited yet explicit manner than traditional versions. Margaret Peterson Haddix's novel *Just Ella,* narrated in the first person by Ella Brown, like McKinley's *Rose Daughter,* explores the role of oral storytelling within the confines of the written mode of storytelling. A revision of "Cinderella," *Just Ella* begins after the traditional story ends. Ella, renamed Princess Cynthiana Eleanora as befits her new position at the castle — and to hide her true origins — spends her days learning how to be a proper princess, something she has no desire to do, particularly since it limits what she can do, from lighting her own fire in the morning to going outside to helping one of her tutors who is having a stroke. But because she thinks she loves the prince, she is willing to endure the training. Ella is also aware that there is no place for her to go if she leaves the castle since she has left her stepmother's home and has no intention of returning to it, even if she were welcome.

When her religion tutor has a stroke, his son Jed replaces him and Ella gains one of her first true friends at the castle, the other being Mary, a servant close to her age who promises to keep her informed of the tutor's condition when no one else will. During this time, she also grows curious about the rumors about her, for several people, including Mary, mention magic and fairy godmothers around her but refuse to elaborate when she questions them. Finally Jed tells her that one of the stories about how she came to be at the castle says that she escaped from her stepfamily's home and arrived at the castle with the help of a fairy godmother. Here, as in the storytelling in *Rose Daughter,* rumor and speculation and elaboration have created new versions of a story, but in this case the narrator of the novel is the participant in the tale, all versions of it, and it is she who sets the record straight as the old woman does in McKinley's novel. Ella tells her version of the story to Jed during one of their lessons, explaining that all she wanted was to attend the ball, not to ensnare the prince. There is no fairy godmother or magic involved, just Ella's own initiative. She finds her mother's old wedding dress and alters it for the ball, and tricks a glassblower into creating the infamous slippers and giving them to her. Without transportation to the ball, she is forced to walk there in her father's old boots before changing into the uncomfortable slippers. Not wanting to arrive at the castle entrance on foot, however, she pays a carriage driver to drive her up to the entrance, and he offers to drive her back if she comes back at midnight. When she does run away at midnight, she feels a slipper crack and leaves it behind so that it doesn't break while she's running in it. The prince then tracks her down through the slipper and whisks her away to the castle.

Even knowing that her "true" story will not replace the gossip versions in the castle, Ella confides in Jed, who will believe her, and who in fact admires her for her initiative and strength. She is also unaware that her view of the story does not take into account the prince's side of it. As she becomes more and more disillusioned by the restricted life at the castle and less enamored of the prince, however, she begins to wonder about why he chose her. When she learns that what she had thought was a romantic ball was in fact a ruse to get all the women in the kingdom to the ball so that the prince's advisers could choose him a mate — and that the beautiful women were separated immediately from the less attractive ones, who were sent to a second ball — Ella is horrified. Her disillusionment increases when she learns that the prince does not love her, though she is also relieved by the discovery because she has realized she does not love the prince either. In her naiveté, she tells the prince that she has no wish to marry him, a move that lands her in the dungeon until such a time as she changes her mind.

But Ella's strength, the same strength that brought her to the ball in the first place, does not fail her. She refuses to let others control her life and thus her story. With the help of Mary, who brings her a shovel, she digs her way out of the dungeon and castle grounds though the "crap hole" then makes plans to leave the area so that the prince cannot find her. Her journey takes her to the border of the land where Jed has been sent, in acceptance of his long-standing request, to take care of the refugees from the kingdom's war with Suala. Just before she reaches Jed, as she is hiding in a field from the Prince's troops, she overhears another story about herself, this time relating how she has finally married the prince. Confused and knowing the story is false, she continues her journey when the way is clear. Upon reaching Jed's camp, she relates the newest part of her story to him, including how she overheard the story of the wedding. Jed, overwhelmed once again by her strength, declares his love for her and asks her to marry him, a move that equally stuns Ella. It has been clear to the reader almost since Jed's introduction to the story that he has been in love with Ella and that she, had she known it, was also in love with Jed, and the reader naturally expects her to accept his proposal and live happily ever after. But Haddix is unwilling to tie her character to such a fate so quickly, just as she was unwilling to make her a passive version of Cinderella, and Ella refuses Jed's proposal and asks that he give her six months to decide.

During those six months, Ella becomes the refugee camp's physician, learning the trade from some of the books she took from the library at her stepfamily's house. She also comes to realize that she loves Jed as he loves her. Before the end of the six months, Jed is called back to the castle to take up the position of priest to the king following his father's death. He leaves Ella in charge of the camp and returns, planning to convince the king to allow one of his brothers, who would rather have this position, to take over so that he can return to the camp. In addition, he takes the opportunity to try to broker peace between the kingdoms. While at the castle, he also learns the "true" story behind the marriage, and it is presented through the letter he sends to Ella, telling her that it was one of her stepsisters who married the prince after his advisers decided it would be easier to take another woman from the same household than to track down Ella and force her to marry him. Because she was heavily veiled during the carriage ride after the wedding, no one knew that the brides had been switched. Again, the story's truth has been discovered, but it is no match for the story that is being passed around the kingdom. Haddix is using storytelling conventions to reveal how the reality, the source of the stories, becomes covered and changed as more people learn of the story and pass it around. Though she is not dealing with a story many generations old, as McKinley was with the story of Longchance, Haddix is still dealing with how stories are told and Ella's story truly resembles the results of the "gossip" game that Vande Velde compares folktales to in *The Rumpelstiltskin Problem*.

Haddix also refuses to allow her storyteller the pat ending that has been created for her. At the end of the novel, Ella does not know when Jed will be able to return to the camp, though she does know that she loves him, but she also does not wallow in loneliness waiting for him. This refugee camp, at which she arrived looking much like a refugee herself, has become home for her, something she has not had since her father's death. She has a place here, a role that fits her far better than the seemingly idyllic role that has been created for her in the stories. Ella has made her own happiness, and no matter what happens with her and Jed, she is her own person with a job to do. The end of the novel emphasizes this fact, for Ella's final words are "I turned from my window and went back to work" (218). There is no traditional happily ever after for Ella, yet now that she knows who she is and where she belongs, she can be content with her life, a work in progress.

Both McKinley and Haddix present their folktale revisions to focus on the development of the traditionally passive main character, and the more limited yet more specific point of view allows readers to understand better what is happening with these characters, who are much stronger than their traditional counterparts. Most novelized revisions of folktales make the strength of the main character a focus, whether the character chosen to be the focal point is the traditional protagonist or antagonist. And while the more limited point of view would theoretically limit the reader's understanding of the story by narrowing the focus, in fact most of the novels do the opposite. Many revisions contain storytelling and thus present not only a revision of a particular tale but also some kind of reflection on how storytelling works, much as McKinley and Haddix do in their works. Folktale revisers appear very conscious of what they are doing with canonical stories and of where they fall within the storytelling tradition, so it is natural to expect them to reflect on that tradition as they rework it. The narrative techniques that they employ emphasize that reflection.

While the majority of authors of long, unillustrated revisions follow standard storytelling techniques of fiction, Donna Jo Napoli employs an unusual narrative technique in her novels. With the exception of *The Prince of the Pond: Otherwise Known as De Fawg Pin* and its sequels, Napoli's revisions, whether the narratives are in first or third person, are presented in present tense. Most of the narratives—those in *Beast, The Magic Circle, Crazy Jack, Breath,* and *Sirena*—are in first person. *Spinners,* written with Richard Tchen, is in third person from the points of view of the Rumpelstiltskin character and Saskia, the miller's daughter's character. *Zel* is narrated in both first and third person, the witch character narrating in first person while Zel (Rapunzel) and Konrad's (Zel's love interest) points of view are presented in third person. The three points of view alternate by chapter, as do the two points of view in *Spinners.* Though present tense usage in narratives is not unusual in certain situations, including dialog and "timeless" statements ("the train always arrives at nine"; "beautiful weather is always a cause for celebration"), the consistent use of it in a fictional text as Napoli presents it is uncommon.

In her article "Spinning New Tales from Traditional Texts: Donna Jo Napoli and the Rewriting of Fairy Tale," Hilary S. Crew calls Napoli's first-person, present-tense technique "an immediate-engaging narrative" based on Andrea Schwenke Wylie's work (78) and explains that in this narrative form "Protagonists are situated in a timeframe that can be defined as continuous-present rather than time-past. While the anonymous narrator of traditional fairy tales, as external narrator, positions readers in a predominantly, objective stance, Napoli's use of immediate-engaging narrative enables readers to identify with the subjective thoughts and feelings of characters who are subjects of their own narration" (78-9). Later in her essay, Crew makes reference to *Zel* and *Spinners*, calling those narratives "plural narratives" (81)—*Zel* containing an "immediate-engaging narrative" in it — but does not discuss verb tense in regard to the third person narratives. Presumably for Crew, the present tense has a similar effect in third person as the "immediate-engaging narrative" of the first person narratives, making the stories more present, more "immediate."

While the use of present tense has often been considered a way of bringing immediacy — "continuous-present" — to narratives, not all critics believe this effect to be accurate in description. Suzanne Fleischman, in *Tense and Narrativity: From Medieval Performance to Modern Fiction*, labels this narrative technique Historical Present (HP) and explains that it is traditionally seen

> as a device to dramatize narration and render it more vivid. This view has validity insofar as it is founded on the visualizing property of the PR [Present], which in ordinary language is primarily a descriptive tense, and on the ability of the PR to offer a mimetic representation of speech. These two properties together motivate use of the PR as a grammatical vehicle for performance, for *representation*. Less compelling is the second component of the traditional HP argument — that the effect of vividness produced by the HP derives from its ability to draw events out of the past and bring them into the present, since, other things being equal, what is present is more salient than what is not present. Yet representation need not entail "presentification" [285].

Fleischman continues, indicating that there is a "fallacy of linking the HP (or NP [Narrative Present]) to the minus-interpretation (presentness) rather than the zero-interpretation (timelessness) of the PR tense. It is the temporal neutrality of the PR that allows it to substitute for the P [Past], or for any tense that makes explicit reference to time" (285-6). Crew's description of Napoli's narratives as "continuous-present," in other words, would be more aptly described as "timeless" for Fleischman, and this idea of a "timeless" narrative works well within the folktale tradition, for folktales themselves, though each version is rooted culturally within a specific timeframe, have a timeless feel to them in terms of their characters and themes. This timelessness has allowed the stories to continue being passed through generations, the opening line of "once upon a time" emphasizing this nebulous timeframe, even though the traditional written narratives are usually presented in past tense.[5]

Napoli's stories are not all set in unknown times and places, however. *Crazy Jack*, for example, is set in "north-central England in the early 1500s" according to the Acknowledgements page; *Beast* begins in Persia and moves to France, though no time is specified; *Zel* is set in Switzerland in the mid-1500s. The novels without specific settings contain enough other clear details to give the reader a sense of the timeframe and location, usually the European Renaissance. Yet despite these clear past settings, Napoli's work does have the timeless feel that Fleischman talks about in her text, and this feel tightens the connection between the traditional story and the revisions, which present much more specific detail than traditional versions. *Crazy Jack*, her revision of "Jack and the Beanstalk," begins with a conversation between nine-year-old Jack and his father:

> Father sets a seed bag at the start of my row. "Go easy. Make the bag last the whole furrow."
> "I will."
> He smiles. "You know how almost as well as I do." He takes another seed bag, balances it on his shoulder, and walks as he plants. His hands squeeze the cut corner of the bag; seeds pour in a thin, steady stream. Other farmers carry only half a bag worth of seeds in baskets slung from their necks; no one works as hard as Father.
> I cup my hands together. When Father first taught me how to make a funnel of my palms, I was only four and his hands were huge around mine [1–2].

The narrative here is clearly in present tense with the exception of the flashback, which is by necessity in past tense. While it is natural to assume that present tense equals present time, this is not always the case. In grammar, present tense can be used to refer to any time — present; past ("so yesterday we're at the park"); future ("tomorrow we leave at eight") — as well as to no time (the habitual — "flowers are pretty"; "I like traffic lights"). Is it not possible then that the use of present tense in narrative can be something besides a representation of present time? Napoli's use of present tense could in fact be less about the timeliness of the events —

making them appear to happen as they're being narrated — than about making the events more vivid for the reader, something that present tense does inherently as Fleischman points out. The timeframe of the narrative is irrelevant here; what is important is the vividness of the story and how Napoli creates that vividness through her tense usage.

Later in *Crazy Jack*, Jack relates his father's death:

> Lightning flashes and for several seconds I can see him, climbing steady and straight-backed. He doesn't look down. Lightning flashes again as Father stops and raises his face to the water of the skies. He sings loud and louder. And he steps out into white air.
> Silence.
> Not even a shout [41].

That is the end of the chapter and the narration by the nine-year-old Jack. On the next page comes the next chapter title "Seven Years Later," and the narrative begins with the sixteen-year-old Jack being woken by his mother. This abrupt shift from child to teenager comes with no transition, though eventually Jack does recollect some of events that happened during this time in flashbacks. It is at this place, and in other similar types of time transitions in other Napoli novels (such as the three-year gap between Zel being cast out of the tower and the novel's resolution) that cast the strongest doubt on the argument for present time (or "continuous present" as Crew calls it). If the timeframe for these narratives is the present, then these transitions would need to be explained most fully, particularly since the characters spend time recalling events between the narrative sections. If these events are important enough to recall in a flashback, then surely they're important enough to show as they happen, in the same present time. However, if the vividness of the moments is what is important, not the timeframe, then it is possible to see the narratives as timeless — exempt from the strictures of present time — and the time gaps then work as they do for more standard past-tense narratives. Narration in present tense is then a technique that allows readers to feel the vividness of the narrative's events without a concern for the timeframe, and it explains how Napoli can bring life to Renaissance times and to her characters without time confusion. Her use of the present tense gives vividness to her revisions that storytellers would have been able to accomplish in an oral telling event such as Dundes describes in his essay, and it does so in both first and third person.

In *Zel*, for example, some of the most vivid description comes from Zel's point of view after she has been left in the tower alone, save for brief daily visits from Mother, for two years. Her isolation has rendered her nearly insane, and she has difficulty distinguishing reality from "visions." One day she stands on the ledge of the tower to throw a paper bird she has fashioned:

> She kisses the paper bird. "Be my soul." She leans as far out as she dares and waits. A wind comes. Oh, merciful nature. Zel lets her bird fly. Over the pines and away and...
>
> Oh! Zel teeters and catches her balance. A man on horseback has come riding from the north. The paper bird swoops. The horse rears. The man jumps to the ground and picks up the paper bird. He looks Zel's way. He waves the bird. He shouts words that are blown back into his mouth. His horse is Meta [whom Zel once helped attend before being locked away].
>
> Zel is spellbound. This vision is new and so real, it hurts. It moves. Horse and man disappear into the pines. Zel jumps into the tower room, her arms clasped across her chest. She hugs her own ribs in terror [160-1].

Zel's fear for her own sanity is clear here. She has longed to see Konrad on his horse Meta for so long that it seems impossible that he is here. His appearance at the foot of the tower later just confuses her further, and she will not believe he is real until he climbs her hair and joins her in the tower. As with *Crazy Jack*, the present tense narrative brings the events a vividness that a past tense would not have, without necessarily being a representation of present time. What the use of present tense does is enhance the emotionalism of the text, bringing another layer of connection to well-known stories, and in this sense the narrative structure serves to recreate some of the emotional response that the oral storyteller would have generated during a performance.

No matter in what manner the narrative is presented for these longer revisions—first or third person, past or present tense — one of the most common elements in them is how storytelling works. McKinley and Haddix, as well as the majority of revisers, examine storytelling by imbedding it as a tradition in their texts, revealing ways in which stories are passed in cultures even as they work within that same tradition. Napoli's texts at times bring in other stories, as in the use of the *Aeneid* in *Beast* or, more significantly, the way that Saskia, the miller's daughter, in *Spinners* is forced to cobble together the story of her parentage — she is actually Rumpelstiltskin's daughter in this revision — and the reasoning behind Rumpelstiltskin's demand for her child. In this case, she learns the truth but is unable to get Rumpelstiltskin to admit it, leading to the inevitable unhappy ending for Rumpelstiltskin and, because she now knows the truth, for Saskia. In many of these revisions, "truth," the real stories, are unable to come to the forefront, for society has chosen to accept a certain version of the story and is unwilling to listen to the true origins. The true origins, in fact, become merely another version of the story that storytellers can work with to fashion their own version of the story, just as these new folktale revisers are doing with their own revisions. And while these revisions, written not performed, cannot hope to achieve the physicality of a performance, their reflexiveness and developed narratives offer something that oral performances cannot. Further, Naopli's present tense narratives, with their immediacy and vividness, bring the audience a fascinating bridge between the oral and the written. Napoli's narratives are representations of storytelling performance, as Fleischman would say, and so they differ from texts such as *Rose Daughter* and *Just Ella* because they are storytelling events as well as novels. The novels are the bridge between the orality of true traditional storytelling and written stories, for they embody the vividness, the representative nature of the oral event, while being in a written form.

8

Folktale Revisions on Film

Folktales have long been a popular subject adapted by filmmakers. Moving picture pioneer George Albert Smith created a version of "Cinderella" in 1898, and in 1899 Georges Méliès also directed a short version of "Cinderella" titled "Cendrillon." In 1901, Méliès directed a version of "Bluebeard" and "Little Red Riding Hood" as well as several other less known folktales. In 1909, he directed a second version of "Cinderella" called "Cinderella Up-to-Date" followed by a third version in 1912 whose English title is "Cinderella or the Glass Slipper." "Beauty and the Beast" has also been recreated on film since 1899.[1] Though most of the early versions are shorts, once full-length features became standard, so did feature-length versions of folktales. The animated features created by Walt Disney are undeniably the best known film versions.

Though many different folktales have been made into film forms, it would be impossible to discuss all of them here. Rather than trying to cover all films, this analysis will focus primarily on several film and television revisions of "Cinderella," both shorts and feature-length. Short film revisions do not focus on developing characters because their length does not allow for development. As with short written folktale revisions, short film revisions of folktales lean toward humor rather than the drama of their longer counterparts. There are a couple of ways in which short films are created. First, they can be original pieces created as part of a series of folktale revisions, such as *Fractured Fairy Tales*, which aired as part of *Rocky & Bullwinkle & Friends*[2] and HBO's *Happily Ever After: Fairy Tales for Every Child*, among other series. But short film revisions are more often created as episodes of established cartoons, such as *Hello*

Kitty, Looney Tunes, Betty Boop, and *The Flintstones,* to name just a few.[3] In these revisions, the writers create revisions that utilize familiar cartoon characters within the framework of familiar folktales. The results tend to be humorous in nature.

   Fractured Fairy Tales, the series whose name is often applied to all humorous revisions of folktales, parodies traditional folktales. Thus Cinderella is a lazy woman, first shown lounging on a couch and reading a magazine, and her stepsisters work as cleaners in town. When her fairy godmother appears, Cinderella expects her to make everything perfect for her. But the fairy godmother has other ideas: she has Cinderella sign an agreement saying she will sell cookware by midnight in exchange for a life of luxury. Cinderella ends up at the ball because she believes the prince will be able to afford the cookware and allow her to keep the glamour her godmother has given her. The prince too is not the ideal of the traditional tales. Instead, he is desperate to get his creditors off his back. His advisor tells him to go to the ball to find a rich heiress. Not surprisingly things do not go as either character plans, and Cinderella ends up back at her stepsisters' house in the same situation she started in. But, as in the traditional versions, the prince arrives at the house. Cinderella once again expects the fairy tale ending, but the prince is not there to claim her. Instead he wants to sell her brushes. Other *Fractured Fairy Tales* are similar in nature, using the name of the folktale and a few of the traditional characters or elements and then reworking the tale in a humorous vein that incorporates elements of modern life with the traditional.

   Other short film versions take characters from established cartoons and combine them with plots of folktales. "Poor Cinderella" (1934) uses Betty Boop as Cinderella, and much of the cartoon follows the traditional folktale, but the transformation of Cinderella's clothes from rags to ball gown sexualizes her — with first the ragged dress disappearing and then her underclothes shrinking until they are very brief before being covered by a ball gown that reveals a lot of leg. It is very much Betty Boop playing Cinderella. Similarly "Cinderkitty" from *Hello Kitty* incorporates the characters of this show into roles that suit their usual behavior. Hello Kitty is naturally the Cinderella figure, and the two antagonistic cats, Fangora and Catnip, are the stepmother and sole stepsister. Grandmother Kitty becomes the fairy catmother while Tuxedo Sam, the penguin, is the prince. Other characters from the cartoon — Chip the seal and Grinder the bulldog — play new secondary characters.

   This revision not only adjusts the characters to incorporate regu-

lar characters from *Hello Kitty,* who are playacting in "Furry Tale Theater," but it also modernizes the story. Cinderkitty wants to be a wide
receiver for the school football team, but she settles for trying out as a
cheerleader in the hope that she'll win the prince's affection as he is planning to choose the head cheerleader to be his princess. Her fairy catmother helps her get to the football field. However, her stepsister causes
her to trip and lose her sneaker in the midst of what had been a successful routine. Cinderkitty runs off, but her catmother convinces her to
return. This time she is given the opportunity to be the wide receiver
when the starting receiver Chip is injured. Naturally she is successful in
her new role and wins the admiration of the prince though she runs off
before he can say much to her. In the tradition of "Cinderella," this
prince searches for the girl who fits the sneaker and finds Cinderkitty
cleaning in the chimney at her stepmother's home. With each of the
episodes of "Furry Tale Theater," similar adaptations occur: the main
characters in the cartoon take on roles similar to their established personality traits in the cartoon series. The other folktale revisions also
present similar modernizations, whether it's the use of TVs instead of a
spindle in "Sleeping Kitty" or the incorporation of a pizza delivery man
in "Kitty Locks and the Three Bears."

By contrast to the short films, feature length films are often self-
contained — not part of a series — and, though they may contain some
humor, lean toward the dramatic, much as longer written folktale revisions contrast with shorter written versions. There are numerous feature-
length versions of "Cinderella" that have been created for stage and
screen in addition to Disney's 1950 animated classic: *The Glass Slipper*
(1955), a ballet starring Leslie Caron; *Hey Cinderella* (1969), the Muppet version; *Rodgers and Hammerstein's Cinderella* (1965 and 1997); *The
Slipper and the Rose* (1975), starring Richard Chamberlain; *A Tale of
Cinderella* (1996), a stage production based on an Italian version of the
story; *Ever After: A Cinderella Story* (1998), starring Drew Barrymore;
and *A Cinderella Story* (2004), starring Hilary Duff.

One of the difficulties of creating feature-length films from very
short texts is the need to add material to make the story fit the necessary length. For romantic folktales such as "Cinderella," "Snow White
and the Seven Dwarfs," and "Sleeping Beauty," one way in which material is added is through the introduction of the male love interest much
earlier than in the written tales. In most full-length film revisions of
romantic folktales, the lead love interests meet, become obsessed with
each other, and must find and identify each other again during their tra-

ditional meeting place from the written folktale. Many variants of "Cinderella," with the notable exception of Walt Disney's 1950 classic, follow this pattern. Further, the prince's role is often greatly increased in these feature-length versions, and this more visible prince tends to be in conflict with his parents, particularly his father, over the need to marry and produce an heir.

Though the manner in which the love interests meet often varies in these "Cinderella" revisions, the result for most versions is the same — to present chemistry between the prince figure and the Cinderella figure. For example, in the 1955 ballet version *The Glass Slipper*, Prince Charles encounters Ella when he's walking through the woods to cool off after an argument with his father. The characters are antagonistic at first but eventually form an interest in each other, though the prince does not reveal that he is the prince, pretending instead to be the cook's son. The 1965 production of *Rodgers and Hammerstein's Cinderella* has the Prince stopping at Cinderella's house where she offers him water. This offering comes before she knows that he is prince, though she discovers that he is royalty during the same scene. Jim Henson's Muppet version *Hey Cinderella*, though shorter than most of the versions at fifty-two minutes, follows a similar pattern with Cinderella meeting Prince Arthur Charming in the garden of the palace when her dog runs there. They hit it off instantly, but Arthur does not reveal himself as prince, pretending instead to be the gardener.

The Slipper and the Rose, starring Richard Chamberlain, follows a slightly different pattern. Both Prince Edward and Cinderella see each other, but they don't meet until the ball. The revision *A Tale of Cinderella*, though based on an Italian version of the story, follows a similar pattern with Cinderella and the prince meeting in the square near Cinderella's house. They are attracted to each other immediately, though they do not know each other's name and the prince does not reveal that he is the prince. The 1997 update of *Rodgers and Hammerstein's Cinderella*, like its 1965 counterpart, introduces Cinderella and the prince almost immediately. This time the prince helps Cinderella pick up the packages she'd been carrying for her stepmother and stepsisters after she is nearly trampled by a carriage. The prince, pretending to be an average man, makes fun of royalty and royals' self-centered nature, but Cinderella defends them. They are both attracted to each other, and the prince tries to pick Cinderella up through flattery, saying she must want to be treated like a princess; Cinderella's response is that she wants to be treated like a person. When they part at the end of this first meeting, the prince knows Cinderella's name, but she does not know who he is. Finally, *Ever After* shows the early meeting of Prince Henry and Danielle de Barbarac when she, believing him to be a horse thief, knocks him from his horse with a well-thrown apple. She finds out moments later that he is royalty, and it is eventually Danielle who pretends to be someone else, taking on her mother's name when next she sees the prince at the castle where she has gone to repurchase a servant sold by her stepmother. Most of these versions of "Cinderella" have at least one of the main characters pretending to be someone else: often it is the prince disguising that he is noble, though in *Ever After* it is Danielle taking on a higher station, one that her stepmother has essentially stripped from her by making her a servant.

Part of the reason that the prince character wants to disguise his nobility is because his parents, primarily his father, are pressuring him to marry and produce an heir. It is for this reason that they plan the ball. This element of the films conflates the Grimm version of the story in which "the king had decided to sponsor a three-day festival, and all the beautiful young girls were invited so that his son could choose a bride" (Zipes, *Great Fairy* 469), and the Perrault version in which "the king's son decided to hold a ball and to invite all the people of quality" (450). Further, the film versions almost all show him to resent and resist this plan, something he does not do in the traditional versions. The ball is a decided point of argument between king and prince that leads in *The Glass Slipper* and *The Slipper and the Rose* to the main characters running into each other (or in the case of *The Slipper and the Rose* seeing each other). In other cases, the resistance to the ball comes after the prince meets Cinderella and decides he is in love with her, or because he believes be should be able to choose his own mate. In *Ever After*, the ball, which is scheduled to honor the visiting Leonardo da Vinci (the fairy godmother figure in the film), becomes the place of compromise for father and son when the king offers to let his son choose someone by midnight at the ball or become engaged to Princess Gabriella of Spain. Regardless of the reason for the ball, the prince is resistant to an arranged marriage. This resistance is a decidedly modern sentiment, one that the traditional versions of the story do not begin to hint at.

The development of the prince's character in these films demands depth, and this depth is usually created through the prince's early meeting with Cinderella and his resistance to his father's will. In *The Slipper and the Rose*, the problem with the prince's resistance is shown to be more than just an irritation to parents concerned with their son's happiness.

Though the prince's father is aggravated by his son's resistance to find a mate, he forces the issue because their small kingdom needs an alliance with another kingdom to ensure that it will continue to exist and thrive with the help of allies. This need for allies is so crucial that even after Cinderella and Prince Edward are reunited, the king and his advisers convince Cinderella that she must sacrifice her love to save the kingdom. Only a second intervention by the fairy godmother allows for the happy ending of the traditional tale, and since this genre demands happiness for all, the bride planned for Prince Edward falls for one of his cousins and the kingdom is saved.

Political intrigue also plays a part in *Ever After*, in which Danielle is revealed to be a commoner at the ball and rejected in one of the least traditional revisions of the story. After his hopes of marrying Danielle are squashed, Prince Henry plans a political alliance with Princess Gabriella of Spain, who is miserable at the thought of marrying him. This time, however, there is no fairy godmother and the prince himself decides against this political alliance. The political problems are not resolved as neatly in this version as in *The Slipper and the Rose*, but it is clear there are no political hard feelings when the wedding is canceled. All ends happily. The developed role of the prince in these tales may be a way for modern filmmakers to reduce the class distinctions of the traditional tales in which the prince's worthiness is established through his title. Because modern audiences are less likely to accept the prince merely because he is a prince, many filmmakers develop his character, turning him into a character as worthy of Cinderella as she is of him. The prince becomes a "normal" person, with all of the foibles and problems of normal people in these films, even while he maintains his title.

In addition to the expanded role of the prince, the fairy godmother also tends to play a larger role. Though often still a motherly or grandmotherly figure, she can also be portrayed by younger, more glamorous actors, such as Whitney Houston's portrayal in the 1997 version of *Rodgers and Hammerstein's Cinderella*. Her character, on seeing Cinderella's shock at her appearance, asks if she was expecting "some old lady in a tutu sprinkling fairy dust." The fairy godmother in *The Slipper and the Rose* is similarly disdainful of the popular costuming of fairy godmothers, commenting that the traditional outfits are "unsuitable costume[s] for a grown woman." The magical abilities for some of the fairy godmothers is also suspect or limited: in Rodgers and Hammerstein's 1997 version, she has problems creating Cinderella's coach initially; in *Hey Cinderella* she spends the beginning of the film having problems turning the pumpkins into a carriage; in *The Slipper and the Rose*, she borrows power to send Cinderella to the ball, explaining that it will only last until midnight; in *A Tale of Cinderella*, the fairy godmother has problems with her wand, a spoon.

The fairy godmothers are less overt in *The Glass Slipper* and *Ever After*. In *The Glass Slipper* she is an old woman who is something of a village outcast. She befriends Cinderella and helps her get to the ball without the flashy magic of most fairy godmothers, though her power is hinted at when a pumpkin and mouse are shown after Cinderella leaves the ball and her carriage crashes. The narrator at the end of the film confirms her identity for the audience. *Ever After*, however, has no traditional fairy godmother. Instead, the visiting dignitary Leonardo da Vinci takes on that helper role along with the servants at Danielle's home. They costume her and assure that she gets to the ball in time. Da Vinci also chastises the prince for wasting his opportunity at true love after the unexpected and unpleasant outcome of the ball. Unlike the other versions, in which magic is possible, this film is about how "Cinderella" could have happened during this time period; it is examining the "true" roots of the tale.

Another trend in the films over the past several decades is the increasingly feminist portrayals of Cinderella. In the 1955 ballet *The Glass Slipper*, though Cinderella is "feisty," she is ultimately a weak character, though not as weak as the Cinderella in the 1965 Rodgers and Hammerstein musical. She is also quite weak in *Hey Cinderella* (1969) and *The Slipper and the Rose* (1975). The versions from the 1990s all present a stronger Cinderella. Cinderella in *A Tale of Cinderella* (1996) stands up to her stepmother and refuses to return the amulet with which the stepmother has bewitched Cinderella's father.[4] In addition, the 1997 version of *Rodgers and Hammerstein's Cinderella*, as well as presenting a racially diverse cast, makes Cinderella stronger than the 1965 version. That strength is encouraged by the fairy godmother. And *Ever After* contains a Cinderella both mentally and physically strong. Danielle spars wittily with Prince Henry but also has the strength to carry him when given the chance to "have anything [she] can carry" after they are surrounded by gypsies. Later she also shows the strength to escape the sexual assault of Monsieur le Pieu, who has bought her from her stepmother following the ball.

A final trend in feature-length versions of folktales is their reflexive or metatextual nature. Each film makes reference at some point to fairy tales or elements of fairy tales. The film with the strongest reference to fairy tales is *Ever After*, which opens with the Grimm brothers going to visit an old woman. This woman brings up their version of "Cinderella" and they defend this version. She then produces a glass slipper and invites them to listen to the "real" version of the story, which she starts with the traditional "once upon a time" opening. Other film versions are less explicit in their references to folktales. *The Glass Slipper* is presented with a narrator who does not hesitate to comment about aspects of the story, or to let the audience know who characters truly are, as in the case of the fairy godmother. In *The Slipper and the Rose*, the fairy godmother not only takes care of Cinderella but is responsible for the creation of other tales. At one point in the film she is shown writing the stories for Scheherazade. She also compares her life to that of Hans Christian Andersen. In addition, Prince Edward, at the height his despair after losing Cinderella a second time, comments that it's "only in fairy tales the prince marries the lady of his choice."

Both of the Rodgers and Hammerstein versions contain smaller references to folktales. The 1965 version features the prince explaining that he does the "usual things" of princes, including rescuing princesses and slaying dragons; the 1997 version has the fairy godmother commenting on the expectations people have of fairy godmothers as well as on how the midnight rule isn't hers, showing that she is part of a larger tradition even though she may not dress the part. In *A Tale of Cinderella*, the references are made often through the father, who wants to dress Cinderella for the ball "just like the stories." This stage version also sets the events up through a secondary character telling the story of how Cinderella lost her mother and her father remarried. Finally, *Hey Cinderella* takes the references from folk literature into classic children's texts. It opens with the fairy godmother's problems transforming pumpkins, playing with the audience's expectations of the fairy godmother. Later in the film, she makes reference to Pinocchio, whom she thinks she left in the whale. Then Cinderella's shoes are changed to ruby slippers before they become glass, an interesting reference to the film *The Wizard of Oz*. This classic is referenced again at the end. The fairy godmother, after accidentally making Cinderella vanish, returns her to the prince, and Cinderella, in response to the question of where she had been, responds, "I think it was Kansas."

Though all of these film versions of "Cinderella" possess similar traits, they also all present a new spin on the traditional tale. The film *A Cinderella Story* (2004), while it contains parallel elements to the more traditionally-set feature film versions, presents "Cinderella" from a decidedly more modern perspective. Like the other films examined, *A*

Cinderella Story has love interests who know each other prior to the traditional meeting at the ball. In fact, Sam, the Cinderella figure, and Austin, the prince figure, attend the same high school. Not surprisingly, Austin is the popular football captain and student body president while Sam is the smart outcast just trying to survive schoolwork and her stepfamily. This film adds a modern twist to their meetings, however, for both Sam and Austin are prospective Princeton University students who meet in a chat room under different names about a month before the main action of the story begins, where they discover that they have much in common. Another similarity between *A Cinderella Story* and other Cinderella films is the tension between Austin and his father. The tension in this version stems from the expectations Austin's father has—sending Austin to USC on a football scholarship and then having him help manage the family's car wash business[5]—and Austin's desires—going to Princeton and becoming a writer. The film also contains the stronger role of the fairy godmother figure Rhonda, who manages the diner owned first by Sam's father and now her stepmother. Rhonda is more of a fixture in Sam's life than any of the other fairy godmothers, appearing in the opening of the film at Sam's eighth birthday party, and like da Vinci's character in *Ever After*, she is not magical. In fact she is one of the most practical, realistic characters in the film.

Aside from the modern setting of this film and the resulting adaptations of the text (such as the loss of the slipper becoming the loss of the cell phone), there are a number of other differences between *A Cinderella Story* and other film versions. One of the most noticeable differences is in the narrative. While both *The Glass Slipper* and *Ever After* also use a frame narrative to present the main story, in those two films the narrator comes from a different place or time than the characters in the main story. In *The Glass Slipper*, the narrator is an unknown male who is not associated with the story at all while in *Ever After* the narrator is the great great granddaughter of the main characters. The narrator of *A Cinderella Story*, however, is Sam, the Cinderella figure herself. This change from a distant character to one participating in the story is an interesting twist and enhances the feminist nature of this film. Cinderella has not only become a modern woman planning her education at a major university, but she has come forward to claim her story in the first person. The use of the first person in this film underscores the events in the story and the strength of this Cinderella. While Sam does put up with the abuse of her stepfamily, she reveals that she does so because Fiona, her stepmother, is her key to affording Princeton. Though Sam does need the encouragement and help of Rhonda and the other helper characters from the diner to meet Austin at the Halloween homecoming dance, it is ultimately her decision to go to that dance. It is also her decision to move out of her stepmother's house after her stepsisters reveal her identity publicly and her stepmother gives her a fake rejection letter from Princeton. And it is her words to Austin that free him from following his father's expectations, for she confronts him after she decides to move out of her stepmother's house, calling him a coward for not doing what he truly wants to do with his life. After Sam's confrontation with Austin, during the final seconds of the Homecoming game, he leaves the field and his father's expectations to claim Sam and a destiny of his choosing. Cinderella has liberated both herself and her prince from a life of misery.

In addition to the very strong feminist message of *A Cinderella Story*, the way in which it reflects on folktales is quite different from the other film versions. While the plot of the story is a clear parallel to "Cinderella" despite different character names and some other alterations, the references to fairy tales come not as comparisons to the characters but to the way in which fairy tales have influenced Sam and this modern society. Though Sam's narration begins, "Once upon a time in a far away kingdom lived a beautiful little girl and her widowed father" and the film shows a beautiful, sweeping landscape ending with an aerial view of a magnificent castle, the image of the fairy tale is broken immediately when the castle is revealed to be part of a snow globe and Sam comments that the "far away" isn't actually far away but the San Fernando Valley. A short time later, she furthers the split between her story and folktales by commenting, "Unfortunately, this was no fairy tale." While Sam is telling the back story, she reveals that her father read fairy tales to her from a collection. As they are discussing the story, Sam's father tells her, "Fairy tales aren't just about finding handsome princes. They're about fulfilling your dreams and about standing up for what you believe in." He also tells her that "this book contains important things that you may need to know later in life." The implication is that the stories' morals will help Sam as she grows up, but his words contain a literal message as well, one that becomes clear late in the film when Sam finds the will her father has hidden in the book. After her father's death in an earthquake, Sam is left in her stepmother's care. In her narrative, Sam comments, "from then on the only fairy tales in my life were the ones I read about in books." There is frequent reference throughout the film to reality versus dreams or fairy tales.

While there is never any doubt that Sam is the Cinderella figure, she does not go by that name except when she is the mystery woman at the ball. The name Cinderella works as a generic type rather than the character's actual name or mocking nickname. It is interesting to note that Sam does earn a nickname in the same way that the Cinderella characters in the other films (and in the traditional tales) do. Because she works so much at the diner, she is called "Diner Girl," and when her stepsisters and the popular girls unmask her at the end of the film, they do so using this nickname. The name Cinderella, however, has become associated with beauty, mystery, and glamour rather than with a girl covered in ashes because she sleeps near the fireplace. This change in meaning reveals how this story has been absorbed into modern culture and how just a beautifully dressed, mysterious woman can become Cinderella without all of the problems that the traditional figure has encountered. Yet while this interpretation may be the way the tale has been internalized by many of the characters, the film shows that despite this internalization, Cinderella must still suffer because this Cinderella, no matter her nickname, does suffer like her counterparts.

The story "Cinderella" also becomes the means by which Sam's stepsisters and the popular girls reveal who Austin's Cinderella is. They create a skit based on "Cinderella" (combined with "The Frog Prince") at the Homecoming rally and expose Sam, "Diner Girl," as Cinderella. It is after this skit that Sam takes full control of her life, and her part in this Cinderella story, by quitting her job, moving out of her stepmother's house, and eventually confronting Austin. When he joins her in the stands at the football game and they kiss, Sam's narrative returns, and she comments that "what I remember most [about that day] is I got my prince." Shortly thereafter she discovers the will her father had left hidden in her book of fairy tales and remarks, "My dad was right. The fairy tale book did contain something important." The film ends with Austin returning Sam's cell phone as if it were a slipper and Sam saying that she and Austin "lived happily ever after — at least for now." Unlike the other film versions of "Cinderella," which present the tale as if it were a true historical story, *A Cinderella Story* parallels "Cinderella" in several ways but also shows how the folktale has been absorbed into modern culture. It is both a Cinderella story and a commentary on Cinderella stories.

By contrast, Walt Disney's *Cinderella* differs greatly from the other "Cinderella" films, particularly in terms of the development of the prince character. In fact, the prince plays no role in Disney's *Cinderella* until the ball, where he is initially shown bored with the other women and then enthralled by Cinderella. His first lines do not come until he sings his response to Cinderella while they are dancing. His role, in fact, appears reduced in this version compared to the traditional written versions, for it is not the prince who scours the country looking for the maiden to fit the slipper after the ball but the Grand Duke. Only at the wedding does the prince reappear. Instead of the prince, the characters developed in this film are the animal helpers, particularly the mice, and the king, whose desire to find his son a bride leads to the ball — without any objection made by the prince. The development of animal or other traditionally secondary characters is a trademark of Disney film revisions. *Snow White and the Seven Dwarfs* is arguably about the dwarfs more than Snow White, just as *Sleeping Beauty* is more the three fairies than the princess. Yet in both Disney's *Snow White and the Seven Dwarfs* and *Sleeping Beauty*, the prince character does see or meet the princess character before the traditional meeting place. It is only in *Cinderella* that the prince's character is not developed.

All of the previously discussed film revisions of "Cinderella" maintain the traditional gender roles of the characters. *Cinderfella*, however, switches those traditional roles so that Cinderella is male, Fella played by Jerry Lewis, and the prince becomes a princess. Aside from the reversal of gender roles, this revision contains several other notable differences even as it parallels the traditional plot of "Cinderella." First, Fella, who is never called Cinderfella in the film, is described as "ordinary," not "tall, handsome, and clever" like his princely counterparts or graceful and sweet like the traditional Cinderella. Further, this film is a Jerry Lewis vehicle in many ways, containing long sections full of physical comedy the likes of which do not appear in other Cinderella films.[6] While Fella is definitely abused by his stepfamily, some of the problems he encounters stem from his own personal foibles.

Like *A Cinderella Story*, *Cinderfella* is a modernization, set in the late 1950s California in this case, and though clearly a Cinderella story itself, also comments on the role of folktales in society. In the second meeting between Fella and his fairy godfather, the fairy godfather reveals that Fella has been "chosen to rectify all the great wrongs brought about by the original story," blaming women, the original "reporters" of the story, for those wrongs. He is upset because these women not only made the fairy godfather into a fairy godmother but also because their version has been internalized by society and caused women, tired of waiting for their "Prince Charming," to marry second best. The women, the fairy godfather says, then negatively compare their husbands to their ideal and neither of them ends up happy as a result. Fella, by taking Cinderella's role, is supposed to reverse the process, making the men dissatisfied with the women instead of the other way around. The hope is that the new story will balance out the old and that men and women will be satisfied with each other as they are and not long for an ideal. Though this is the stated plan for the newly created tale, that thread is lost by the end, for the audience only sees the successful pairing of Fella and Princess Charming[7] and not the subsequent effect, if any, on society, and there is not return of the fairy godfather to offer an epilogue.

The role of Princess Charming is more like that of the Disney film, for she and Fella do not meet formally prior to the ball, though he does watch her arrive at his home and startle her the night before the ball.[8] Yet there is still some need, as in most feature film revisions, for these characters to earn each other. Once Princess Charming finds Fella again, he refuses to accept her love because he is not a "person"—someone of importance—and she is. Princess Charming tries to convince him that she is as normal as he, but he runs off, only to return a short time later, apparently having synthesized her words. There is no exchange of dialog after that, only the words "And they lived happily ever after" across the screen. As with many of the other versions of "Cinderella," there must be some additional problem for the main characters to overcome. In *Cinderfella*, it is a brief problem, and one that comes after the ball rather than before it, but it still works to show that these characters deserve each other at the end. Like *A Cinderella Story*, *Cinderfella* acts as a modern reflection of folktales and their place in society while it simultaneously recreates that same folktale.

The length of film revisions, like the length of written revisions affects how the revision is presented in terms of tone. Feature-length films demand more development of characters, particularly the main romantic leads, and modern resistance to class distinctions means that characters are no longer accepted merely because of their title or position in society, though there is still awareness of class differences. Thus in the "Cinderella" revisions discussed above, the prince's character must suffer and prove worthy of Cinderella, just as she does for him. The two exceptions to the development of the prince character—Disney's *Cinderella* and *Cinderfella*—do not develop that character because the focus is less on the romantic relationship than on other things—the helper characters' role in the case of the Disney film, and the gender switch in the case of *Cinderfella* (and the plan to alter how folktales are perceived in society by making that switch). But when the romance is the focus of the film, the characters must earn their happiness.

Film revisions of folktales, like their written counterparts, take traditional folktales and rework them to fit the new medium through which they can be disseminated. Each time a new method of distributing story comes about, folktales are one of the first types of stories spread, and each new medium adapts and continues to adapt folktales to this medium, first as "faithful" representations—traditional versions—and then as revisions. This is true of written versions of folktales and equally true of the film and television industry, which continues to create versions and revisions of folktales to captivate new and varied audiences.

9

Revising the Folktale Tradition

Neil Gaiman, in his poem "Instructions," offers guidelines for folktale characters to follow throughout their journey. The poem begins with the folktale character, the "you" of this second person poem, being sent into the story, the folktale, through a gate, down a path, and into a house. As the poem continues, the instructions guide the character through a house, warning, "Take nothing. Eat nothing" (8) before advising the character to aid any "creature" that asks for help, if it is possible to give that aid. The poem is rife with the stock elements of folktales, from the journey to unknown places, to the characters such as mysterious old women, princesses and enchanted animals, to difficult tasks, yet it does not itself rework or retell any specific tale, though reference is made to several. The effect of Gaiman's poem is not to comment about a single tale by revising it, but to reveal some of the innate features of folktales, and Gaiman does this by revealing the "instructions" to survive the journey a hero takes on a folktale, from entering the path, to meeting and negotiating with various helper characters on the journey, to accomplishing the given task, to returning home. Gaiman reveals the formula of the folktale and exhorts the folktale character and the reader to "Trust your heart, and trust your story" (53). Like many modern fantasy writers, Gaiman has written a work that both acts as type of new folktale and analyzes the folktale tradition.

The folktale tradition, though originally an oral one, evolved into written tradition once tales began to be compiled, published, and republished. As the folktale was becoming more and more popular, authors such as Hans Christian Andersen, George MacDonald, Oscar Wilde, and others in the nineteenth and early twentieth centuries began to create original, literary folktales that emulated the tales compiled from the oral tradition. Though these tales were influenced by the traditional folktale form and elements—and sometimes even by specific tales—they were ultimately original in nature, and, in some cases, especially for Andersen, literary folktales such as "The Little Mermaid," "The Emperor's New Clothes," and "The Ugly Duckling," among others, have become so well known that they are often mistaken for traditional oral folktales.

Contemporary children's literature has continued the folktale tradition in several directions. In many cases, specific tales are revised in various forms, as in the case of *Ella Enchanted*, a Cinderella retelling by Gail Carson Levine, and the many revisions by Donna Jo Napoli (*Beast, Zel, The Magic Circle*) and Robin McKinley (*Beauty, Spindle's End, Rose Daughter*). This type of revision has been the focus of the most of the chapters in this book. Another manner in which the folktale tradition has evolved is in high fantasy novels by authors such as JRR Tolkien and Ursula K. LeGuin. Though these authors do not revise particular tales, they are clearly influenced by folktales and folk literatures. The worlds that many high fantasy authors create contain characters common in the folk tradition, from elves and goblins to witches, wizards, and other enchanted creatures, and the main characters follow similar quests for identity through strange and often threatening, enchanted lands much as the characters in folktales. Gaiman's instructions would work as well for characters in high fantasy as they do for characters in folktales.

Though both of these offshoots of the folktale tradition are important avenues of study, the focus of this chapter is on a third way of exploring and expanding folktales. In these stories, there is not a revision of a specific tale or the creation of a new world that contains elements of other folktales. Rather, the authors create new tales that respond clearly to the folktale tradition without revising a single tale. There are three ways in which this type of story manifests itself: as new tales in the vein of Andersen and MacDonald without reference to other tales in the tradition; as new tales that incorporate elements of specific other tales either explicitly or implicitly; and as new tales that have a modern or nontraditional setting yet contain elements that are part of the folktale tradition and also comment on that tradition. Often the new tale is a response to a perceived problem with traditional tales. New tales that contain strong female characters as a response to the perceived weakness of females in traditional tales are particularly common. These types of revisions can be found in both picture books and novels for children and young adults (and even extend into adult literature).

An excellent example of a new tale that uses the folktale tradition without referencing specific tales is Robert Munsch's picture book *The Paper Bag Princess*. This tale reverses traditional gender roles and does away with the common bloody conflict resolution in traditional folktales. In Munsch's tale, when the main characters Princess Elizabeth and Prince Ronald are introduced, the readers are led to expect these characters to fall into the traditional folktale roles because they read that the beautiful Princess Elizabeth "lived in a castle and had expensive princess clothes" and "was going to marry a prince named Ronald." Those expectations are dashed almost immediately by the narrative when the antagonist, a dragon, "smashed her castle, burned all her clothes with his fiery breath, and carried off Prince Ronald." Now rather than the traditional helpless female being rescued by the dashing, brave and strong male, it is Princess Elizabeth, clad in the only clothes she can find, a paper bag, who rushes to the captured prince's rescue. And unlike traditional stories in which the dragon must die, in Munsch's tale, Elizabeth outsmarts the dragon by wearing him out with physical challenges that leave him "so tired he didn't even move."

As the dragon sleeps, Princess Elizabeth helps Prince Ronald escape. Unlike the liberated Elizabeth, however, Ronald expects his fiancée to be the perfect stereotypical princess, and he rebukes her, saying, "you're a mess! You smell like ashes, your hair is all tangled and you are wearing a dirty old paper bag. Come back when you are dressed like a real princess." None too impressed with Ronald's attitude, Elizabeth describes Ronald's impeccable attire then declares, "You look like a real prince, but you are a bum." The story concludes "They didn't get married after all." This conclusion, as with almost the entire story, reverses folktale traditions. Munsch's story incorporates the elements of traditional folktales, including the setting and the stock characters and events, but the gender reversals serve to question the traditional roles of males and females in folktales while the change in the confrontation with the antagonist questions the need for a bloody and violent outcome.[1] No specific folktale is alluded to or mentioned in this tale; rather, it is the tradition as a whole that is being examined here and revised to incorporate new sensibilities.

Other authors take a different tack than Munsch in revising the folktale tradition by creating a new tale that contains implicit and sometimes explicit references to popular traditional folktales. E.D. Baker's trilogy of novels *The Frog Princess*, *Dragon's Breath*, and *Once Upon a Curse* all center around the same main character, first-person narrator Princess Emeralda or Emma, and her relationship with Prince Eadric. The first novel, *The Frog Princess*, is a revision of the story "The Frog Prince," and though the original tale is altered significantly — most notably when Emma, upon kissing Eadric in frog form, herself transforms into a frog — it is ultimately still a version of "The Frog Prince," just as *Ella Enchanted* by Gail Carson Levine and *Just Ella* by Margaret Peterson Haddix are versions of "Cinderella" no matter how altered.

Once Emma has recovered her human form at the end of *The Frog Princess*, the new tales begin, but they are not tales that rework a single fairy tale as the first novel does. Instead, using family problems established in *The Frog Princess*, Baker creates new challenges for Emma to fix that are stock problems in folktales but not associated with a specific tale. In *Dragon's Breath*, Emma is on a quest to find the ingredients needed to reverse a curse that transformed her Aunt Grassina's love interest into an otter; in *Once Upon a Curse*, the quest is to find the source of and then reverse a family curse that makes all of the women in Emma's family turn into evil witches if they touch a flower after they turn sixteen. Both stories are engaging and, though original in terms of the specific reasons for the quests, present standard folktale elements within the quests. Emma must find specific magical ingredients to change Haywood the otter back into a human, most notably a vial of breath from a green dragon in *Dragon's Breath*, and her travels take her to different lands and lead to encounters with unusual magical characters, including mermaids, enormous spiders, winged horses, and, of course, dragons. Similarly, in *Once Upon a Curse*, Emma must travel to learn the root of the curse on her family. Her manner of learning the curse is less common to folktales because she travels back in time to see the curse being cast, but the events aside from the magical time traveling all resemble the typical events in folktales, from fighting magical foes such as harpies and dragons, to following gift giving protocol at major events — the curse is laid after a fairy does not receive her gift along with the rest of the guests. At the end of each novel, the main problem is resolved happily, though both *The Frog Princess* and *Dragon's Breath* also end with the problem for the next novel coming to the forefront.

What is more interesting about these novels than the expected plots and happy resolutions, however, is the way Baker incorporates other traditional folktales and folktale characters both implicitly and explicitly. This incorporation begins with the first novel of the series when Emma and Eadric, still frogs, are trapped in a witch's cabin. As Eadric sleeps thanks to a sleeping draught given to him, Emma, talking to the bat Li'l Stinker, learns that the potion is a popular one when Li'l asks, "What do you think those witches used to help Sleeping Beauty and Snow White get all that beauty rest? A full vial will knock you out for a hundred years or more" (79). Later, when Eadric appears unable to wake up, Li'l offers a possible solution, saying, "I suppose you could try the remedy used on those nitwits Snow White and Sleeping Beauty" (97), a solution that Emma is reluctant to try since the first kiss she and Eadric exchanged resulted in her being transformed into a frog. But, given the conventions of this folktale world, Emma does kiss him again, and her kiss wakes him from his magical slumber. Despite having to use the same remedy as that used in the other tales, Emma is disdainful of this tradition, and there is a clear lack of respect for the popular heroines who must rely on princes to wake them. Emma is a more liberated folktale heroine, and, like Princess Elizabeth in Munsch's tale, is the one to save the prince in this situation, though in this case she is not rebuked by Eadric for her pains, though Eadric does believe in the traditional gender roles, for throughout the trilogy he claims that Emma will need him to help protect her.

Later in this same book, Baker alludes to "Hansel and Gretel" when she talks about the Old Witches' Retirement Community where Emma's grandmother, afflicted by the family curse, lives in a gingerbread house. And a reference to "Cinderella" appears at the end of the book after Emma and Eadric have returned to their human forms. Emma rejects the notion of marrying Prince Jorge, the suitor her mother has chosen for her, and comments that "if he's lucky, maybe [he'll] find the perfect woman for him, one who wears the same size shoes he does" to which Eadric responds, "His feet are kind of small. It might take him awhile to find her" (213). Though not explicit references like those to "Snow White and the Seven Dwarfs" and "Sleeping Beauty," these are clearly referring to specific tales, and, in the case of "Cinderella," it is another disdainful reference.

It is in the other two novels, however, that Baker really weaves in traditional tales. In *Dragon's Breath*, the reader learns that, though Emma's grandmother lives in a gingerbread house, she is not the witch from "Hansel and Gretel." Instead, Aunt Grassina, searching for the grandmother, recounts the story of another former inhabitant of the retirement community "who had some children visit for a few days. One of them shoved her in her own oven and slammed the door shut. All that was left of her were some charred bones" (36). When Emma asks what happened to the children, she is told, "Not a thing. They said she was going to eat them, and claimed it was self-defense" (36). As with the references to popular folktales in the first book, this folktale reference takes a different point of view, in this case siding with the wicked witch from "Hansel and Gretel," though the children remain unnamed. Later in this novel, after Emma, Eadric, Grassina, and Haywood have tracked the missing witches to a remote island where they have been stripped of their memories (which have been placed in jars by a wizard), Baker makes reference to Snow White's wicked stepmother, who is one of the witches on the island. The witch's jarred memory recounts some of her tale, as do the witch from the tale "Diamonds and Toads" and Emma's grandmother. Placing these tales side by side emphasizes the folktale quality of Baker's new tale through its similarity to other more popular ones. However, unlike the "Hansel and Gretel" witch referred to earlier, these witches are not seen in a positive light.

As *Dragon's Breath* continues, reference is made to "Jack and the Beanstalk" as Emma and Eadric look for the husk of a magic bean and run into the vendor at the magic market who traded the beans for a cow named Milky White — homage to Stephen Sondheim's musical *Into the Woods*. And when Emma and Eadric are in frog form again and visiting the dragon king with his grandson, whom they've saved from a giant spider web, they get a glimpse of his horde, which he is sorting by color. The red pile contains numerous folktale artifacts, including "[a] red riding cape lined with a wolf skin," "[a] half dozen pairs of dancing shoes" and "a blooming rose [trembling] beside a restless magic carpet woven in every imaginable shade of red" (203). Though none of these artifacts plays an important role in the story, they do serve to emphasize the folktale nature of this new story, implying that Emma and her quest are part of a larger tradition.

In the final novel in the series, *Once Upon a Curse*, Baker branches the folkloric connections to other types of mythological creatures. When Emma and Eadric travel back in time to learn the source of the curse, and the act that can undo it, they encounter dragons again, but also harpies and a vampire, and in the main time in which the story is set, they have frequent encounters with ghosts. In addition, a more modern literary folktale reference is made in a scene in which Emma deliberately spills wine on a witch. The witch is angered enough to threaten to curse Emma, but the witch's sister scolds her, saying, "It's just a little wine. You aren't going to melt" (159), a reference to *The Wizard of Oz*.

This last novel is less concerned with other tales, though, than it is with Emma completing her quest to break the family curse and to resolve her relationship with Eadric, whom she has decided not to marry unless she can undo the curse. It is also the novel in which Emma not only comes to understand her power as the Green Witch of her kingdom, a title she inherits from her Aunt Grassina, but also masters that power. And though Emma is in many ways caught in a world in which traditional folktale expectations rule, she is able to manipulate them to her benefit and show herself to be both a strong and powerful witch and princess even though she starts off as a dispirited princess who chafes at the role her mother is trying to confine her to. By finding a balance between what she wants to do—practice magic—and what she is born to be—a princess—Emma survives her folktale.

Rebecca Lickiss' main character in *Never After*, Lady Vevila, like Emma in Baker's trilogy, chafes at the restrictions of her role in the kingdom. Lickiss' novel, however, weaves together many different popular folktales into a new tale, as well as a new way of looking at many of the popular tales incorporated into the novel. Lickiss opens the novel with the traditional beginning "Once upon a time" and then takes her readers to the main setting of the novel, a castle that has been asleep for so long that briars have grown up around it, though "A small path, just wide enough for a man to pass, had been recently cut through the decidedly unpicturesque bramble" (1–2). This path to what the reader expects to be the castle holding Sleeping Beauty has been cut by Prince Althelstan, but he is surprised by what he finds there. After kissing every possible woman who might be the princess he's looking for, he discovers that there "had to be a transcription error" in the story that has brought him to the castle because instead of a sleeping princess, he finds three sleeping princes, "And he wasn't about to kiss those three" (3). As Althelstan ponders the transcription error and grows frustrated, the reader learns of the decayed state of the castle, which, though it has kept the occupants in an enchanted sleep, has undergone the ravages that one hundred years will cause to a building.

When he realizes that he is not the one who can break the curse, he decides to convince his cousin Lady Vevila to come kiss the princes to wake them because he has found amid all of the slumbering people "a young woman sitting off by herself in a chair" (4), whom he believes is a princess and whom he wants to marry when she wakes. Under an edict that his father has placed on him saying that he must marry a princess and there being a dearth of princesses in the land presently,[2] this sleeping woman seems to be the answer to his problems if he can just wake her. Lickiss' reversal of the traditional role of the prince waking the sleeping princess with a kiss is the first indication that the folktale tradition is being set on its head. The introduction of Lady Vevila is the next indication, and it is Vevila who, more than any other character, challenges the gender roles of the traditional weak princess waiting to be saved. The granddaughter of two kings and "first cousin once removed" of Althelstan, Vevila is much sought after as a mate by princes in this land lacking princesses, but she has no interest in marrying anyone. She attempts to escape the dance once, and after it is finally over decides to run away to seek the adventure she craves. She has no interest in helping Althelstan when he discovers her but is convinced to go once he threatens to return her home if she doesn't agree. Althelstan has also enlisted the aid of a trio of magicians to try to break the curse if Vevila cannot.

Once they reach the castle again, the true problems begin, and what began as a version of "Sleeping Beauty" widens to incorporate several other tales. The first one brought in is "Rumpelstiltskin," for when Vevila tries to kiss the princes, the witch Urticacea, who claims to be the princes' fairy godmother, refuses to allow Vevila to kiss them until she proves that she is a princess. The "princess test" she devises is to have Vevila spin straw into gold, something both women know is impossible, though the witch is clever enough to convince the magicians and Althelstan that it is possible, playing off their lack of knowledge about spinning by drawing the analogy between spinning wool into silk and "straw, such as grows out of the earth, into thin ribbons of gold, such as is dug out of the earth" (30). The greedy men, eager to be convinced, ignore Vevila's cry that "You can't spin wool into silk!" (30) and lock her in a room with straw to spin.

Understandably furious, Vevila is vowing revenge on all of them when the Rumpelstiltskin character arrives. Though this "very short man" (32) remains nameless until near the end of the novel as he does in the traditional story, he helps Vevila to "pass" the test, not by spinning straw into gold, but by replacing the straw with gold and quartz. In return, he demands that she promise him an unnamed favor to be collected at a later time. Vevila is naturally suspicious of this bargain, but agrees despite the potential pitfalls because "a nebulous promise would make a good excuse for anything she wanted to get out of. What prince would want to marry her, knowing she owed an odd, ill-dressed, little man an unnamed favor?" (37). Vevila is always considering the best way to avoid doing what is expected of her — marrying well, having children, and living a sheltered life of luxury. The next day when the others return to the room, they are all willing to believe that Vevila spun the straw into gold except Urticacea. The witch uses the quartz, which Vevila claims was spun from stray bits of hay, as an excuse to extend this "princess test" for two more nights, thus forcing Vevila into the same three-night spinning task as the miller's daughter from "Rumpelstiltskin." Displeased, Vevila makes numerous attempts to escape, having decided that kissing the princes isn't worth the hassle of passing the witch's test.

As the day passes, two new popular folktales are brought into the novel. The first occurs when the narrative moves to follow the Rumpelstiltskin character to a swamp where he is talking to some unseen creature later revealed to be the frog from a version of the story "The Frog Prince." Throughout the novel as the narrative shifts from character to character, Rumpelstiltskin is seen conversing cryptically with the frog as he plots to have Vevila break the spell on the frog. The second new popular folktale brought into the novel is revealed with the arrival of Berengaria, a young woman claiming to be a princess. Urticacea again refuses to let her kiss the princes until she passes a princess test and so devises a different test, this time the one from "The Princess and the Pea."

Not surprisingly, neither of the two princess tests follows the expected path of the traditional folktales upon which they are based, though they both result in the women being "proven" princesses. For Berengaria, who knows that she is being tested but not what the actual test is, the test poses a further challenge, for she is not entirely sure she's really a princess. All she knows of her background is that she was raised by a spinster who, in one of the stories of her background, told her that she was "the lost daughter of the last king of Perideridia" (97), and even if this story is true, "Her knowledge of princesses was limited to bedtime stories and hearsay" (97). As she stares at the twenty mattresses, twenty feather beds, and twenty silk blankets piled high without a ladder to get her to the top, she tries to determine what the test is and finally decides that "A true princess would climb to the top of the bed and sleep up there, rather than on the floor, ladder or no" (98). The result of her efforts are injuries that make her almost incoherent the next day because she falls as she is climbing as well as when she finally gets to sleep at the top of the bed. Althelstan, the wizards, and Urticacea are all horrified when they find her so injured the next day, and the men are irate when they learn that the witch had placed a pea under the mattress to test Berengaria. Urticacea, while forced to admit that Berengaria has passed this test, remains puzzled, murmuring, "But under all those mattresses?" (118) as she helps them escort Berengaria to a new room to recover before she tries to kiss the princes awake.

While Berengaria is struggling with her bed, Vevila, in the midst of another escape attempt, trades a second promise with the still-unnamed Rumpelstiltskin for him to exchange the straw for gold again. Rumpelstiltskin is clearly smitten with Vevila and gives her "a small hand-pick and shovel" because, he tells her, "I thought you'd like something useful" (106). And though he too wants Vevila to stay to wake the princes—and then to kiss the frog—he does not try to stop her from leaving, saying, "You should be whoever you want to be" (106). He is the only character in the novel who understands Vevila's frustration with her station in life. Later, as he's talking to the frog, he describes her as a "strong-willed woman" who will "do the job" he needs her to do (133). And then, after an apparent qualm from the frog, Rumpelstiltskin says, "there's no law that says that just because she kisses someone she has to marry him. Even if the someone she kisses is under some sort of a spell.... That's just a convenient way to end all the folktales" (134). This explicit reference to folktales and their endings separates this woven collection of tales from the others, even though this novel fits in the genre. Rumpelstiltskin questions the reliability of folktale rules even while he is in some ways bound by those rules, most notably the need for a true princess' kiss to break curses.

Yet another popular folktale is introduced to the novel back at the castle. While Vevila continues to work on her escape—now using the gifts Rumpelstiltskin gave her to help dig the mortar from around a stone—and while Berengaria is sleeping, a woman arrives at the castle and, after some confusion, invites Althelstan, the wizards, and Urticacea to a ball for her "princess" daughters, whom she wants to marry princes. This woman, the Dowager Queen Dulcamara, and her invitation initiate the Cinderella tale, for she is the stepmother and her daughters the stepsisters from "Cinderella." The preparation for the ball does not follow traditional means, however, for the wizards are the ones who scramble to create appropriate dress and transportation for them and eventually cast spells on a pumpkin and several animals to accomplish their goal, much as Cinderella's fairy godmother does in the traditional tale. The Cinderella character, later identified as Lady Amelanchier Ceneritious, in the brief glimpse given of her before the ball, does not seek help to get to this ball. Instead, she has created her own gown, scoffing about wishing as she dresses: "Wishing had gotten her nowhere, which is why she'd taken matters into her own hands. She might as well have wished for a fairy godmother to do all this for her" (179). Here she reveals herself to be nearly as strong as Vevila. Lickiss has once again emphasized the strength and resourcefulness of the women in this novel.

All of the woven tales come together the next day when Urticacea is caught trying to steal away with the princes. When Vevila is revealed as the only true princess, Berengaria admitting that she didn't feel the pea in the bed and Lady Amelanchier Ceneritious declaring her stepsisters to be frauds, she kisses the princes awake, but only after extracting the promise of a favor from each of the other characters present — at the behest of Rumpelstiltskin. As the princes awaken, Vevila and Berengaria are transported to the swamp with Rumpelstiltskin, and Vevila also kisses the frog to transform him back to his human form. This prince, who turns out to be Rumpelstiltskin's brother, tries to claim Vevila as his wife, but she refuses and they convince him to take Berengaria, who is enthralled by the prince, instead. Rumpelstiltskin, having already tried to get Vevila to marry him, tells his brother, "You tell everyone this princess kissed you, and you make is sound good and convincing" (229), thereby setting up a very different version of this folktale.

Vevila also manages to get out of marrying one of the three princes she has awoken by pairing all three off with Lady Amelanchier Ceneritious and her stepsisters. She is not able to escape marriage entirely, however, because she is forced to choose between returning to the castle with King Abelardann and marrying someone of her parents' choosing or marrying Rumpelstiltskin, who tells her, "If you marry me, you will marry a prince, making your relatives happy; and your life will be filled with adventure and excitement" (247). By agreeing to this proposal, Vevila is able to fulfill part of her duty — to marry royalty — but also gets to do as she wants, have adventure in her life. The end of the novel, like the beginning, falls into the expected trope of the folktale, and the final words of the novel are "And they all lived happily ever after" (261), as is expected from this type of story.

Ultimately, *Never After*, like Baker's trilogy, is a feminist reworking of the folktale tradition. Lickiss uses Vevila as the reluctant, liberated princess who, naturally, is the only one with the confidence to believe she is a princess — and to convince others that she is one. She is, as a result, the only one who can break the curses in the novel. Yet even some of the less confident women — Lady Amelanchier Ceneritious and Berengaria in particular — are more independent than their counterparts in the traditional tales. Similarly, the tales themselves are shaped in such a way that they either reverse or somehow alter the gender roles, whether it is making the sleeping princess become three princes or throwing the ball for husbands to woo the women. Even the witch Urticacea, who is looked down upon by the wizards for not being educated in magic as they are, manages to lay a curse on them that they are unable to lift, and only Vevila is able to figure out the true cure, though, as part of her revenge on them, she won't allow Rumpelstiltskin to tell them the cure, arguing, "They're wizards, and heading for Recondite University [where they were educated and now work]. They're smart; surely they'll figure it out. And you are a wild, barbarous wizard. They don't like that sort of thing at the University" (259). The wizards, traditionally seen as all-powerful and good, have been reduced to figures of mockery while Rumpelstiltskin, arguably the oddest of the characters and a traditional antagonist, is the closest the novel comes to a hero and equal to Vevila the heroine. Though Althelstan, based on the opening of the novel, is set up to be the hero, in fact he becomes a secondary character who, while getting the woman he wants in the end, does so only because his home is away from the castle where most of the action takes place, his saving grace for Princess Jaquenetta, who does not want to be in charge of cleaning and repairing everything. For most of the novel, Althelstan is mocked as a foolish, love-sick, egotistical prince, and Vevila spends much time reviling him. Lickiss has created a new tale from traditional folktales much like Baker did in her trilogy; the main difference is in how much more Lickiss incorporates those traditional characters into her story.

Unlike Baker and Lickiss' reworking of the folktale form within the same setting as traditional tales, the third manner in which writers create new tales that respond to the folktale tradition involves the use of a modern story that is in some way transformed into a folktale. Vivian Vande Velde's novel *A Well-Timed Enchantment* begins with a modern setting. The main character Deanna, bored and resentful at being dragged to France for the summer and angry about her parents' divorce, finds herself and Oliver, a cat whom she saved from some local dogs, at an old well in the countryside. In her misery, she begins to make a wish then stops and accidentally drops her watch into the well. This accident causes the well water to rise, and a hand shoots out of the well to pull Deanna in, and Oliver follows. When she wakes, Deanna discovers that she has been brought back in time by two elves, though they object to that term, saying, "*Elves* has such ridiculous connotations—don't you think?—helping shoemakers and such" (18). Here the first reference to traditional folktales is made, and the reader is led to see them as separate from the rest of the story. But this story follows some of the traditional lines of folktales. Deanna's aborted wish, it is revealed, is what opened the portal, and her dropping her watch has led to potential problems because it is a device that does not belong in this time — near 1066. As a result, Deanna has been brought back in time to retrieve the watch and stop the potentially devastating changes from occurring. Her quest is odd as folktales go, but it is still within that framework: she must complete this task within twenty-four hours with the help of Oliver, whom the elves turn into a human, albeit one who is learning human niceties. During this quest, Deanna will encounter several traditional figures of folktales, including knights, a wizard, and a castle setting.

There are also further references to folktales that Vande Velde uses as a contrast to the realities Deanna encounters. The first comes when, on trying to determine where to go to get the watch, Oliver points to a "road, paved with red polka-dot linoleum and marked with a flashing road construction arrow" (25). Recounting the events of the day, Deanna says, "Wishing well.... Elves. Next thing you know, we'll be meeting a frog demanding kisses" (25). She is forced to explain the folktale reference to Oliver, but he is oddly literal in his interpretation of her words and assures her that "Most likely, there won't be any story characters here" (26). This statement from one of the characters who most closely resembles a folktale character in the novel is nicely ironic and serves simultaneously to disconnect the characters from folktales — at least in their minds — and to connect them for the reader.

The next connection to folktales comes with Deanna's first sight of the castle, which "was not what Deanna had anticipated. She had assumed something along the lines of Sleeping Beauty's Castle in Disneyland, where she had gone with her parents last summer; but Sir Henri's family home was small as castles go and built of rough stone" (45). This reference is very modern in its nature and once again serves to separate Deanna and what she encounters from what she knows from folktales. Of course, this same castle that she thinks is small is large enough for her to get lost in, and as she is talking about the castle's size with Lady Marguerite, she makes reference to "Hansel and Gretel" by saying, "Any bigger and I'd have to drop breadcrumbs," a comment that confuses her hostess, who can only reply, "I suppose if you really want to ..." (84). This folktale reference, unlike the previous ones that separated Deanna from the tradition, actually connects her to it by casting her as one of the lost children in "Hansel and Gretel."

This connection to folktales that Deanna casually makes also colors how she looks at the world around her. Even though she sees difference between what folktales have led her to expect in this time period and the reality, she continues to make judgments based on storybook expectations. Her reading of Sir Henri's sons, both knights, and of Algernon, the wizard and Sir Henri's brother, are the clearest example of snap judgments. When she meet Baylen and Leonard, Henri's sons, at the beginning of the novel, she is impressed by them and their knightly prowess, and even though they continually show themselves to be buffoons, she trusts them to help her on her quest, a trust that ultimately fails her when Baylen tries to stop her completing her quest in order to play a petty prank on his brother.

Similarly, her initial meeting with Algernon leads her to a snap judgment that he is the antagonist and must be the one hindering her on her quest. This judgment is based largely upon his appearance. Vande Velde writes, "He had a shaven head, dark bushy eyebrows, and a velvet gown of midnight blue, sprinkled with embroidered stars. He carried a staff with a fist-sized crystal ball" (46). Algernon's appearance, capped off by a smile "showing more teeth than a weekday-afternoon game-show host" (47) puts Deanna off even further. Her distrust only increases throughout the novel as she spies on him and discovers more about him, such as his room, whose contents are mostly invisible, that make her trust him even less. Much of what Deanna experiences in this time shows her that folktales are not true. Yet she is greatly influenced by them, so much so that it is not until time is almost up that she can accept that Algernon is not evil and that he actually wants to help. Once she accepts his different role, she can admit that she was "Wrong: she had been wrong about everything. She had seen only what she expected to see and had refused to let anything else sink in" (184). Her expectations are caused by her experiences with folktales. Once she realizes that people do not always fit the role they appear to fit, she is able to complete her quest.

The next problem arises with Oliver, who has adapted to being human and does not want to be a cat again. Before Deanna can demand he remain human, however, the elves transport them back to the well and modern time, in the same forms they started the story in. Deanna is angered at the elves' callous disregard of feelings and declares that "Making shoes is all you're good for!" (226), referencing "The Shoemaker and the Elves" once more. Then, feeling defeated, she begins to wish again and hears the well gurgle behind her. Her original unarticulated wish, before her trip back in time, had been for her parents to be back together, but even as she starts to make this wish again, she realizes "you can't go wishing happiness on other people...; you've got to make your own" (227). With this realization she sees Oliver again and, even knowing the problems that will likely arise if he does turn human, she "leaned over the well and wished" (228). Though the outcome of the wish is not revealed, what is clear is that Deanna has finally done something of her own choosing to try to prove wrong Oliver's comment that "No matter what you do, I'm not going to change into a prince" (223).

This third type of revision of the folktale form does still possess the elements of folktales, but it transports them to the modern time. The characters in this type of revision, unlike the other types discussed, are influenced heavily by the popularity of folktales in modern life, and though they may not live in the traditional folktale world, the characters can still be part of their own folktale. Such is the case with Deanna, who in the end is much like the princess of "The Frog Prince" trying to transform a beast into a man. Vande Velde's novel also possesses a lighter feminist message than the other books discussed, for Deanna in many ways longs for someone to make decisions for her, yet she is also offended by Sir Henri acting as if women are not as strong as men. This ambivalence about gender roles is likely the result of the modern nature of Deanna's character and her home time. The characters living in times that resemble the traditional folktales are trapped in their gender roles, forcing writers to show them rebelling against the strictures of this male dominated time (as in the case of Vevila particularly). Characters from a more modern setting, particularly the late twentieth through the twenty-first centuries, come from a more liberated time and thus feel less need to chafe against gender constraints. Deanna in Vande Velde's novel bristles at the way Sir Henri treats women, but she does not rebel, for she does not plan to stay in that time and does not need to worry about her actions being restricted as Vevila and even Emma in Baker's trilogy do.

All of the examples here represent different ways in which the folktale tradition is reworked by modern authors, yet all of them are simultaneously expanding on the folktale tradition and questioning its rules, Gaiman's "Instructions," along the way. Just as Gaiman creates a tale and explores its rules, so do these contemporary authors. Even while these authors revise the folktale tradition, they are still bound by some of its same restrictions so that readers can see its connections to the very tradition they are revising. These new tales act as the contemporary literary folktale, a conscious, self-referential genre that expands and comments on the folktale tradition.

10

The Adult Connection

Maria Tatar, in *The Hard Facts of the Grimms' Fairy Tales*, comments that "Exactly when the function of folktales shifted from amusement for adults to the edification and diversion of young children is not clear" (23). She continues, explaining that

> folktales were still very much adult fare in sixteenth-century France. In certain parts of Germany, the art of composing and narrating folktales persisted as a widespread custom among adults up to the time of the Franco-Prussian War in 1870. But as industrialization gradually curtailed the need for the kinds of collective household chores and harvesting activities that had created a forum for oral narration, folktales as a form of public entertainment for adults died out. There may still exist many pockets of culture — both rural and urban — in which oral performance of tales and songs thrives, but on the whole it is safe to say that the nineteenth century witnessed a steady decline in the once intense preoccupation of adults with folktales [23].

Though Tatar is talking about the oral telling of tales, adult preoccupation with folktales also waned in written works with the exception of those who collected them or who created original tales. These collections and new creations would usually be marketed for children, however, so the primary audience of folktales if not the tale tellers remained children. Yet despite the shift from adult to child audiences, tales for adults have never completely disappeared from the folktale landscape, as Tatar indicates, and this is equally true for folktale revisions.

Though it may seem natural for children's literature to contain a wide assortment of folktale revisions, literature written for adults also contains a vast amount of revisions in all different forms and genres, from narrative fiction to poetry to drama, and from fantasy to romance to mystery and even erotica, some literary, some not. Direct revisions of tales are popular, but equally popular is the metaphoric use of specific folktales and folktale elements and characters. This use of the folktale in literature for adults serves to reclaim the folktale form for its mature audiences, who have never really lost touch with the tales, even though the tales are considered children's literature. And though the manner of revision can be similar to revisions in children's literature, whether it's through the use of a first person narrator or a postmodern or feminist presentation, the revisions for adults often explore areas of these popular folktales not appropriate for children. As with children's literature, settings for folktale revisions vary, from traditional to specific historical periods, to modern to futuristic, as do themes explored in revisions. There are also different points of view from which the story is told.

The particular tales revised can also vary greatly. For example, "The Three Little Pigs" is a popular tale for revision by children's authors, but it does not get great treatment in literature for adults. "Cinderella" is popular in both children's and adult literature, as is "Little Red Riding Hood." "Sleeping Beauty," however, is a tale that, though revised in children's literature on occasion —*Princess Sonora and the Long Sleep* by Gail Carson Levine and *Sleeping Ugly* by Jane Yolen, for example — is much more commonly revised in young adult and adult literature. The tale itself, with its sexual nature, has lent itself to varied revisions, many of which look to a version of the tale older than the Perrault or Grimm versions— Giambattista Basile's "Sun, Moon, and Talia." This is the version in which the Sleeping Beauty character Talia is woken when one of the twins she has borne after the king finds her sleeping and has sex with her sucks the piece of hemp or flax from her finger. Some revisions of "Sleeping Beauty," while not focused on the Basile text, fixate on other sexual elements of the story such as comparing the spindle or distaff to a penis. Other revisions of "Sleeping Beauty" avoid the sexual nature of the tale and focus instead on the metaphor of the sleeping woman who must be woken from some kind of stupor or slumber not produced by an enchantment. Those Sleeping Beauty characters must become aware of something within their life for their story to end successfully.

It is, of course, impossible to analyze all revisions of "Sleeping Beauty" since there are several dozen novel revisions for adults alone, as well as many short stories, poems, and plays, but examining several revisions will illustrate how folktale revisions for adults are often constructed. Robert Coover's postmodern novel *Briar Rose* has the unspecified, archaic-feeling setting of most folktales. It begins, however, with a prince trying to wend his way through the briars, which "part like thighs" while "the silky [rose] petals caress his cheeks" (1). Immediately there is a sexual element to the story, an element that is continued through the entire revision, primarily from the point of view of the prince and the crone or fairy, though also on occasion in the passages from the Sleeping Beauty character's point of view. The point of view shifts from the prince to the Sleeping Beauty character to the crone in short passages written in third person present tense, making the story feel immediate and ongoing, an important element in this revision, which seems to be more about how stories are created than "Sleeping Beauty" itself.[1]

Each character focuses on one main thing. For the prince, it is reaching the princess and waking her, not for her sake but for his: "He has undertaken this great adventure, not for the supposed reward — what is another lonely bedridden princess? — but in order to provoke a confrontation with the awful powers of enchantment itself. To tame mystery. To make, at last, his name" (1). The prince character is obsessed with making his name, with earning a place in history, and as he becomes increasingly tangled in the briars, he fears he will become like all the dead princes whose bones he can hear in the briars, "their names unmade, forever-aftered into the ignominious anonymity of the nameless dead" (40). This obsession with making his name is a nice irony in the revision, for in traditional versions of the tale the prince remains nameless despite his success in waking Sleeping Beauty.

The Sleeping Beauty character by contrast is focused on her dreams and a desire to wake that remains unfulfilled. She is in a constant loop of dreaming and forgetting:

> None remembered of course, no memory of her dreams at all, each forgotten in the very dreaming of them as though to dream them were to erase them. And yet, so often have her dreams revisited fragments and images of dreams dreamt before, a sort of recognizable architecture has grown up around them, such that, though each dream is, must be, intrinsically unique, there is an ambient familiarity about them all that consoles her as a memory might [5].

These dreams are fed to her by "a loving old crone, hideously ugly and vaguely threatening" (6) and most often involve her searching out the crone and being told some kind of story, frequently the story of which she is a part.

The crone character is the most aware of the others, and her first words are a response to the final thought of the Sleeping Beauty character in the previous section: "Well, old crone. Ugly. Thank you very much. Has that smug sleeper paused to consider how she will look and smell after a hundred years, lying comatose and untended in an unchanged bed? A century of collected menses alone should stagger the lustiest of princes" (6). The crone, or bad fairy as she's often called, tends to Sleeping Beauty's practical needs while also giving her the dreams she experiences. She weaves the story of "Sleeping Beauty" in numerous varied ways that largely lean toward the Basile version with the rape and the children, yet each time she recounts a version of the story, Sleeping Beauty tries to reject it, claiming, "It doesn't sound right. It's not like a real story" (41). In addition, during the tales the crone tells, Sleeping Beauty frequently interjects questions and concerns about the unfolding events. She has no memory of previous stories, even though she has a sense of déjà vu with the telling, asking, "Have I heard this story before?" (27) quite frequently. The crone herself varies the stories with each telling "for her own sake more than her auditor's" (56) since she, like the Sleeping Beauty figure, is caught in the enchantment even though she is the originator of that enchantment. The alterations are those of the storyteller refining tales to keep them fresh and interesting, and reflect the orality of the folktale tradition of which these characters are a part. The violence and sex and even incest that are a part of her stories also reflect the wider nature of traditional audiences — adults as well as children.

In addition to the crone telling the stories to Sleeping Beauty in her dreams, by the end of the story she seems also to be intruding on the prince's thoughts conflating her thoughts with his when they both think of "a door that is not a door" (69, 71). The crone at this point is weaving a story for herself involving the prince until she grows weary of it and "unravels the knots, loosing thread from thread, and, allowing her hump to rise once more, her hide to horrify, her multitude of breasts to fall, commences to spin again" (72). There is no doubt that this crone is conscious of her role as storyteller.

Folktales are further reflected on in other places in this novel when the prince thinks of the stories he has heard that have led him to his quest and his desire to make his name known in future stories. The Sleeping Beauty character constantly struggles against the variants of her story and hopes to wake from it, though by the end she wonders if "the fairy's spell [binds] her not to a suspenseful waiting for what might yet be, but to the external reenactment of what, other than, she can never be" (85).

She despairs that she will be forever caught in her dreams. And the crone on numerous occasions reflects on tales. She is "a caster of spells and a manipulator of plots" (33), and casts Sleeping Beauty as part of a larger group of "sisters" who were "locked away in iron towers, lamed and stuck in kitchens, sent to live with savage beasts. They had their hands and feet cut off, were exiled, raped, imprisoned, reviled, monstrously deformed, turned to stone, and killed. Even worse: many of them had their dreams come true" (31). Later she explains why she tells the stories containing "infanticide and child abuse, abandonment, mutilation, mass murder and cruel executions"—because she "wants to prepare her moony charge for more than a quick kiss and a wedding party" (60). At this point too, the crone reflects on what it means to be a good or bad fairy. Later she assigns both roles to herself, though the conventional good and bad distinctions are reversed: "The good fairy's boon to this child, newborn, was to arrange for her to expire before suffering the misery of the ever-after part of the human span, the wicked fairy in her, for the sake of her own entertainment, transforming that well-meant gift to death in life and life in death without surcease" (80-1). The entertainment she refers to is that of telling stories to Sleeping Beauty in her dreams. And at the end of this short novel, the crone remains in charge, for the story has looped back to a prince arriving at the briars and the Sleeping Beauty figure dreaming of being awoken. There is no closure, only a continuation of a story that has worked its way into Western culture and has been shaped and reshaped and continues to be shaped and reshaped. Coover's novel is about the cycle of storytelling and how, despite changes made by storytellers in different situations, the heart of the story remains and is repeated.

Emma Donoghue's book *Kissing the Witch: Old Tales in New Skins* also reflects on storytelling and the role of women in storytelling and is set in a standard timeless but archaic-feeling time, but the approach is very different from Coover's novel. Donoghue's book contains the first person retellings of twelve different folktales, including "Sleeping Beauty," all woven together with a question followed by the stock phrase "Will I tell you my own story? It is a tale of" something. Each tale is told to a main female character from the previous story except for the first story "The Tale of the Shoe," a retelling of "Cinderella" told by the Cinderella figure. Though often categorized as a series of thirteen short stories, each a revision of a particular tale, *Kissing the Witch* can also be seen as a novel containing thirteen different narrators, each tied to a character in a previous story. Further, because each narrator tells her story following the interaction with the previous narrator and because the stories are nested within each other, the book can also be seen as being a story with one primary narrator — the unnamed Cinderella figure — who as part of her own story relates the other stories, which have been passed down from one woman to another until they have reached Cinderella. This technique is similar to that of the embedded narratives of Mary Shelley's *Frankenstein* and Joseph Conrad's *Heart of Darkness*, and shows the nature of storytelling and how stories travel through time from one woman to another. The use of the first person narrators also hints at a "true" or "real" basis for the stories, for though each of the stories is recognizable as a folktale, each also alters the plot of the traditional tale significantly.[2] Thus it is that the Cinderella figure, having won the heart of the prince in her story, discovers that it is not the prince she wishes to spend her life with but the fairy godmother figure, who, unlike the traditional fairy godmothers, does not practice magic.

This revision combines the Grimm and Perrault versions since it contains both the hazel tree representing Cinderella's mother and a fairy godmother, and there are three balls. The revision diverges from the traditional versions in the end, when the Cinderella figure tosses her remaining slipper aside with the comment "He'll find someone to fit, if he looks long enough" (8). There is also a major difference in how the Cinderella figure is depicted in the revision compared to more traditional texts. It is her grief over her mother's death in this revision that makes her work so hard, for working helps her cope with her loss. At the end of her story, in the connection passage between the two tales, the Cinderella figure asks her fairy godmother, "Who were you before you walked into my kitchen?" and receives the answer "Will I tell you my own story? It is a tale of a bird" (9). The fairy godmother's voice then recounts her story — a revision of "Thumbelina." In turn, the bird that she rescues tells her story: she is Beauty from "Beauty and the Beast." The passage of stories continues.

Donoghue's revision of "Sleeping Beauty," "The Tale of the Needle" is sandwiched between revisions of "Donkeyskin" and "The Little Mermaid." In the "Donkeyskin" revision, "The Tale of the Skin," the Sleeping Beauty figure is the seamstress who creates the magnificent dresses for the narrator as she tries to put off her father's advances, and at the end of her tale the Sleeping Beauty figure asks to hear the story of the woman in the tower who teaches her to spin.

"The Tale of the Needle" presents "Sleeping Beauty" through a nonmagical lens. The Sleeping Beauty figure, the narrator, is born a princess who is coddled and protected by her parents who had "thought for sure they were barren" (168) and so revere her that they allow her to do no work and dress her hands in "gold mesh" gloves from "the very first day of life" (169). The narrator reflects on her ability to make the servants freeze until she clicks her fingers to make them "slump into ordinary life again, like grumbling giants woken from their sleep of ages" (168). She also remarks on the aged feel of the castle and her understanding of her life:

> I was content, I suppose, though having no basis for comparison I couldn't be sure. It felt more like sleep than joy. The manor had a drowsy air to it. Even the fire seemed lazy as it ate away at the logs. Whenever I asked a question that began with why, I would be told that things were done just as they had always been done for a hundred years before [169-70].

Here Donoghue takes the element of sleep and applies it to Sleeping Beauty's life during childhood. When she becomes an adolescent, the Sleeping Beauty figure becomes increasingly dissatisfied with the limits placed on her and finally begins exploring. Like the Sleeping Beauty of the traditional tale, she finds the tower and sneaks up to it where she encounters "an old woman I had never seen before, her hands moving in and out of her song" (176). This woman is spinning thread and as she talks with the Sleeping Beauty figure, she mocks her innocence and urges her to "Wrap your hands around the length of [the distaff] now.... And she howled with laughter as if at some joke I had missed" (177). As with many revisions for more mature audiences, the distaff and spindle (and even the tower) are compared to a penis and are a new experience for the Sleeping Beauty figure, who has just reached puberty.[3]

The sexual element in this revision, though present, is brief, and the conversation between the Sleeping Beauty figure and the old woman continues with the woman encouraging Sleeping Beauty to try out the spinning, telling her she has "long spinster's fingers" and is "made for it" (179). The Sleeping Beauty figure is reluctant to try spinning, however, because she has been told that "I am delicate" and "I must not do any sort of work" (178). She is torn between what she has always been told and what she could do—work, get her hands dirty, play. As she is considering sitting at the wheel and wondering if the servants are "scouring the house for me" (180), the old woman tells her, "Wake up, princess.... clapping her hands in front of my nose" (180). The Sleeping Beauty figure sits at the wheel and begins to spin, and "There was a long moment of glorious whirling, and then I felt the needle drive itself into my finger. I screamed like a baby" (180). As the old woman laughs at her, the Sleeping Beauty figure has a temper tantrum and threatens to have the woman beheaded, to which the woman responds, "But what a mess that would make" (181). The Sleeping Beauty figure is shocked by this woman's refusal to treat her with kid gloves, and this shock is life-changing:

> My head felt as if it were about to break open like an egg.
> The old woman gave me a most peculiar smile.
> I heard feet pounding on the stairs, and a call that sounded like my name. I turned to the door and pulled the bolt across. All of a sudden I felt quite awake [181–2].

At this point she returns to the spinning wheel and asks politely to be taught how to spin. Just as Donoghue makes Sleeping Beauty's childhood her time of sleep, so she turns the pricking of the finger and the meeting with the old woman into the moment of waking. It is the wound, the first hurt, that awakens this Sleeping Beauty and makes her actively choose to learn the skill that has caused her first injury.

There is no magic involved in this revision — or, for that matter, in any of the revisions in *Kissing the Witch* — instead, the tale's focus is on how overprotective parents can damage a child and how fruitless that overprotection is, for, despite everything that the Sleeping Beauty figure's parents do to protect her, she manages to find something to cause her injury, as well as offer her fulfillment. While most revisions of "Sleeping Beauty" do contain the element of the enchanted (or at least mysterious) sleep, there are some such as this one in which the sleep is a metaphor for not living and the waking is representative of living or of being aware. Donoghue's revision of "Sleeping Beauty" (and her other tales) also show the importance of passing on folk skills such as spinning, as well as tales, for once "I had got the knack of [spinning] I asked, Who were you before you came to live in this tower?" and the old woman responds by telling her "tale of a voice," in which she has the role of the Little Mermaid (183). Storytelling, and the woman's role in storytelling, is the primary focus of the novel as a whole, and each individual story has a point of its own.

Like Donoghue's novel, Sheri S. Tepper's novel *Beauty* interweaves several traditional tales, and there is some analysis of storytelling, but the true focus of this novel is Beauty's role as "all our hope" for the future, as the fairy Carabosse writes in her Foreword to Beauty's journal. Tepper's novel is presented as a rendering of the main character Beauty's journal and annotated throughout by Carabosse, "the fairy of clocks, keeper of the secrets of time" (Foreward), who keeps watch over Beauty throughout her life. She is also the fairy who placed "the curse" that "*the duke's daughter would be pricked by a spindle and fall into and enchanted sleep* [on her sixteenth birthday]. *All that about the hundred years and the prince is pure invention. I never said the child would die ...*" (32, emphasis in original). However, Beauty believes that the modified curse is "When Duke Phillip's beautiful daughter reaches her sixteenth year, she shall prick her finger upon a spindle and fall into a sleep of one hundred years, from which she will be wakened by the kiss of a charming prince" (31-2) thanks to the content of a letter from her mother, who left her when she was an infant. She discovers this letter not long before she turns sixteen when she is forced to move to the tower room in which her mother was locked after she bore Beauty. Prior to discovering this letter, Beauty has never known much about her mother or the curse because no one in the household will discuss them with her. The details are something of a shock to her, sharpened by the fact that her sixteenth birthday is close at hand. The reader, like Beauty, assumes that the curse is directed toward her and that her sleep is imminent. However, upon her sixteenth birthday, it is her maid and half sister Beloved, born on the same day as Beauty and who bears a strong resemblance to Beauty, who pricks her finger and falls into an enchanted sleep that also puts the entire area governed by Beauty's father to sleep. Only Beauty and her cat escape from the enchantment because Beauty is wearing a magical invisibility cloak she had fashioned with some thread found in a box her mother left behind. This cloak protects them "because we were cloaked in magic and invisible to the enchantment" (66). It is at this point that what had appeared to be a fairly straightforward revision of "Sleeping Beauty" becomes something entirely different, for Beauty embarks upon a series of journeys spanning over one hundred years, the length she believes is the limit for the enchantment. This is also the point at which the novel shifts from something that might suit older children to aspects for more mature audiences. Prior to her journeys, she was a teenager in medieval England, but she quickly becomes a jaded adult thanks to her experiences.

Though the setting of the story begins in April 1347 in England rather than the vague folktale past of Donoghue and Coover, the opening of the story still has a traditional feel to it. That traditional feel is altered when Beauty is whisked away into the future by a film crew "recording the vanishment of magic from England" (73). The crew takes her to their time, the late twenty-first century, when the earth's natural resources have been nearly depleted and Tepper's ecological message begins to emerge. The narrative starts to revolve around the problems in the modern world and the way in which natural resources are being used by the earth's population. Beauty moves from her original fourteenth century to the twenty-first to the late twentieth where she is educated at a high school and begins college. She becomes the victim of the violence and degradation of this society when she is raped by one of the men who had helped her leave the twenty-first century. This rape precipitates her return to the fourteenth century through the use of seven league boots that she had made, like her cloak of invisibility, from magic thread in the box her mother left her. Back in her own century, though three years later than she was last there, she learns that she is pregnant and orchestrates a marriage for herself so that her child will not be illegitimate.

Throughout the course of the novel, Beauty uses the boots to move in and out of human time, as well as in and out of different worlds, whether Faery, a version of Hell, or Chinanga, a world created by Carabosse. She leaves her daughter, whom she sees as a reflection of her rapist father, behind with her surrogate father and searches for her mother in Chinanga; she moves on to Faery when Chinanga disappears; and she then returns to the fourteenth century to discover that it is 1467 and that her daughter Elladine, now in her late teens, is the Cinderella figure of the folktale. Beauty herself takes on the role of fairy godmother, helping her to get the prince. Her daughter, however, does not have the disposition of the traditional tale's Cinderella — Beauty continues to associate her with her father — but that disposition does not matter for long, for Elladine dies giving birth to her daughter, a child "White as snow.... Red as blood. Black as death" (289). This child, named Galantha or Snow Drop, is Snow White. She, in turn, bears a son, Giles Edward Vincent Charming, who becomes the prince who finds Rapunzel as well as the Frog Prince and ultimately the prince who wakes Beloved from her hundred years of sleep.

Throughout the entire rather convoluted plot, several themes emerge. The first major one is the eco-commentary about the twentieth century and where Tepper speculates it is heading. In fact, Beauty's role is to preserve the beauty of all the creatures of the world, something she does at the end of the novel by, in a fashion comparable to Noah only on a grander scale, having her great grandson Giles Edward and several of the Bogles from Faery collect specimens of all the flora and fauna of the earth and storing it in the stasis of the enchanted castle until such time as "life will come again" (462). But even should there never be a time when they are disenchanted, she reflects, "Then everything is here. Sleeping. Dreaming, perhaps, of what might have been. Perhaps others, on some other world will catch the dream, will wake from it astonished at its marvel, at its complicated wonder. Perhaps someone or something will dream who can create once more" (463). The wish for a return to Eden, or at least to a time when people did not waste natural resources, is what spears her actions at the end of the novel. It is at this point that Carabosse tells her that the burning she has felt in her chest all her life is a miniature of all that she has collected, placed there by Carabosse and Israfel, another fairy. Beauty is the hope for the world because she carries inside her everything beautiful and natural in the world, a miniature paradise. Carabosse comments, "In the beautiful is Beauty, and in Beauty, beauty" (461). Tepper uses the name Beauty to represent the character's role as the keeper of all things natural.

A second theme that comes up is that of nature versus nurture and how genes are passed along. Each of the children until the great grandson is associated directly with the father. Thus Elladine is as evil as her rapist father Jaybee, whom she never met, and Galantha is kind but self-centered like her father Charme. Even Giles Edward is similar to his biological father, the courtier Vincent with whom Galantha has an affair. Vincent and his son Giles Edward are two of the few positive male characters in this novel in which men are frequently violent or insane or otherwise unlikable. Giles Edward is also the only relation in whom Beauty sees a reflection of herself. Her dislike of the two girls is justified by her refusal to see herself in them, though she does wonder if her abandonment of Elladine shapes her to be the unpleasant woman she becomes. Ultimately, she decides that the problem stems from Jaybee and not herself. Yet she does not attribute her own behaviors and personality with either her father or her mother, one of whom had abandoned her and the other who had barely acknowledged her existence. This aspect of the novel is uneven and contradictory.

What is the most interesting aspect of the novel thematically is the way that storytelling and folktales are explored. From the opening, the reader is led to believe that Beauty will be Sleeping Beauty because that is what Beauty believes. When Beloved becomes the victim of the curse instead, there is some question about Beauty's role in the story. Later she takes on the role of characters from two other stories: the fairy godmother in "Cinderella" and the princess (however aged) in "The Frog Prince" who restores the prince to his human form. She is also, like the fairies she meets and lives with, including her mother, aware that she is in the folktales at their origins, for her experience in the twentieth century exposed her to Walt Disney's versions as well as written collections of tales. She discusses folktales with Puck, one of the Bogles who aids her throughout the novel, when she realizes that her daughter Elladine is Cinderella, and he asks her, "Did you think the stories were made up?" (261). Puck compares folktales with "how legends gather around some people. There is the truth about a man, and then the part truths that gather afterward, and then the myths that follow later yet. A legendary man tends to have legendary sons. Power attracts power, so power gathers. It is one of the truths of magic" (261). Puck's comparison explains how Beauty's line is full of folk figures, but it also leaves her to wonder what aspects of the tale she knows will be real. This question exists in all of the folktales that come about during the course of the novel, including Beauty's original story. It is only at the end of the novel that it becomes clear that Beauty is a Sleeping Beauty, just not the expected one. Beloved takes on the traditional role, for after just over one hundred years of sleep, she is removed from the enchanted area to be woken by Giles Edward. In her place the now aged Beauty finishes her journal, removes her magical cloak, and lies down with Giles, the love of her life, also aged, having been brought to the enchanted area years earlier when he fell ill during their short time together.[4]

She is finally able to rest now that her quest to protect nature has been accomplished. Beauty does not escape "the curse"; instead, she delays its onset for herself to accomplish the task the fairies set for her when she was born. At the end of the novel, she reflects on the curse: "That time, so long ago, I would not allow the Curse to touch me. I did not want to spend a hundred years sleeping. I thought it unworthy of me.... I evaded it. I escaped it, so I thought. Escaping destiny is not so easy as that" (463). She is destined to be Sleeping Beauty and so returns to the original role she and the reader expected her to play, though it is Beloved's version of the story that will be immortalized in the Sleeping Beauty tales Beauty learned in the twentieth century. Tepper has given her versions of the "truth" behind the stories (as Puck calls them), and the readers already know the half truths and myths that remain. The interweaving of folktales is similar to Donoghue's in *Kissing the Witch*, though in this case the folktales are literally related while for Donoghue they are passed down through the characters who are not kin but who are connected nonetheless. And like Coover and Donoghue's revisions, Tepper's presents much darker, more mature elements of the tales, removing them from their place in the nursery to a historical place, full of the realities of adult life and all of its conflicts.

Orson Scott Card's novel *Enchantment*, like Tepper and Donoghue's novels, interweaves a variety of folktales for a more mature reading audience. In Card's case, however, the tales added to "Sleeping Beauty" are primarily Russian and Jewish. And like Tepper, Card employs time travel in his text, though his use of time travel is very different from Tepper's. Written in third person, the point of view of the novel is primarily Ivan Smetski, a doctoral candidate in Old Slavonic languages and folklore, though there are parts of the narrative told from other main characters' points of view. The story opens when he is a boy living with his parents in Kiev in the Soviet Union. They spend time at a cousin's house in the Carpathian Mountains while they are waiting for the papers to allow them to flee the Soviet Union and travel to the United States. During this visit, while he is in the woods, Ivan discovers a woman lying in a clearing scattered with leaves. He is frightened away from her by a mysterious creature that is under the leaves, but he is unable to forget completely this experience.

Many years later, he returns to Cousin Marek's house after spending time in the now democratic Kiev researching for his dissertation. On a jog through the woods one day, he comes upon the sleeping woman again and discovered that she is on a pedestal surrounded by a pit containing a giant bear. Unwilling to leave her to the mercy of the bear, who threatens Ivan by hurling rocks at him, Ivan, a successful long distance runner, races around the pit until he tires out the bear. Then he leaps the pit and lands on the pedestal with the sleeping woman, wondering about his actions all the while. Previously he had reflected, "After all the fairy tales he had read and studied, the one possibility he had never entertained was this: That they might be true, or have some basis in truth. That the world might actually admit such possibilities as giant magical bears that could throw stones, as enchanted women who could lie forever in a coma..." (51–2). When he reaches the sleeping woman, he further reflects on her role: "he knew her as an icon, as the princess of the fairy tales. She was asleep because of some evil charm placed upon her by a jealous rival, a powerful witch who hated her. Had her finger been pricked by the sharp point of a spindle? Who knew which details of the old stories might be true?" (58). Like other folktale revisions, this one is clearly self-referential, though in Card's novel, the main character is more conscious of folktales and their roles and background than most because he is a scholar of the tales as well as someone surrounded by them in his culture. He is also likely the only person from the modern world who could succeed in breaking the spell, which in this case involves not just waking the Sleeping Beauty character with a kiss but asking her to marry him in Proto-Slavonic, a language he can understand because he has studied Old Church Slavonic. The breaking of the spell, which also casts the bear away, however, is just the beginning of this story.

Ivan learns from Katerina that The Widow had claimed the lands ruled by Katerina's father until Katerina married, and "Then she had the Great Bear pursue me. He drove me here, where I could run no farther. I fell asleep and he guarded me, until you came and gave me your oath, setting me free of him" (62-3). When he realizes that The Widow Katerina mentions is Baba Yaga, he is shocked, thinking, "If unconsciously he was looking for fairy tales, he had stumbled upon the mother lode" (63). He tries to explain that she has been asleep for a thousand years, but she tells him she was driven there that same day. This is where Card brings in time travel, for the reader learns through the Baba Yaga passage that follows this section that she had put "both Bear and the princess in a place cut loose from time" (65). The bridges that Katerina and Ivan see once the bear has disappeared lead to their respective times, and only when they hold hands can they see each other's bridge. Katerina insists that Ivan accompany her across the bridge, and thus begins his experience around 900 CE in Taina, a society that has long been dead in his own twentieth century. As he is walking naked through the village, having lost his clothing as he crossed the bridge, he reflects on his expectations of Sleeping Beauty's world compared to this reality:

> Yet even as he recognized and admired the medieval village he expected, Ivan had to wrestle with a completely different set of expectations, courtesy of Walt Disney. Wasn't it Sleeping Beauty he had kissed? Then where was the magnificent palace? Never mind that Disney's version of the story was set in some weird combination of the sixteenth and nineteenth centuries—Ivan couldn't help being let down at seeing—and hearing, and smelling—such a coarse reality instead of a magical dream [90].

He is forced to adjust to this much different world and is torn between his fascination at getting first-hand experience in a time he has studied for so long and his feelings of inadequacy and frustration with how little he fits in and how little respect he is given because he is not built like the other men and does not possess the same strength and fighting skills. In fact, when he is being taught swordplay, he is barely able to wield the sword because he lacks the upper body strength of the rest of the men.

Amid Ivan's learning about the reality of life around 900 CE, there are the continued problems with Baba Yaga, who, though her spell has been broken, has not given up her plans to possess Taina as she has taken over the surrounding villages. Eventually the danger to him and Katerina is so great that, shortly after they marry, they are forced to return to Ivan's time in an attempt to escape Baba Yaga. At that point Katerina realizes the difficulty Ivan must have had adapting to her culture and time because she is having similar difficulties with customs and language. Unfortunately, Baba Yaga follows them and they are forced to make plans to evade her in the twentieth century. They also devise a plan to defeat her when they return to the tenth century, eventually returning to Katerina's time with a few modern designs for weaponry that can be made using materials from the tenth century. The folktales that they are part of follow them through the times, and Ivan comes to realize that he is the Ivan of popular Russian folktales, and unlike the versions of "Sleeping Beauty" by Coover, Donoghue, and Tepper, Card's revision ends with a satisfactory, happy ending in which the Sleeping Beauty figure and her prince live happily ever after, have a family, and move freely between the two time periods.

Though it contains an odd contrast of modern and traditional settings, *Enchantment* is undeniably "Sleeping Beauty" combined with Baba Yaga and other Russian and Jewish tales,[5] with a focus on the post-kiss rather than the sleep or the backstory as many of the other revisions do. Card's novel also has more of a focus on Ivan, the prince figure, than most revisions, though the point of view does shift among many other characters, including Baba Yaga, Katerina, and Ivan's parents. As with the novels by Coover, Donoghue, and Tepper, Card's also contains elements that differ from children's revisions. Because there is no spindle or distaff, there is none of the ribald joking about that sexuality, though there are some considerations of sex once Ivan and Katerina marry and negotiate their relationship within that marriage. The more intellectual analysis of folktales and their role in society and in Ivan's life is what really makes this novel stand out as more mature than others. While many children's novels have a reflexive or metatextual element to them, they do not usually explore them in such depths, including their origins, their role in society, and the way they have traveled through time to their present form. Ivan, as both the prince character and a scholar of folklore, is in a unique position to understand and analyze how what he is doing is shaping the materials he will study.

Emily Dalton's novel *Wake Me with a Kiss*, like Card's novel, follows the more traditional happily ever after ending of folktales. This ending is expected, however, because the novel is part of the Harlequin American Romance Once Upon a Kiss miniseries in which popular folktales and myths are rewritten as modern romances. What is interesting about these types of revisions — and there are several imprints that have published folktale based miniseries — is how the authors bring the folktales into the modern world. Dalton's novel is set in the 1990s in Atlanta, Georgia. Her main characters are Aurora Dawn McBride — nicknamed Rorie and Briar Rose — and Phillip Fairchild, the "Perfume Prince." Rorie lives with her three godmothers, Dahlia, Daisy, and Daffodil "Daffy" Farley, who are expert gardeners. All of these names are interesting plays with the traditional elements of "Sleeping Beauty." These sisters have a younger half sister, Delphinia, who represents the evil fairy out to get not just Rorie but also her own sisters. Rorie and her godmothers live in an old Victorian house complete with a turret that Rorie uses as an office. The front door of this house is difficult to reach because of the literal maze of vegetation at the end of which stands Dragon, a giant sheepdog who guards the door. The main conflict of the story is Phillip and Delphinia's desire to get the secret formula for the godmothers' fertilizer. Phillip has earned the approval of the godmothers and is given three tests to earn the formula, while Delphinia plans to steal the formula with the help of a servant. Ultimately, the reader learns that the godmothers are setting up Phillip and Rorie, something that Rorie resists for most of the novel.

Despite the similarities of the names, the setting, and the godmothers, the story bears little resemblance to the plot of "Sleeping Beauty" until near the end of the novel when, as Delphinia and her chauffeur attempt to steal the volatile fertilizer, the chauffeur drops the bag containing it. It explodes and knocks Rorie unconscious. She lies comatose in the hospital for several days with Phillip at her side worrying about her. It is then that his mother visits and, recognizing Rorie, who looks like her late mother, tells him that he and Rorie had met as children and that their mothers had speculated that they "were destined to be married" (230). After his mother leaves, Phillip remembers a comment Rorie had made about being woken with a kiss, and he says to her, "You said this was your favorite way to wake up, Briar Rose.... So don't disappoint me" (233). When his kiss does not garner an instant response, he is dis-

couraged, but as Delphinia returns and tries to get Phillip to go in with
her on the sale of the fertilizer recipe, Rorie not only wakes but threatens to throw a vase at Delphinia is she doesn't leave Phillip alone. Like
the Sleeping Beauty of traditional tales, Rorie is woken by her prince,
but she is a much stronger woman who stands up for herself and her
prince than the traditional heroine.

   Though Dalton's novel can hardly be called literary, it does show
an interesting modern spin on "Sleeping Beauty" that combines the
stock characteristics of the modern romance novel with the elements of
the traditional folktale. There are godmothers with near magical powers, a prince, a princess, and an evil character. Further, there is a mysterious sleep — Rorie's coma — which ends as if by magic when Phillip
kisses her. Spinning, the skill banned in the traditional tale, is also
brought into the novel because Rorie runs her own business designing
hand knit sweaters for which she spins the wool. The novel is more based
on the Disney film version than the written versions by the Grimms,
Perrault or Basile. There are also, as in other revisions of a more literary nature, references made to folktales and the folktale tradition, such
as Phillip's thought that Rorie "would rather kiss a frog than kiss the Perfume Prince" (55) and Rorie's thought about the back garden, which
"seemed like an enchanted forest from a fairy tale" (65). And when
Phillip comes upon Rorie spinning in the turret by candlelight, he muses,

> Her hair fell over her shoulder like spun gold.
> *Spun gold.* Hell, had he somehow stepped into a fairy tale? [98].

Later, when Rorie and Phillip finally go on a date, she thinks of the night
as "the fulfillment of a dream, a fairy tale" (181) and decides "to give in
to the fairy tale a little bit longer. She'd deal with reality tomorrow"
(189). Finally, when Rorie is in a coma at the end, Dahlia comments,
"She's a real sleeping beauty" (227), and Delphinia snidely echoes that
comment when Rorie threatens her: "So the sleeping beauty has finally
awakened" (237). After Delphinia leaves, Rorie tells Phillip her dream:
"It was kind of like my own life, only exaggerated. You know, like a fairy
tale" (238), recounting a dream that is remarkably like the Walt Disney
film version of "Sleeping Beauty."

   The main difference between this revision and many of the others
is that though the characters compare their lives to folktales, they do not
see themselves as the origination of the tale — something clearly done by
Coover, Tepper, and Card. Instead, they are similar and parallel to the
stories they know. The adult element of Dalton's novel, aside from the

fact that it is a Harlequin imprint marketed for late teens and adult women, is the sexualized nature of the story. Though the actual tale is not sexualized, the novel itself contains sexual elements, just not as ribald as most. The older age of the main characters — Rorie is almost ten years older than the traditional Sleeping Beauty character — also lends this novel to the adult category, much like the revisions by Tepper and Card, whose characters are either older during the main part of the story or age throughout the story.

Philip Margolin's novel *Sleeping Beauty* differs completely from the other novels discussed. Though this novel is, like Dalton's novel, completely modern in setting, the story "Sleeping Beauty" is used as a metaphor for two characters in the story. The novel is the story of a true crime writer Miles Van Meter and his book *Sleeping Beauty*. In his book, dealing with a serial rapist and killer who put his sister Casey into a coma, it is Casey who is the Sleeping Beauty figure because she has been in a coma, with no indication if she will ever wake, for many years. Yet there is also a second Sleeping Beauty figure in the part of the novel retelling the events of Van Meter's book: Ashley Spencer whose parents are both thought to have been murdered by the same person who put Casey into a coma. Though never directly called Sleeping Beauty, and though never in a literal sleep, Ashley spends several years of her life hiding from the killer and further time avoiding Miles' book. Once she does read his book, she is woken to the truth of the murder case and realizes that the wrong man has been convicted. Casey, on the other hand, is directly compared to Sleeping Beauty by Miles when he tells Ashley that his father "fooled himself into believing that Casey would wake up from her coma like Sleeping Beauty. But the children's fable and his dream are both fairy tales" (179). Because this novel uses the character Sleeping Beauty metaphorically, there is the assumption that the reader is familiar with the tale and also that making the allusion is enough. Many adult novels use folktales in this manner. Ed McBain's series of Matthew Hope novels, starting with *Goldilocks*, also uses the tales metaphorically, though his comparisons to folktales in *Goldilocks* is more overt than Margolin's references in *Sleeping Beauty*.

For most adult novels, the focal point is the construction of story and how the characters fit into the stories, whether they are originators of the tales or comparable to the traditional story. Even the use of metaphor in Margolin's novel is focused on the story because in the case of Miles' true crime book, he is constructing his story around his sister and Ashley (who turns out to be his niece) while Margolin's main story

revolves around Ashley's story being constructed and then her decon-
struction of Miles' book, which lead to the reconstruction of the story
with the true criminals caught and convicted. All of the adult revisions
contain themes and elements more advanced than in children's revisions. For many, it is the sexualized nature of the story, though for some,
such as *Enchantment* and *Wake Me with a Kiss*, which are slightly less
sexualized, the difference may be the older age of the main characters,
pulling them away from adolescence and thus from an age with which
the child reader can easily relate. This is why "Sleeping Beauty" is used —
the tale is one about the maturing of the main character, and many adult
revisions look at the character's life after waking or at the sexual matu-
ration.[6] A tale such as "The Three Little Pigs," very commonly revised
in children's literature, while showing the title characters moving away
from home, a mature theme, have the element of animal characters,
which appeals greatly to children. And a tale such as "Cinderella," popular in both adult and children's literature, has the theme of the under-
privileged child making good, something that appeals to children and
adults alike, but also has the more mature possible themes explored for
adults, such as the question of whether the prince is an ideal mate. Some
revisions, including Tanith Lee's "When the Clock Strikes" and Tepper's
section about Cinderella in *Beauty*, also point to the possibility that the
Cinderella character is actually the antagonist, plotting for her future and
planning to ensnare the prince for her own reasons. The adult revisions
reclaim the tales for their original audience, bringing back some of the
darker elements that were sanitized out as they were brought into the
realm of the nursery.

Conclusion: Reweaving
the Folktale Tradition

This book opened with Vivian Vande Velde's comment in *The Rumpelstiltskin Problem* that "Rumpelstiltskin" "makes no sense" (viii). The question that must be asked after the analyses in the preceding chapters is "Do modern folktale revisions make sense of the folktale tradition?" The answer, of course, is complex.

For some authors, particularly the ones who revise folktales with an eye toward humor, such as Mike Thaler and Roald Dahl, the goal of the revision is not necessarily to make sense of the tale but to show how the tale doesn't makes sense by focusing attention on the very places where the tales fail for a contemporary audience. Thus for Thaler in *Cinderella Bigfoot*, Cinderella's small feet and wicked stepfamily come under scrutiny while Dahl in *Revolting Rhymes* questions Goldilocks' innocence and Little Red Riding Hood's weakness, as well as whether she is trustworthy. Vande Velde similarly questions Goldilocks' innocence in *Tales from the Brothers Grimm and the Sisters Weird*, as well as the role of many traditional folktale characters. Even as she tries to "make sense" of "Rumpelstiltskin," answering the many questions she posed about it in *The Rumpelstiltskin Problem*, she pokes fun at the characters she doesn't understand, usually the miller, but also the king and the miller's daughter on occasion. The humor in these folktale revisions often precludes sense being made of the tales, but it does shine a spotlight on where and how the traditional tales do not make sense.

Other authors, however, struggle to make sense of the tales for their audiences in a serious manner, maintaining the tone of the traditional versions and exploring the places where the tales do not make sense. The results are varied. In feminist revisions, for example, the focus is naturally on gender roles and how traditionally weak characters can be explained and/or empowered. For Gail Carson Levine in *Ella Enchanted*, this means excusing Cinderella's passiveness by placing her under a fairy's curse that she must struggle to break. For Jane Yolen in *Sleeping Ugly*, it means contrasting Plain Jane with Princess Misrella to show that beauty is not as important as personality. For Diane Stanley in *Rumpelstiltskin's Daughter*, it means having Hope outsmart the king. Feminist revisions look to address the perceived sexism in traditional folktales, thus making sense of the tales for modern girls and women.

Other types of revisions make sense of folktales in different manners. Novel-length revisions in particular explore character motivation in a number of ways, including through a feminist lens. In these novel-length revisions, whether presented in first or third person point of view, the development of character and point of view helps to make sense of any number of characters. Usually it is the traditional protagonist, as in the case of Robin McKinley's *Beauty* and *Rose Daughter*, Margaret Peterson Haddix's *Just Ella*, and E.D. Baker's *The Frog Princess*, but traditional antagonists have their points of view explored as well. The use of the traditional antagonist's point of view allows the reader to understand if not excuse the actions of these typically flat characters. Donna Jo Napoli accomplishes this rounding in her novels *Beast*, "Beauty and the Beast" told from the Beast's perspective; *Spinners*, with its balanced point of view between Rumpelstiltskin and the miller's daughter; and *The Magic Circle*, told by Hansel and Gretel's witch. The development of character is one of the most effective ways to "make sense" of traditional folktales, for it allows contemporary readers to understand how events in folktales can occur.

Like novel-length revisions, short folktale revisions can also revise the point of view to present the tale from the traditional antagonist's point of view. Both Jon Scieszka in *The True Story of the 3 Little Pigs* and Alvin Granowsky's *The Unfairest of Them All/Snow White* and *That* Awful *Cinderella/Cinderella*, among others, employ this technique for exploring the elements of traditional folktales that don't "make sense." Though the presentation of this different point of view may not always convince the reader of that character's innocence in the tale, it does allow for a better sense of how the events in the tale happen.

Feature-length film revisions similarly explore the motivation of characters, often rejecting the role that love at first sight plays in traditional tales. While Cinderella and her prince may be instantly attracted to each other, even in love, most films force them to earn each other's affection in some manner. For *Ever After*, they meet secretly on several occasions and seem to have earned that love only to have it tested again at the masquerade. Prince Henry must prove that he is worthy of Danielle's love throughout the film. Most of the other film revisions require similar tests of the characters' strength and worthiness.

Even revisions that look toward the entire folktale tradition struggle to make sense of that tradition — its character types, the reasons for their actions, their likely resistance to their prescribed roles. Again feminism often comes into play here with authors reshaping gender roles in various ways, from Robert Munsch's *The Paper Bag Princess*, with Princess Elizabeth refusing to marry Prince Ronald, to Rebecca Lickiss' character Lady Vevila in *Never After*, chafing at her role and eventually finding a way to fulfill her role while retaining her freedom.

Regardless of how folktales revisions are shaped, the main element that ties them together is their intertextuality. Even though not all folktale revisions must be read with the traditional version in mind, they are all best understood when placed alongside the traditional texts, or of the generic conventions in the case of revisions of the form. Because contemporary authors are making sense of the folktale tradition, parallels to that tradition are vital. The intertextuality adds substance to the analyses of these contemporary texts, which reweave the folktale tradition using the threads of the oral and written folktale traditions.

Notes

1. The Folktale Revision as a Form

1. This tale is also often categorized as a fairy tale because of the magical elements involved.

2. In *When Dreams Came True: Classical Fairy Tales and Their Tradition*, Zipes does offer the translation art tale without commenting on it, but he continues to use the label fairy tale to discuss the literary tradition of folktales.

3. It should be noted that even today adaptations of children's books occur on a nightly basis, for even though parents may use a specific written version of a folktale to read their children, often they are both performing and adapting the text, whether to remove objectionable elements, shorten the text, make the story more engaging, or otherwise alter the text in front of them. I am indebted to Charlotte Amaro for pointing out this act of retelling to me.

4. Maria Tatar, in *The Hard Facts of the Grimms' Fairy Tales*, discusses this combination of oral and literary, placing the Grimms' tales on a spectrum halfway between "oral folktales" and "printed literary texts" (33). She then differentiates *folktales* and *folk tales*, the former being "the entire class of traditional oral narratives," and the latter "its naturalistic subset" (33). The *folk tale* differs from the *fairy tale*, which Tatar defines as being "reserved for all narratives set in a fictional world where preternatural events and supernatural interventional are wholly taken for granted" (33). Fairy tales can be both oral and literary, and the Grimms' collection is a combination of folk tales and fairy tales.

2. Humor in Folktale Revisions

1. Picture books are usually published without page numbers. As a result, unless page numbers are given in the books, none will be cited.

2. This revision is also included in *The Rumpelstiltskin Problem*.

3. It is interesting to note that folktales are frequently used in advertising campaigns for a variety of products, including ESPN ("Cinderella"), food items ("Goldilocks and the Three Bears"), investing ("The Frog Prince") and even foot spray ("Cinderella").

4. They were originally published individually in small hardbacks of approximately 100 pages each. They can also be found in two three-tale collections in paperback, *The Princess Tales, Volume One* and *The Princess Tales, Volume Two*.

5. Ethelinda threatens to take away

Myrtle's "punishment" to get her to help Rosella, which leads to the question of why she doesn't just take away Rosella's "reward" to help her.

6. See Chapter 7 for an analysis of her narrative technique.

3. Cultural and Regional Folktale Revisions in Picture Books

1. Specifically, the picture book tradition in the United States, and, to a smaller extent, Canada and Great Britain.

2. Though *Mufaro's Beautiful Daughters* is often considered a Cinderella tale, in fact it more closely resembles "The Kind and Unkind Girls" type (AT480), perhaps best known from the tale "Toads and Diamonds."

3. Her other revisions include *The Three Little Javelinas*, *Dusty Locks and the Three Bears*, and *Cindy Ellen: A Wild Western Cinderella*.

4. This is not the only time that "Little Red Riding Hood" and "The Three Little Pigs" are combined. Roald Dahl also combines them in his book *Revolting Rhymes*, though the character that crosses over in his revision is Little Red Riding Hood, not the wolf.

5. They are, respectively, a "Hawaiian way of preparing raw fish"; "pudding made of baked or steamed grated taro and coconut milk"; and "pig that has been baked in an underground oven."

6. Artell's revision is the only one that depicts Little Red Riding Hood as something other than human. In Jim Harris' drawings, she and her family are white geese, though the text itself does not specify whether they are supposed to be human or geese.

4. Breaking the Picture Book Rules

1. Nikolajeva and Scott, in discussing endpapers in picture books, note that

though both endpapers are usually "either white or neutral," "a growing number of picturebook creators have discovered the possibilities of endpapers as additional paratexts that can contribute to the story in various ways" (247). The method Levine uses, beginning and ending the story on the endpapers, is one of the most unusual of the methods of utilizing the endpapers.

5. Feminist Folktale Revisions

1. These strong women who are defeated reveal the need people felt to discredit strong female characters. The implication behind the use of wicked witches and evil stepmothers is that women who have power are corrupt and must be stopped so that women who are passive (Snow White, Rapunzel) can be protected from their influence and remain pure and part of the ideal of womanhood.

2. Several years later she also published *Mightier Than the Sword: World Folktales for Strong Boys*, a collection of tales in which the heroes are revered for their intelligence rather than their brawn. Though not a feminist collection of tales, it is certainly a collection in which modern ideas of gender are challenged and boys who do not fight are more important than those who do.

3. Some of the tales in these collections are also revisions of tales and will thus fit in the final group, to be discussed presently.

4. For a longer discussion of this type of tale, see Chapter 9, which examines ways in which authors have revised the folktale tradition as a whole.

5. There are also tales that switch the gender roles in the opposite manner, making a boy the main character that is typically the girl. This switch occurs most often with revisions of "Cinderella" such as Helen Ketterman's *Bubba the Cowboy Prince: A Fractured Texas Tale* and Babette Cole's *Prince Cinders*. In both of these ver-

sions, the protagonist plays the role of the abused child forced to do all of the chores and not allowed to attend the ball. Though there is no crying from these characters, they both are given the opportunity to go to the ball by a helper character and win the princess character without any active attempt on their part. There are other, more humorous, aspects to these revisions as well.

6. "Beauty and the Beast" and its counterparts are the main exceptions to this rule.

7. In fact many revisions of "Cinderella" question the validity of the "love at first sight," sometimes making the love a result of a spell (as in the case of Tanith Lee's "When the Clock Strikes") or questioning the strength of the love in a post "happily ever after" scene (as in the musical *Into the Woods*).

6. Postmodern Folktale Revisions

1. Scieszka is not the only author to create this new, first person voice for the traditional antagonist. Alvin Granowsky, in his Point-of-View series (discussed briefly in chapter 4), uses the traditional antagonists almost exclusively in the revision side of his flip books, and in most of these first person retellings, the narrators simultaneously make a case for themselves and dismantle that case through the manner in which they present their point of view. This is particularly true in the "Snow White and the Seven Dwarfs" revision *The Unfairest of Them All* told from the stepmother's point of view. In this narrative, though she tries to show herself as a doting stepmother, she also shows herself to be quite vain and thus undermines her own arguments. What is interesting about Granowsky's series is that he presents two versions of the story within a single book, something fitting for postmodern revisions and the concept of authorization as presented by Bacchilega.

2. Other authors have presented multiple versions of the same tale as well. Alvin Granowsky, mentioned above, presents two different versions, one traditional, one a revision, in each of his books. Robin McKinley has published two novel revisions of "Beauty and the Beast," *Beauty* and *Rose Daughter*. Vande Velde's book, however, with its six versions, is one of the most dramatic cases of an author presenting a tale in multiple voices.

7. Narrative in Folktale Revisions

1. In the same article referenced earlier, Dundes comments, "One should be able to investigate the nature of fairy tale book illustrations, but one should realize that one is dealing with a derivative, printed art-form, part of a literary and commercial tradition which is at least one full step removed from the original oral tale" (265). The removal from the oral tale is undeniable, but the artwork is not always derivative, and in fact the variety of traditional folktales published in picture book format shows that artists are in many ways following in the same path that the oral tellers used to, for previous picture book artists influence new ones and each picture book, while differing from past versions, reveals the influence, much as tale telling would have done orally. Storytellers would hear a tale and adapt it to their own style while keeping the heart of the tale in tact. The same can be argued about picture books. Claire Malarte-Feldman's article "Folk Materials, Re-Visions, and Narrative Images: The Intertextual Games They Play" examines this artistic connection.

2. It does not always remain the same text, however, for different author/illustrators choose different textual versions than each other as well as different illustration styles. Often the author retranslates or otherwise "adapts" the traditional tale as well.

3. McKinley has an earlier revision of "Beauty and the Beast" called *Beauty* that

is told in first person from Beauty's point of view.

4. There are several more traditionally named characters, such as Jack and Aubrey Trueword, the sons of the Squire, and two of the cats that act as guides for Lionheart and Jeweltongue.

5. There may be the occasional use of Historical Present in the traditional versions, but edited compilations often remove this usage from the stories in order to make the stories appear more literary. A traditional storyteller, however, is likely to use the Historical Present within the story. This technique is also sometimes called Conversational Historical Present, defined by Nessa Wolfson in her article "A Feature of Performed Narrative: The Conversational Historical Present" as "the use of the historical present tense specifically in narratives which occur in everyday conversational interactions" (215), though a traditional storyteller is more likely to be seen as using Historical Present because storytelling is usually a more formal situation than everyday conversations.

prince in addition to Cinderella's godmother.

5. The business is Big Andy's and has the motto "The Car Wash King," an interesting way that Austin is further tied to his role of prince.

6. There are occasions in which some Cinderellas are shown falling or otherwise uncoordinated, but these situations are usually caused in some way by the stepfamily, whereas Lewis' Cinderfella is inherently klutzy.

7. She is sometimes called Charmant.

8. Though there is still a ball in this revision, it is hosted by Cinderella's stepmother and stepbrothers for Princess Charming, who is visiting them in California. This change is an interesting one, for it is Rupert, one of Fella's stepbrothers, who is throwing the ball in an attempt to woo Princess Charming (and marry her for her money) rather than her throwing the ball to find a mate. There is some speculation by the media covering the event that Princess Charming is looking for a mate, but she never confirms it.

8. Folktale Revisions on Film

1. Information gathered from Internet Movie Database <www.IMDB.com>.

2. This program was also titled *Rocky and His Friends*, *The Rocky and Bullwinkle Show*, and *The Bullwinkle Show* at various times in its history.

3. Some children's shows, notably *Sesame Street* and the Muppets, have hour-long revisions. *Hey Cinderella*, one of the Muppet revisions, is discussed with the feature-length films, though it could arguably be read as a hybrid of the feature-length and short film, for it contains character development but also leans toward humor and the incorporation of familiar characters such as Kermit the Frog.

4. This version of "Cinderella" contains the only lasting father figure, who is eventually able to break away from his evil wife and cast her from his house. This version also features a godfather for the

9. Revising the Folktale Tradition

1. The book is not long enough to grapple with the possibility that once the dragon recovers his energy he will be looking for revenge, though that seems a likely possibility since he was outmaneuvered by a princess.

2. In later scenes between Althelstan's parents, it is revealed that this edict was made because King Abelardann feared Althelstan would marry Vevila. When Queen Tarax tells him that "Vevila wouldn't have Althelstan, not even for all Portula and Regenweald," the king wonders if it's "too late to revoke that pronouncement" (45).

10. The Adult Connection

1. This use of present tense is similar to Donna Jo Napoli's style discussed in Chapter 7.

2. The exception is the final story, which is about the power of witches and how they can come about that power.

3. It is interesting to note that *Kissing the Witch* is generally considered a young adult text, like Jane Yolen's *Briar Rose*, though both have very mature themes and elements and easily fit under the umbrella of adult literature. The line between young adult and adult books is somewhat fluid.

4. Giles, for whom she names her great grandson, moves in and out of her life from her childhood. They are separated just before her sixteenth birthday, but meet up again each time she returns to the fourteenth century, finally finding some happiness together when they are in their eighties.

5. The Jewish tales come into play when Ivan and his family convert to Judaism in order to escape the Soviet Union, planning to get permission to move to Israel, but change planes to a new direction once they are out of the Soviet Union.

6. There are many other revisions of "Sleeping Beauty" for an adult audience that could have been discussed here, including Jane Yolen's novel *Briar Rose* and A.N. Roquelaure's trilogy *The Claiming of Sleeping Beauty*, *Beauty's Punishment*, and *Beauty's Release*, as well as many poems and short prose revisions.

Bibliography

The following bibliography begins with a list of traditional folktale collections then presents contemporary folktale revisions listed first by anthology and then by individually published tales. The bibliography mixes revisions for children and adults, indicating adult revisions in parentheses after the citation. Additional information about the revisions, if necessary, is presented in brackets. Following the list of written revisions is a list of film revisions and then a list of critical sources.

Traditional Collections

Andersen, Hans Christian. *A Treasury of Hans Christian Andersen*. Trans. Erik Christian Haugaard. Garden City, NY: Doubleday, 1974.

Cole, Joanna. *Best-Loved Folktales of the World*. New York: Doubleday, 1982.

Grimm, Jacob, and Wilhelm Grimm. *Grimm's Complete Fairy Tales*. New York: Doubleday, n.d.

Heiner, Heidi Anne. *SurLaLune Fairy Tales*. 1998–2005. 25 Sept. 2005. <http://www.surlalunefairytales.com/index.html>. [This exceptional web site contains numerous annotated traditional folktales as well as information about folktale revisions.]

Lang, Andrew, ed. *The Blue Fairy Book*. 1889. New York: Dover, 1965.

_____. *The Brown Fairy Book*. 1904. New York: Dover, 1965.

_____. *The Crimson Fairy Book*. 1903. New York: Dover, 1967.

_____. *The Green Fairy Book*. 1892. New York: Dover, 1965.

_____. *The Grey Fairy Book*. 1900. New York: Dover, 1967.

_____. *The Lilac Fairy Book*. 1910. New York: Dover, 1968.

_____. *The Olive Fairy Book*. 1907. New York: Dover, 1968.

_____. *The Orange Fairy Book*. 1906. New York: Dover, 1968.

_____. *The Pink Fairy Book*. 1897. New York: Dover, 1967.
_____. *The Red Fairy Book*. 1890. New York: Dover, 1966.
_____. *The Violet Fairy Book*. 1901. New York: Dover, 1966.
_____. *The Yellow Fairy Book*. 1894. New York: Dover, 1966.
Nye, Robert. *Classic Folk Tales from Around the World*. London: Bracken, 1994.
Opie, Iona, and Peter Opie. *The Classic Fairy Tales*. New York: Oxford UP, 1974.
Saltman, Judith. *The Riverside Anthology of Children's Literature*. 6th ed. Boston: Houghton, 1985.
Tatar, Maria M. *The Classic Fairy Tales: Texts, Criticism*. Norton Critical Ed. New York: Norton, 1998. [also contains numerous revisions]
Yolen, Jane. *Mightier Than the Sword: World Folktales for Strong Boys*. Illus. Raul Colón. New York: Harcourt, 2003.
_____. *Not One Damsel in Distress: World Folktales for Strong Girls*. Illus. Susan Guevara. New York: Harcourt, 2000.
Zipes, Jack. *The Great Fairy Tale Tradition: From Straparola and Basile to the Brothers Grimm*. Norton Critical Ed. New York: Norton, 2001.

Anthologies

Ada, Alma Flor. *Dear Peter Rabbit*. Illus. Leslie Tryon. New York: Aladdin, 1994.
_____. *With Love, Little Red Hen*. Illus. Leslie Tryon. New York: Atheneum, 2001.
_____. *Yours Truly, Goldilocks*. Illus. Leslie Tryon. New York: Aladdin, 1998.
Beaumont, Jeanne Marie and Claudia Carlson, eds. *The Poets' Grimm: 20th Century Poems from Grimm Fairy Tales*. Ashland, OR: Story Line P, 2003. (Adult)
Block, Francesca Lia. *The Rose and the Beast: Fairy Tales Retold*. New York: Harper, 2000.
Broumas, Olga. *Beginning with O*. Yale Series of Younger Poets vol. 72. New Haven, CT: Yale UP, 1977. (Adult)
Carter, Angela. *The Bloody Chamber and Other Stories*. New York: Penguin, 1979. (Adult)
_____. *Saints and Strangers*. New York: Viking, 1985. (Adult)
Cashorali, Peter. *Fairy Tales: Traditional Stories Retold for Gay Men*. New York: Harper, 1995. (Adult)
Coover, Robert. *Pricksongs & Descants: Fictions*. New York: Grove, 1969. (Adult)
Dahl, Roald. *Revolting Rhymes*. Illus. Quentin Blake. New York: Bantam, 1983.
Datlow, Ellen, and Terri Windling, eds. *Black Heart, Ivory Bones*. New York: Avon, 2000. (Adult)
_____, eds. *Black Swan, White Raven*. New York: Avon, 1997. (Adult)
_____, eds. *Black Thorn, White Rose*. New York: AvoNova, 1994. (Adult)
_____, eds. *The Green Man: Tales from the Mythic Forest*. New York: Firebird-Penguin, 2004. (Adult)
_____, eds. *Ruby Slippers, Golden Tears*. New York: AvoNova, 1995. (Adult)
_____, eds. *Silver Birch, Blood Moon*. New York: Avon, 1999. (Adult)
_____, eds. *Sirens and Other Daemon Lovers*. New York: Eos-Harper, 1998. (Adult)

_____, eds. *Snow White, Blood Red*. New York: AvoNova, 1993. (Adult)

_____, eds. *Swan Sister: Fairy Tales Retold*. New York: Simon, 2003.

_____, eds. *A Wolf at the Door and Other Retold Fairy Tales*. New York: Simon, 2000.

Donoghue, Emma. *Kissing the Witch: Old Tales in New Skins*. New York: Harper, 1997. (Adult — sometimes categorized as Young Adult)

Dunn, Carola, Karla Hocker, and Judith A. Lansdowne. *Once Upon a Kiss: Fairy Tale Regency Romances from Three Favorite Authors*. New York: Zebra, 1999. (Adult)

_____. *Once Upon a Time: Fairy Tale Regency Romances from Three Favorite Authors*. New York: Zebra, 1998. (Adult)

_____. *Once Upon a Waltz*. New York: Zebra, 2001. (Adult)

Fredericks, Anthony D. *Frantic Frogs and Other Frankly Fractured Folktales for Readers Theatre*. Illus. Anthony Allan Stoner and Joan Garner. Westport, CT: Teacher Idea P, 1993.

French, Vivian. *Aesop's Funky Fables*. Illus. Korky Paul. London: Hamish Hamilton-Puffin, 1997.

Galloway, Priscilla. *Truly Grim Tales*. Toronto: Stoddary, 1995.

Gaiman, Neil. *Smoke and Mirrors: Shorter Fiction and Illusions*. New York: Perennial, 1998. (Adult)

Garner, James Finn. *Once Upon a More Enlightened Time: More Politically Correct Bedtime Stories*. New York: Macmillan, 1995.

_____. *Politically Correct Bedtime Stories: Modern Tales for Our Life & Times*. New York: Macmillan, 1994.

Goldman, Leslie. *Dora's Favorite Fairy Tales*. Illus. A & J Studios. New York: Scholastic, 2004.

Gorman, Ed, and Martin H. Greenberg, eds. *Once Upon a Crime*. New York: Berkley Crime Prime, 1998. (Adult)

Greenberg, Dan. *Fractured Fairy Tales Fractions & Decimals*. New York: Scholastic, 2005.

_____. *Fractured Fairy Tales Multiplication & Division*. New York: Scholastic, 2005.

Hallett, Martin and Barbara Karasek, eds. *Folk & Fairy Tales*. 3rd ed. Orchard Park, NY: Broadview, 2002. [mix of traditional and revisions]

Hartwell, David G. *Masterpieces of Fantasy and Enchantment*. Garden City, NY: Doubleday, 1988. (Adult)

Hawkins, Colin and Jacqui. *Fairytale News*. Cambridge, MA: Candlewick, 2004.

Hay, Sara Henderson. *Story Hour*. 1961. Fayetteville, AR: U of Arkansas P, 1998. [poems]

Jacobs, A.J. *Fractured Fairy Tales*. New York: Bantam, 1997.

Jasheway, Leigh Anne. *Bedtime Stories for Dogs*. Kansas City: Andrews and McMeel, 1996.

Lansky, Bruce, ed. *Girls to the Rescue Book #1: Tales of Clever, Courageous Girls from around the World*. New York: Meadowbrook, 1995.

_____. *Girls to the Rescue Book #2: Tales of Clever, Courageous Girls from around the World*. New York: Meadowbrook, 1996.

_____. *Girls to the Rescue Book #3: Tales of Clever, Courageous Girls from around the World*. New York: Meadowbrook, 1997.

_____. *Girls to the Rescue Book #4: Tales of Clever, Courageous Girls from around the World*. New York: Meadowbrook, 1998.

_____. *Girls to the Rescue Book #5: Tales of Clever, Courageous Girls from around the World*. New York: Meadowbrook, 1998.

_____. *Girls to the Rescue Book #6: Tales of Clever, Courageous Girls from around the World*. New York: Meadowbrook, 1999.

_____. *Girls to the Rescue Book #7: Tales of Clever, Courageous Girls from around the World*. New York: Meadowbrook, 2000.

_____. *Newfangled Fairy Tales: Classic Stories with a Funny Twist Book #1*. New York: Meadowbrook, 1997.

_____. *Newfangled Fairy Tales: Classic Stories with a Funny Twist Book #2*. New York: Meadowbrook, 1998.

Lee, Tanith. *Red as Blood, or Tales of the Sisters Grimmer*. New York: Daw, 1983. (Adult)

Little, Denise, ed. *Twice Upon a Time*. New York: Daw, 1999. (Adult)

Looney Tunes: Your Favorite Looney Tunes Storybook Collection. Franklin, TN: Dalmation P, 2003.

Maguire, Gregory. *Leaping Beauty and Other Animal Fairy Tales*. Illus. Chris L. Demarest. New York: Harper, 2004.

Martin, Justin McCory. *12 Fabulously Funny Fairy Tale Plays*. New York: Scholastic, 2002.

McKinley, Robin. *The Door in the Hedge*. New York: Berkley, 1981.

McNaughton, Colin. *Who's Been Sleeping in My Porridge?: A Book of Wacky Poems and Pictures*. Cambridge, MA: Candlewick, 1990.

My Big Book of Fairy Tales in Rhyme! Illus. Jan Lewis. London: Tucker Slingsby, 2004.

Once Upon a Fairy Tale. New York: Viking, 2001. [with CD]

Once Upon a Kiss: Fairy Tale Regency Romances from Three Favorite Authors. New York: Zebra, 1999. (Adult)

Once Upon a Waltz: Three Stories of Fairy Tale Love. New York: Zebra, 2001. (Adult)

Pugliano, Carol. *Easy-to-Read Folk and Fairy Tale Plays*. New York: Scholastic, 1997.

Rae, Jennifer. *Dog Tales*. Illus. Rose Cowles. Berkeley: Tricycle, 1998.

Scieszka, Jon. *Squids Will Be Squids: Fresh Morals, Beastly Fables*. Illus. Lane Smith. New York: Viking, 1998.

_____. *The Stinky Cheese Man and Other Fairly Stupid Tales*. Illus. Lane Smith. New York: Viking, 1992.

Sexton, Anne. *Transformations*. New York: Mariner, 1971. (Adult)

Shepard, Aaron. *Folktales on Stage: Scripts for Reader's Theater*. Los Angeles: Shepard, 2004.

Szereto, Mitzi. *Erotic Fairy Tales: A Romp through the Classics*. San Francisco: Cleis, 2000. (Adult)

Thurber, James. *Fables for Our Time and Famous Poems Illustrated*. New York: Harper, 1939. (Adult)

Tyler, Alison, ed. *Naughty Fairy Tales from A to Z*. Garden City, NY: Venus, 2003. (Adult)

Vande Velde, Vivian. *Tales from the Brothers Grimm and the Sisters Weird*. New York: Dell Yearling, 1995.

Viorst, Judith. *If I Were in Charge of the World and Other Worries.* Illus. Lynne Cherry. New York: Aladdin, 1981. [contains section called fairy tales with four poems in it]

Walker, Barbara G. *Feminist Fairy Tales.* New York: Harper, 1996. (Adult)

Wolf, J.M. *Cinderella Outgrows the Glass Slipper and Other Zany Fractured Fairy Tale Plays.* New York: Scholastic, 2002.

Zipes, Jack, ed. *The Outspoken Princess and the Gentle Knight: A Treasury of Modern Fairy Tales.* Illus. Stéphane Poulin. New York: Bantam, 1994.

_____, ed. *Spells of Enchantment: The Wondrous Fairy Tales of Western Culture.* New York: Viking, 1991. [some of content is for adults]

Specific Tales

In addition to the most popular folktales by the Grimms and Perrault, this list includes a few non–Western tales and others that are not well known, as well as some legends and fables. Though the list is fairly comprehensive, it cannot hope to list every folktale revision published.

Ali Baba/Arabian Nights

Dokey, Cameron. *The Storyteller's Daughter.* New York: Simon Pulse, 2002.

Tremblay, Carole. *Mary Baba and the 40 Sailors.* Illus. Dominique Jolin. Trans. Catherine Solyom. Saint-Lambert, PQ: Dominique, 1998.

Beauty and the Beast (including East of the Sun, West of the Moon)

Baker, Jennifer. *The Rose.* New York: Scholastic, 1996.

Baldwin, Rebecca. *Arabella and the Beast.* New York: St. Martin's, 1988. (Adult)

Bevarly, Elizabeth. *Beauty and the Brain.* Silhouette Desire 1130. Blame It on Bob Miniseries. New York: Silhouette, 1998. (Adult)

Bird, Jessica. *Beauty and the Black Sheep.* Silhouette Special Edition 1698. The Moorehouse Legacy Miniseries. New York: Silhouette, 2005. (Adult)

Christenberry, Judy. *Beauty & the Beastly Rancher.* Silhouette Romance 1678. From the Cricle K Miniseries. New York: Silhouette, 2003. (Adult)

Colter, Cara. *Nighttime Sweethearts.* Silhouette Romance 1754. In a Fairy Tale World ... Miniseries. New York: Silhouette, 2005. (Adult)

Dalton, Emily. *Beauty and the Beastie.* Harlequin Regency Romance 59. New York: Harlequin, 1991. (Adult)

Feather, Jane. *The Silver Rose.* New York: Bantam, 1997. (Adult)

Garbera, Katherine. *In Bed with Beauty.* Silhouette Desire 1535. King of Hearts Miniseries. New York: Silhouette, 2003. (Adult)

Grace, Carol. *Beauty and the Big Bad Wolf.* Silhouette Romance 1767. In a Fairy Tale World ... Miniseries. New York: Silhouette, 2005. (Adult)

Hambly, Barbara. *Beauty and the Beast*. New York: Avon, 1989. (Adult) [based on TV series]

Hearne, Betsy. *Beauties and Beasts*. The Oryx Multicultural Folktale Series. Illus. Joanne Caroselli. Phoenix: Oryx, 1993.

Johnson, Janice Kay. *Beauty & the Beasts*. Harlequin Superromance 758. New York: Harlequin, 1997. (Adult)

Kaiser, Janice. *Wilde at Heart*. Harlequin Temptation 429. Lovers & Legends Miniseries. New York: Harlequin, 1993. (Adult)

Lackey, Mercedes. *The Fire Rose*. New York: Baen, 1995. (Adult)

Mason, Jane B., and Sarah Hines Stephens. *Beauty Is a Beast*. The Princess School #4. New York: Scholastic, 2004.

McKinley, Robin. *Beauty*. New York: Harper, 1978.

_____. *Rose Daughter*. New York: Ace, 1997.

Medeiros, Teresa. *The Bride and the Beast*. New York: Bantam, 2001. (Adult)

Napoli, Donna Jo. *Beast*. New York: Antheum, 2000.

Pattou, Edith. *East*. New York: Harcourt, 2003.

Ryan, Taylor. *Beauty and the Beast*. Harlequin Historical 342. New York: Harlequin, 1996. (Adult)

Singh, Nalini. *Craving Beauty*. Silhouette Desire 1667. New York: Silhouette, 2005. (Adult)

Woodiwiss, Kathleen E. *A Rose in Winter*. New York: Avon, 1982. (Adult)

Yep, Laurence. *The Dragon Prince: A Chinese Beauty & the Beast Tale*. Illus. Kam Mak. New York: Harper, 1997.

Bluebeard

Frost, Gregory. *Fitcher's Brides*. The Fairy Tale Ser. New York: Tor-Tom Doherty, 2002. (Adult)

The Boy Who Cried Wolf

Hartman, Bob. *The Wolf Who Cried Boy*. Illus. by Tim Raglin. New York: Putnam, 2002.

Levine, Gail Carson. *Betsy Who Cried Wolf*. Illus. Scott Nash. New York: Harper, 2002.

Perrotta, Anne-Marie, and Tean Schultz. *The Dog Who Cried "Woof!"* New York: Scholastic, 2001.

The Brave Little Tailor

Osborne, Mary Pope. *The Brave Little Seamstress*. Illus. Giselle Potter. New York: Atheneum, 2002.

Chicken Little

Kellogg, Steven. *Chicken Little*. New York: Harper, 1985.

Cinderella/Ashputtle

Bascom, William. "Cinderella in Africa." Dundes, *Cinderella* 148–68.

Baker, Jennifer. *At Midnight*. New York: Scholastic, 1995.

Brucker, Meredith Babeaux, adapt. *Anklet for a Princess: A Cinderella Story from India*. Illus. Youshan Tang. Story by Lila Mehta. Fremont, CA: Shen's, 2002.

Buehner, Caralyn. *Fanny's Dream*. Illus. Mark Buehner. New York: Puffin, 1996.

Burchell, Mary. *Cinderella After Midnight*. 1945. Harlequin Romance 1075. New York: Harlequin, 1976. (Adult)

Christenberry, Judy. *A Ring for Cinderella*. Silhouette Romance 1356. Lucky Charm Sister Miniseries. New York: Silhouette, 1999. (Adult)

Climo, Shirley. *The Egyptian Cinderella*. Illus. Ruth Heller. New York: Harper, 1992.

_____. *The Irish Cinderlad*. Illus. Loretta Krupinski. New York: HarperTrophy, 1996.

_____. *The Korean Cinderella*. Illus. Ruth Heller. New York: Harper, 1993.

_____. *The Persian Cinderella*. Illus. Robert Florczak. New York: Harper, 1999.

Coburn, Jewell Reinhart. *Angkat: The Cambodian Cinderella*. Illus. Eddie Flotte. Fremont, CA: Shen's, 1998.

_____. *Domitila: A Cinderella Tale from the Mexican Tradition*. Illus. Connie McLennan. Fremont, CA: Shen's, 2000.

_____. *Jouanah: A Hmong Cinderella*. With Tzexa Cherta Lee. Illus. Anne Sibley O'Brien. Fremont, CA: Shen's, 1996.

Cole, Babette. *Prince Cinders*. New York: PaperStar, 1987.

Collins, Sheila Hébert. *Cendrillon: A Cajun Cinderella*. Illus. Patrick Soper. Gretna, LA: Pelican, 2000.

Darcy, Lilian. *The Millionaire's Cinderella Wife*. Silhouette Romance 1772. New York: Silhouette, 2005. (Adult)

De la Paz, Myrna J. *Abadeha: The Philippine Cinderella*. Illus. Youshan Tang. Fremont, CA: Shen's, 2001.

Dwyer, Mindy. *The Salmon Princess: An Alaska Cinderella Story*. Seattle, WA: Paws IV, 2004.

Edwards, Pamela Duncan. *Dinorella: A Prehistoric Fairy Tale*. Illus. Henry Cole. New York: Hyperion, 1997.

Feather, Jane. *The Diamond Slipper*. New York: Bantam, 1997.

Garbera, Katherine. *Cinderella's Christmas Affair*. Silhouette Desire 1546. King of Hearts Miniseries. New York: Silhouette, 2003. (Adult)

_____. *Cinderella's Millionaire*. Silhouette Desire 1520. Dynasties: The Barones Miniseries. New York: Silhouette, 2003. (Adult)

Grace, Carol. *Cinderellie!* Silhouette Romance 1775. Fairy Tale Brides Miniseries. New York: Silhouette, 2005. (Adult)

Granowsky, Alvin. *That Awful Cinderella/Cinderella*. Illus. Rhonda Childress and Barbara Kiwak. Austin, TX: Steck-Vaughn, 1993.

Haddix, Margaret Peterson. *Just Ella*. New York: Aladdin-Simon, 1999.

Hayes, Sally Tyler. *Cinderella and the Spy*. Silhouette Intimate Moments 1001. New York: Silhouette, 2000. (Adult)

Hickox, Rebecca. *The Golden Sandal: A Middle Eastern Cinderella Story*. Illus. Will Hillenbrand. New York: Holiday House, 1998.

Hicks, Barbara Jean. *All That Glitters*. Colorado Springs: WaterBrook, 1999.

Hughes, Shirley. *Ella's Big Chance: A Fairy Tale Retold.* London: Bodley Head-Random, 2003.

Jackson, Ellen. *Cinder Edna.* Illus. Kevin O'Malley. New York: Mulberry, 1994.

Jaffe, Nina. *The Way Meat Loves Salt: A Cinderella Story from the Jewish Tradition.* Illus. Louise August. New York: Holt, 1998.

James, Melissa. *Cinderella's Lucky Ticket.* Silhouette Romance 1741. New York: Silhouette, 2004. (Adult)

Johnston, Tony. *Bigfoot Cinderrrrella.* Illus. James Warhola. New York: Puffin, 1998.

Karlin, Barbara. *James Marshall's Cinderella.* Illus. James Marshall. New York: Puffin, 1989.

Kauffman, Donna. *The Cinderella Rules.* New York: Bantam, 2004. (Adult)

Ketterman, Helen. *Bubba the Cowboy Prince: A Fractured Texas Tale.* Illus. James Warhola. New York: Scholastic, 1997.

Knight, Hilary. *Hilary Knight's Cinderella.* New York: Random, 2001.

Krensky, Stephen. *The Youngest Fairy Godmother Ever.* Illus. by Diana Cain Bluthenthal. New York: Simon, 2000.

Lackey, Mercedes. *The Fairy Godmother.* New York: Luna, 2004. (Adult)

Lee, Tanith. "When the Clock Strikes." *Red as Blood* 49–65. (Adult)

Levine, Gail Carson. *Ella Enchanted.* New York: Trophy Newbery, 1997.

Louie, Ai-Ling. *Yeh-Shen: A Cinderella Story from China.* Illus. Ed Young. New York: Puffin, 1982.

Lowell, Susan. *Cindy Ellen: A Wild Western Cinderella.* Illus. Jane Manning. New York: Harper, 2000.

Lum, Darrell. *The Golden Slipper: A Vietnamese Legend.* Illus. Makiko Nagano. New York: Troll, 1994.

Mackenzie, Myrna. *Their Little Cowgirl.* Silhouette Romance 1738. In a Fairy Tale World ... Miniseries. New York: Silhouette, 2004. (Adult)

Maguire, Gregory. *Confessions of an Ugly Stepsister.* New York: ReganBooks, 1999. (Adult)

Mah, Adeline Yen. *Chinese Cinderella: The True Story of an Unwanted Daughter.* New York: Laurel-Leaf, 1999.

Marceau-Chenkie, Brittany. *Naya, The Inuit Cinderella.* Illus. Shelley Brookes. Yellowknife, NT: Raven Rock, 1999.

Martin, Rafe. *The Rough-Face Girl.* Illus. David Shannon. New York: Puffin, 1992.

Mason, Jane B., and Sarah Hines Stephens. *If the Shoe Fits.* The Princess School #1. New York: Scholastic, 2004. [also "Sleeping Beauty"]

Mayer, Marianne. *Baba Yaga and Vasilia the Brave.* Illus. K.Y. Craft. New York: Morrow, 1994.

McMahon, Barbara. *Cinderella Twin.* Silhouette Desire 1154. Identical Twins Miniseries. New York: Silhouette, 1998. (Adult)

Meddaugh, Susan. *Cinderella's Rat.* Boston, Houghton, 1997.

Minters, Frances. *Cinder-Elly.* Illus. G. Brian Karas. New York: Puffin, 1994.

Mitchell, Marianne. *Joe Cinders.* Illus. Bryan Langdo. New York: Henry Holt, 2002.

Mortimer, Carole. *His Cinderella Mistress.* Harlequin Presents 2370. The Calendar Brides Miniseries. New York: Harlequin, 2004. (Adult)

Myers, Bernice. *Sidney Rella and the Glass Sneaker*. New York: Macmillan, 1985.

Perkal, Stephanie. *Midnight: A Cinderella Alphabet*. Illus. Spencer Alston Bartsch. Arcadia, CA: Shen's, 1997.

Perlman, Janet. *Cinderella Penguin or, The Little Glass Flipper*. New York: Puffin, 1992. [based on film *The Tender Tale of Cinderella Penguin*]

Pollock, Penny. *The Turkey Girl: A Zuni Cinderella Story*. Illus. Ed Young. New York: Little, Brown, 1996.

Ross, JoAnn. *The Prince & the Showgirl*. Harlequin Temptation 453. Lovers & Legends Miniseries. New York: Harlequin, 1993. (Adult)

San Souci, Robert D. *Cendrillon: A Caribbean Cinderella*. Illus. Brian Pinkney. New York: Aladdin, 2002.

_____. *Cinderella Skeleton*. Illus. David Catrow. New York: Harcourt, 2000.

_____. *Little Gold Star: A Spanish American Cinderella Tale*. Illus. Sergio Martinez. New York: Harper, 2000.

_____. *Sootface: An Ojibwa Cinderella Story*. Illus. Daniel San Souci. New York: Dragonfly, 1994.

Sathre, Vivian. *Slender Ella and Her Fairy Hogfather*. Illus. Sally Anne Lambert. New York: Yearling, 1999.

Scott, Christine. *Cinderella Bride*. Silhouette Romance 1134. Valentine Brides Miniseries. New York: Silhouette, 1996. (Adult)

Shroeder, Alan. *Smoky Mountain Rose: An Appalachian Cinderella*. Illus. Brad Sneed. New York: Puffin, 1997.

Sierra, Judy. *Cinderella*. The Oryx Multicultural Folktale Series. Illus. Joanne Casorelli. Westport, CT: Oryx, 1992.

_____. *The Gift of the Crocodile: A Cinderella Story*. Illus. Reynold Ruffins. New York: Simon, 2000.

Silverman, Erica. *Raisel's Riddle*. Illus. Susan Gaber. New York: Farrar, 1999.

Silverstein, Shel. "In Search of Cinderella." *A Light in the Attic*. New York: Harper, 1981. 162.

Skinner, Daphne. *My Side of the Story Cinderella/Lady Tremaine*. Illus. Atelier Philippe Harchy and John Kurtz. New York: Disney, 2003.

Steptoe, John. *Mufaro's Beautiful Daughters: An African Tale*. New York: Lothrop, 1987.

Tagg, Christine. *Cinderlily: A Floral Fairy Tale in Three Acts*. Illus. David Ellwand. Cambridge, MA: Candlewick, 2003.

Takayama, Sandi. *Sumorella: A Hawai'i Cinderella Story*. Illus Esther Szegedy. Honolulu: Bess, 1997.

Thaler, Mike. *Cinderella Bigfoot*. Illus. Jared Lee. Happily Ever Laughter. New York: Scholastic, 1997.

Walker, Kate. *The Cinderella Trap*. Harlequin Romance 2957. New York: Harlequin, 1989. (Adult)

Webb, Kathleen. *Cinderella's Shoe Size*. Harlequin American Romance 904. New York: Harlequin, 2001. (Adult)

Whipple, Laura. *If the Shoe Fits: Voices from Cinderella*. Illus. Laura Beingessner. New York: McElderry, 2002. [poems]

Willard, Nancy. *Cinderella's Dress*. Illus. Jane Dyer. New York: Blue Sky, 2003.

The Emperor's New Clothes

The Emperor's New Clothes: An All-Star Illustrated Retelling of the Classic Fairy Tale. New York: Harcourt, 1998. [with CD]

The Emperor's New Clothes as told by Vince Gill. Illus. Carol Newsom. New York: Dutton, 2003. [with CD]

Perlman, Janet. *The Emperor Penguin's New Clothes*. New York: Scholastic, 1994.

The Frog Prince

Baker, E. D. *The Frog Princess*. New York: Bloomsbury, 2002.

Berenzy, Alix. *A Frog Prince*. New York: Henry Holt, 1989.

Bingham, Lisa. *The Princess & the Frog*. . Harlequin American Romance 692. Once Upon a Kiss Miniseries. New York: Harlequin, 1997. (Adult)

Carpenter, Jill, ed. *Of Frogs and Toads: Poems & Short Prose Featuring Amphibians*. Sewanee, TN: Ione P, 1998.

Graff, Laurie. *You Have to Kiss a Lot of Frogs*. Don Mills, ON: Red Dress Ink, 2004. (Adult)

Jump, Shirley. *Her Frog Prince*. Silhouette Romance 1746. In a Fairy Tale World ... Miniseries. New York: Silhouette, 2004. (Adult)

Mitchell, Stephen. *The Frog Prince: A Fairy Tale for Consenting Adults*. New York: Harmony, 1999. (Adult)

Moore, John. *The Unhandsome Prince*. New York: Ace, 2005.

Napoli, Donna Jo. *Gracie: The Pixie of the Puddle*. New York: Dutton, 2004.

_____. *Jimmy, the Pickpocket of the Palace*. Illus. Judith Byron Schachner. New York: Puffin, 1995.

_____. *The Prince of the Pond: Otherwise Known as De Fawg Pin*. Illus. Judith Byron Schachner. New York: Puffin, 1992.

Radford, Sheri. "Kissing Frogs." *Plays* Oct. 1996: 49- . *General Reference Center Gold*. InfoTrac Web. Lake Superior State University. 18 Feb. 2002 <http://infotrac.galegroup.com/>.

Sanders, Glenda. *Dr. Hunk*. Harlequin Temptation 437. Lovers & Legends Miniseries. New York: Harlequin, 1993. (Adult)

Sciezska, Jon. *The Frog Prince Continued*. Illus. Steve Johnson. New York: Viking, 1991.

The Gingerbread Man

Jarrell, Randall. *The Gingerbread Rabbit*. Illus. Garth Williams. New York: Harper, 1964.

The Golden Goose

Levine, Gail Carson. *The Fairy's Return*. New York: Harper, 2002.

Goldilocks

Christenberry, Judy. *In Papa Bear's Bed*. . Harlequin American Romance 701. Once Upon a Kiss Miniseries. New York: Harlequin, 1997. (Adult)

Collins, Sheila Hébert. *Jolie Blonde and the Three Héberts: A Cajun Twist to an Old Tale.* Illus. Patrick Soper. Gretna, LA: Pelican, 1999.

Dealey, Erin. *Goldie Locks Has Chicken Pox.* Illus. Hanako Wakiyama. New York: Scholastic, 2002.

Ernst, Lisa Campbell. *Goldilocks Returns.* New York: Simon, 2000.

Goldilocks and the Three Bears as Told by Pam Tillis. Illus. Jane Chambless Wright. New York: Dutton, 2003. [with CD]

Granowsky, Alvin. *Bears Should Share!/Goldilocks and the Three Bears.* Illus. Anne Lunsford and Lyn Martin. Austin, TX: Steck-Vaughn, 1996.

Laird, Donivee Martin. *Wili Wai Kula and the Three Mongooses.* Illus. Carol Jossem. Honolulu: Barnaby, 1983.

Lester, Helen. *Tackylocks and the Three Bears.* Illus. Lynn Munsinger. New York: Walter Lorraine-Houghton, 2002.

Lowell, Susan. *Dusty Locks and the Three Bears.* Illus. Randy Cecil. New York: Henry Holt, 2001.

Marshall, James. *Goldilocks and the Three Bears.* New York: Puffin, 1988.

McBain, Ed. *Goldilocks.* New York: Arbor House, 1976. (Adult)

Meyers, Cindy. *Rolling Along with Goldilocks and the Three Bears.* Illus. Carol Morgan. Bethesda, MD: Woodbine House, 1999.

Petach, Heidi. *Goldilocks and the Three Hares.* New York: Scholastic, 1995.

Stanley, Diane. *Goldie and the Three Bears.* New York: Harper, 2003.

Tolhurst, Marilyn. *Somebody and the Three Blairs.* Illus. Simon Abel. New York: Orchard, 1990.

Goose Girl

Hale, Shannon. *The Goose Girl.* New York: Bloomsbury, 2003.

Hansel and Gretel

DeLuise, Dom. *Dom DeLuise's Hansel & Gretel.* Illus. Christopher Santoro. New York: Aladdin-Simon, 1997.

Hébert-Collins, Sheila. *'T Pousette et 'T Poulette: A Cajun Hansel and Gretel.* Illus. Patrick Soper. Gretna, LA: Pelican, 2001.

Napoli, Donna Jo. *The Magic Circle.* New York: Puffin, 1993.

Thaler, Mike. *Hanzel and Pretzel.* Illus. Jared Lee. Happily Ever Laughter. New York: Cartwheel-Scholastic, 1997.

Henny Penny

Granowsky, Alvin. *Brainy Bird Saves the Day!/Henny Penny.* Illus. Éva Vágréti Cockrille and Mike Krone. Austin, TX: Steck-Vaughn, 1996.

The Hero of Barletta

Napoli, Donna Jo. *The Hero of Barletta.* Illus. Dana Gustafson. Minneapolis: Carolrhoda, 1988.

The House That Jack Built

Scieszka, Jon. *The Book That Jack Wrote*. Illus. Daniel Adel. New York: Viking, 1994.

Jack and the Beanstalk

Birdseye, Tom. *Look Out, Jack! The Giant Is Back!* Illus. Will Hillenbrand. New York: Holiday House, 2001.
Catanese, P.W. *The Thief and the Beanstalk*. New York: Aladdin-Simon, 2005.
Granowsky, Alvin. *Giants Have Feelings, Too/Jack and the Beanstalk*. Illus. Henry Buerchkholtz and Linda Graves. Austin, TX: Steck-Vaughn, 1993.
Holub, Joan. *Jack and the Jellybeanstalk*. Illus. Benton Mahan. New York: Grosset, 2002.
Kellogg, Steven. *Jack and the Beanstalk*. New York: Harper, 1991.
Laird, Donivee Martin. *Keaka and the Liliko'i Vine*. Illus. Carol Jossem. Honolulu: Barnaby, 1982.
Napoli, Donna Jo. *Crazy Jack*. New York: Delacorte, 1999.
Osborne, Mary Pope. *Kate and the Beanstalk*. Illus. Giselle Potter. New York: Atheneum, 2000.

Jack, the Giant Killer

De Lint, Charles. *Jack of Kinrowan*. New York: Orb-Doherty, 1995. [contains *Jack, the Giant Killer* and *Drink Down the Moon*] (Adult)

The Little Mermaid/Mermaid Tales

Maclay, Charlotte. *Catching a Daddy*. Harlequin American Romance 709. Once Upon a Kiss Miniseries. New York: Harlequin, 1998. (Adult)
Minters, Frances. *Princess Fishtail*. Illus. G. Brian Karas. New York: Viking, 2002.
Napoli, Donna Jo. *Sirena*. New York: Scholastic, 1998.
Viguié, Debbie. *Midnight Pearls*. New York: Simon Pulse, 2003.

The Little Red Hen

Granowsky, Alvin. *Help Yourself, Little Red Hen!/The Little Red Hen* Illus. Jane Manning and Wendy Edelson. Austin, TX: Steck-Vaughn, 1996.
Sturges, Philemon. *The Little Red Hen (Makes a Pizza)*. Illus. Amy Walrod. New York: Puffin, 1999.

Little Red Riding Hood

Amoss, Berthe. *A Cajun Little Red Riding Hood*. New Orleans: MTC P, 2000.
Artell, Mike. *Petite Rouge: A Cajun Red Riding Hood*. Illus. Jim Harris. New York: Puffin, 2001.

Collins, Sheila Hébert. *Petite Rouge: A Cajun Twist to an Old Tale*. Illus. Chris Diket. Gretna, LA: Pelican, 1997.

Ernst, Lisa Campbell. *Little Red Riding Hood: A Newfangled Prairie Tale*. New York: Aladdin, 1995.

Hyman, Trina Schart. *Little Red Riding Hood*. New York: Holiday House, 1983.

Kauffman, Donna. *The Big Bad Wolf Tells All*. New York: Bantam, 2003. (Adult)

Laird, Donivee Martin. *'Ula Li'i and the Magic Shark*. Illus. Carol Jossem. Honolulu: Barnaby, 1985.

Lowell, Susan. *Little Red Cowboy Hat*. Illus. Randy Cecil. New York: Henry Holt, 1997.

Marshall, James. *Red Riding Hood*. New York: Puffin, 1987.

Sanvoisin, Éric. *Little Red Ink Drinker*. Illus. Martin Matje. Trans. Georges Moroz. New York: Delacorte-Random, 2003.

Schmitz, Anthony. *Darkest Desire: The Wolf's Own Tale*. Hopewell, NJ: Ecco, 1998. (Adult)

Viguié, Debbie. *Scarlet Moon*. New York: Simon Pulse-Simon, 2004.

Young, Ed. *Lon Po Po: A Red-Riding Hood Story from China*. New York: PaperStar, 1989.

Zipes, Jack, ed. *The Trials & Tribulations of Little Red Riding Hood*. 2nd ed. New York: Routledge, 1993. [a combination of critical material and various revisions, primarily adult]

Mother Goose/Nursery Rhymes

Garriel, Barbara S. *I Know a Shy Fellow Who Swallowed a Cello*. Illus. John O'Brien. New York: Scholastic, 2004.

Gosling, Gabby. *The Top Secret Files of Mother Goose*. Illus. Tim Banks. North Vancouver: Walrus, 2003.

Lansky, Bruce, ed. *The New Adventures of Mother Goose: Gentle Rhymes for Happy Times*. Illus. Stephen Carpenter. New York: Meadowbrook-Simon, 1993.

McBain, Ed. *Mary, Mary*. New York: Warner, 1992. (Adult)

_____. *There Was a Little Girl*. New York: Warner, 1994. (Adult)

Smith, Linda. *There Was an Old Woman Who Lived in a Boot*. Illus. Jane Manning. New York: Harper, 2003.

The Pied Piper

Mackenzie, Myrna. *The Pied Piper's Bride*. Silhouette Romance 1714. The Brides of Red Rose Miniseries. New York: Silhouette, 2004. (Adult)

Napoli, Donna Jo. *Breath*. New York: Atheneum, 2003.

Pearson, Ridley. *The Pied Piper*. New York: Hyperion, 1999.

Pratchett, Terry. *The Amazing Maurice and His Educated Rodents*. New York: Harper, 2001.

Richardson, Bill. *After Hamelin*. New York: Annick, 2000.

The Princess and the Pea

Auch, Mary Jane. *The Princess and the Pizza*. Illus. Mary Jane and Herb Auch. New York: Holiday House, 2002.

Grey, Mini. *The Very Smart Pea and the Princess-to-Be*. New York: Knopf, 2003.
Haan, Linda de and Stern Nijland. *King & King*. Berkeley, CA: Tricycle P-Ten Speed P, 2000.
_____. *King & King & Family*. English adapt. Abigail Samoun. Berkeley, CA: Tricycle P-Ten Speed P, 2004.
Johnston, Tony. *The Cowboy and the Black-Eyed Pea*. Illus. Warren Ludwig. New York: PaperStar, 1992.
Levine, Gail Carson. *The Princess Test*. New York: Harper, 1999.
Thaler, Mike. *The Princess and the Pea-ano*. Illus. Jared Lee. Happily Every Laughter. New York: Cartwheel-Scholastic, 1997.
Wilkins, Gina. *When It's Right*. Harlequin Temptation 445. Lovers & Legends Miniseries. New York: Harlequin, 1993. (Adult)

The Princess on the Glass Hill

Levine, Gail Carson. *Cinderellis and the Glass Hill*. New York: Harper, 2000.

Puddocky

Levine, Gail Carson. *For Biddle's Sake*. New York: Harper, 2002.

Puss-in-Boots

Huling, Jan. *Puss in Cowboy Boots*. Illus. Phil Huling. New York: Simon & Schuster, 2002.
McBain, Ed. *Puss in Boots*. New York: Warner, 1987. (Adult)

Rapunzel

Charman, Janet. *Rapunzel, Rapunzel*. Auckland: Auckland UP, 1999. [poetry] (Adult)
Jensen, Muriel. *The Prince, the Lady & the Tower*. Harlequin American Romance 669. Once Upon a Kiss Miniseries. New York: Harlequin, 1997. (Adult)
Mason, Jane B., and Sarah Hines Stephens. *Let Your Hair Down*. The Princess School #3. New York: Scholastic, 2004.
Napoli, Donna Jo. *Zel*. New York: Puffin, 1996.
Neggers, Carla. *Night Watch*. Harlequin Temptation 461. Lovers & Legends Miniseries. New York: Harlequin, 1993. (Adult)
North, Mary. *Barbie as Rapunzel: A Storybook*. Photographs by Willy Lew, et. al. New York: Golden Books, 2002.
Roberts, Lynn. *Rapunzel: A Groovy Fairy Tale*. Illus. David Roberts. New York: Abrams, 2003.
Span, Lisa Russ. *Glass Town*. Los Angeles: Red Hen P, 1999. [poems—section labeled "Rapunzel's Clock"] (Adult)
Wilcox, Leah. *Falling for Rapunzel*. Illus. Lydia Monks. New York: Putnam, 2003.

Robin Hood

Granowsky, Alvin. *The Sheriff Speaks/Robin Hood*. Illus. Gregg Fitzhugh and David Griffin. Austin, TX: Steck-Vaughn, 1993.

McKinley, Robin. *The Outlaws of Sherwood*. New York: Ace, 1988.

Springer, Nancy. *Rowan Hood: Outlaw Girl of Sherwood Forest*. New York: Puffin, 2001.

Rumpelstiltskin

Granowsky, Alvin. *A Deal Is a Deal/Rumpelstiltskin*. Illus. Tom Newbury and Linda Graves. Austin, TX: Steck-Vaughn, 1993.

Kilworth, Garry. "Masterpiece." Datlow and Windling, *Ruby Slippers* 33–53. (Adult)

Logan, Leandra. *The Missing Heir*. Harlequin Temptation 433. Lovers & Legends Miniseries. New York: Harlequin, 1993. (Adult)

McBain, Ed. *Rumpelstiltskin*. New York: Viking, 1981. (Adult)

Napoli, Donna Jo, and Richard Tchen. *Spinners*. New York: Puffin, 1999.

Stanley, Diane. *Rumpelstiltskin's Daughter*. New York: Harper, 1997.

Vande Velde, Vivian. *The Rumpelstiltskin Problem*. Boston: Houghton, 2000.

Sleeping Beauty

Card, Orson Scott. *Enchantment*. New York: Del Ray, 1999. (Adult)

Carruth, Hayden. "The Sleeping Beauty (1970–1980)." *Collected Longer Poems*. Port Townsend, WA: Copper Canyon P, 1994. 115–186. (Adult)

Coover, Robert. *Briar Rose*. New York: Grove, 1996. (Adult)

Dalton, Emily. *Wake Me with a Kiss*. Harlequin American Romance 685. Once Upon a Kiss Miniseries. New York: Harlequin, 1997. (Adult)

Davisdon, Avram, and Grania Davis. *Marco Polo and the Sleeping Beauty*. Berkely Heights, NJ: Wildside P, 1988. (Adult)

Dokey, Cameron. *Beauty Sleep*. New York: Simon Pulse, 2002.

Faulkner, Keith. *Sleeping Bronto*. Illus. Graham Kennedy. Surrey, UK: Prospero, 2001.

Hyman, Trina Schart. *The Sleeping Beauty*. New York: Little, Brown, 1977.

Ivory, Judith. *Sleeping Beauty*. New York: Avon-Harper, 1998. (Adult)

Kassirer, Sue. *Barbie: Sleeping Beauty*. New York: Golden Book, 2003.

Keller, Emily Snowell. *Sleeping Bunny*. Illus. Pamela Silin-Palmer. New York: Random, 2003.

Levine, Gail Carson. *Princess Sonora and the Long Sleep*. New York: Harper, 1999.

MacDonald, Ross. *Sleeping Beauty*. New York: Vintage-Random, 1973. (Adult)

Margolin, Phillip. *Sleeping Beauty*. New York: Harper, 2004. (Adult)

McKinley, Robin. *Spindle's End*. New York: Putnam's, 2000.

Medeiros, Teresa. *A Kiss to Remember*. New York: Bantam, 2001. (Adult)

Navin, Jacqueline. *The Sleeping Beauty*. Harlequin Historical 578. New York: Harlequin, 2001. (Adult)

Norris, Rufus. *Sleeping Beauty*. London: Nick Hearne, 2003. (Adult)

Roquelaure, A.N. *Beauty's Punishment*. New York: Plume, 1984. (Adult)
_____. *Beauty's Release*. New York: Plume, 1985. (Adult)
_____. *The Claiming of Sleeping Beauty*. New York: Plume, 1983. (Adult)
San José, Christine. *Sleeping Beauty*. Illus. Dominic Catalano. Honesdale, PA: Boyd Mills P, 1997.
Swanson, Denise. *Murder of a Sleeping Beauty*. New York: Signet, 2002. (Adult)
Tepper, Sheri S. *Beauty*. New York: Bantam, 1992. (Adult)
Yolen, Jane. *Briar Rose*. New York: Tor, 1992. (Adult — sometimes labeled Young Adult)
_____. *Sleeping Ugly*. Illus. Diane Stanley. New York: PaperStar, 1981.

Snow White and the Seven Dwarfs

Barthelme, Donald. *Snow White*. New York: Scribner, 1965. (Adult)
French, Fiona. *Snow White in New York*. Toronto: Oxford UP, 1986.
Granowsky, Alvin. *The Unfairest of Them All/Snow White*. Illus. Mike Krone and Rhonda Childress. Austin, TX: Steck-Vaughn, 1993.
Hébert-Collins, Sheila. *Blanchette et les Sept Petits Cajuns: A Cajun Snow White*. Illus. Patrick Soper. Gretna, LA: Pelican, 2002.
Laird, Donivee Martin. *Hau Kea and the Seven Menehune*. Illus. Carol Ann Jossem. Honolulu: Barnaby, 1995.
Lee, Tanith. *White as Snow*. The Fairy Tale Ser. New York: Tor, 2000. (Adult)
Lynn, Tracy. *Snow*. New York: Simon Pulse, 2003.
Mason, Jane B., and Sarah Hines Stephens. *Who's the Fairest?* The Princess School #2. New York: Scholastic, 2004.
Rolofson, Kristine. *The Perfect Husband*. Harlequin Temptation 425. Lovers & Legends Miniseries. New York: Harlequin, 1993. (Adult)
Sinclair, Elizabeth. *Eight Men and a Lady*. Harlequin American Romance 677. Once Upon a Kiss Miniseries. New York: Harlequin, 1997. (Adult)
Thaler, Mike. *Schmoe White and the Seven Dorfs*. Illus. Jared Lee. Happily Ever Laughter. New York: Scholastic, 1997.

The Three Billy Goats Gruff

Granowsky, Alvin. *Just a Friendly Old Troll/The Three Billy Goats Gruff*. Illus. Michele Nidenoff and Thomas Newbury. Austin, TX: Steck-Vaughn, 1996.

The Three Little Pigs

Amoss, Berthe. *The Three Little Cajun Pigs*. New Orleans: MTC P, 1999.
Asch, Frank. *Ziggy Piggy and the Three Little Pigs*. Tonawanda, NY: Kids Can P, 1998.
Claverie, Jean. *The Three Little Pigs*. Trans. Elizabeth D. Crawford. New York: North-South, 1989.
Collins, Sheilan Hébert. *Les Trois Cochons*. Illus. Patrick Soper. Gretna, LA: Pelican, 1995.
Dunker, Bon. *An Almost True Tale of Three Pigs & a Wolf*. Forks, WA: Z3 Universe, 2000.

Kellogg, Steven. *The Three Little Pigs.* New York, Harper, 1997.
Laird, Donivee Martin. *The Three Little Hawaiian Pigs and the Magic Shark.* Illus. Carol Jossem. Honolulu: Barnaby, 1981.
Laverde, Arlene. *Alaska's Three Pigs.* Illus. Mindy Dwyer. Seattle: Paws IV, 2000.
Lowell, Susan. *The Three Little Javelinas.* Illus. Jim Harris. Flagstaff, AZ: Rising Moon, 1992.
Moser, Barry. *The Three Little Pigs.* New York: Little, Brown, 2001.
Petach, Heidi. *Wee Three Pigs.* New York: Grosset, 2002.
Scieszka, Jon. *The True Story of the 3 Little Pigs.* Illus. Lane Smith. New York: Viking, 1989.
Trivizas, Eugene. *The Three Little Wolves and the Big Bad Pig.* Illus. Helen Oxenbury. New York: Macmillan, 1993.
Whately, Bruce. *Wait! No Paint!* New York: Harper, 2001.
Wiesner, David. *The Three Pigs.* New York: Clarion, 2001.

The Three Spinners

Ernst, Lisa Campbell. *The Three Spinning Fairies: A Tale from the Brothers Grimm.* New York: Dutton, 2002.

Toads and Diamonds

Levine, Gail Carson. *The Fairy's Mistake.* New York: Harper, 1999.

The Tortoise and the Hare

Granowsky, Alvin. *Friends at the End/The Tortoise and the Hare.* Illus. Normand Chartier and Delana Bettoli. Austin, TX: Steck-Vaughn, 1996.
Lowell, Susan. *The Tortoise and the Jackrabbit.* Illus. Jim Harris. Flagstaff, AZ: Rising Moon, 1994.

The Ugly Duckling

Michaels, Lynn. *Second Sight.* Harlequin Temptation 449. Lovers & Legends Miniseries. New York: Harlequin, 1993. (Adult)

Revisions of the Form (but not of a specific tale)

Baker, E.D. *Dragon's Breath.* New York: Bloomsbury, 2003.
_____. *Once Upon a Curse.* New York: Bloomsbury, 2004.
Black, Holly. *Tithe: A Modern Faerie Tale.* New York: Simon, 2002.
Brennan, Herbie. *Faerie Wars.* New York: Bloomsbury, 2003.
Browne, Anthony. *Into the Forest.* Cambridge, MA: Candlewick, 2004.
Brust, Steven. *The Sun, the Moon, & the Stars.* New York: Orb-Doherty, 1987. (Adult)
Cabot, Meg. *The Princess Diaries.* New York: Harper, 2000.

Carman, Patrick. *The Dark Hills Divide*. The Land of Elyon Book 1. New York: Orchard-Scholastic, 2005.

Coville, Bruce. *Into the Land of the Unicorns*. The Unicorn Chronicles: Book 1. New York: Apple-Scholastic, 1994.

Coyle, Carmela LaVigna. *Do Princesses Wear Hiking Boots?* Illus. Mike Gordon and Carl Gordon. New York: Scholastic, 2003.

Delacroix, Claire. *The Beauty Bride*. New York: Warner, 2005. (Adult)

_____. *The Rose Red Bride*. New York: Warner, 2005. (Adult)

_____. *The Snow White Bride*. New York: Warner, 2005. (Adult)

DiCamillo, Kate. *The Tale of Desperaux*. Illus. Timothy Basil Ering. Cambridge, MA: Candlewick, 2003.

Ferris, Jean. *Once Upon a Marigold*. New York: Harcourt, 2002.

Fierstein, Harvey. *The Sissy Duckling*. Illus. Henry Cole. New York: Simon, 2002.

Flynn, Christine. *Prodigal Prince Charming*. Silhouette Special Edition 1624. The Kendricks Camelot Miniseries. New York: Silhouette, 2004. (Adult)

Funke, Cornelia. *Dragon Rider*. Trans. Anthea Bell. New York: Chicken House-Scholastic, 2004.

_____. *Inkheart*. Trans. Anthea Bell. New York: Chicken House-Scholastic, 2003.

Gaiman, Neil. "Instructions." Datlow and Windling, *Wolf at the Door* 30–33.

Goldman, William. *The Princess Bride: S. Morgenstern's Classic Tale of True Love and High Adventure*. New York: Ballantine, 1973. (Adult)

Gray, Margaret. *The Ugly Princess and the Wise Fool*. Illus. Randy Cecil. New York: Henry Holt, 2002.

Gribben, Valerie. *Fairytale*. Montgomery, AL: Junebug, 2003.

Jacobs, Holly. *Once Upon a Prince*. Silhouette Romance 1777. Perry Square: The Royal Invasion! Miniseries. New York: Silhouette, 2005. (Adult)

_____. *Once Upon a Princess*. Silhouette Romance 1768. Perry Square: The Royal Invasion! Miniseries. New York: Silhouette, 2005. (Adult)

Kaye, M.M. *The Ordinary Princess*. New York: Puffin, 1980.

Keyes, Greg. *The Briar King*. The Kingdoms of Thorn and Bone. New York: Del Rey-Ballantine, 2003. (Adult)

_____. *The Charnel Prince*. The Kingdoms of Thorn and Bone. New York: Del Rey-Ballantine, 2004. (Adult)

Kindl, Patrice. *Goose Chase*. New York: Puffin, 2001.

Lake, M.D. *Once Upon a Crime*. New York: Avon, 1995. (Adult)

Levine, Gail Carson. *The Two Princesses of Bamarre*. New York: HarperTrophy, 2001.

_____. *The Wish*. New York: Scholastic, 2000.

Lickiss, Rebecca. *Never After*. New York: Ace, 2002.

Luckett, Dave. *The Girl, the Dragon, and the Wild Magic*. New York: Scholastic, 2000.

Lyons, Judith. *A Texas Tale*. Silhouette Special Edition 1637. New York: Silhouette, 2004. (Adult)

Mackenzie, Myrna. *The Black Knight's Bride*. Silhouette Romance 1722. The Brides of Red Rose Miniseries. New York: Silhouette, 2004. (Adult)

Martin, Rafe. *The Storytelling Princess*. Illus. Kimberly Bulcken Root. New York: Puffin, 2001.

Mason, Jane B., and Sarah Hines Stephens. *Princess Charming*. The Princess

School # 5. New York: Scholastic, 2005. [also contains "Jack and the Beanstalk"]

Matlock, Curtiss Ann. "Once Upon a Christmas." *1993 Keepsake Christmas Stories.* New York: Harlequin, 1993. 9–144. (Adult)

McKinley, Robin. *The Hero and the Crown.* New York: Puffin, 1984.

McWilliams, Judith. *Dr. Charming.* Silhouette Romance 1721. New York: Silhouette, 2004. (Adult)

Meier, Susan. *Twice a Princess.* Silhouette Romance 1758. In a Fairy Tale World ... Miniseries. New York: Silhouette, 2005. (Adult)

Mitchell, N.J.W. *The Adventures of Princess Nightshade.* New York: Writer's Showcase, 2001.

_____. *Fuzbud and the Wizard: A Sequel to the Adventures of Princess Nightshade.* New York: Writer's Showcase, 2001.

_____. *Hannah, the Witch, and the Unicorn: A Sequel to the Adventures of Princess Nightshade and Fuzbud and the Wizard.* New York: Writer's Showcase, 2002.

_____. *The Search.* New York: Writer's Showcase, 2003.

Munsch, Robert. *The Paper Bag Princess.* Illus. Michael Martchenko. New York: Annick, 1980.

Naylor, Phyllis Reynolds. *Alice in Blunderland.* New York: Scholastic, 2003.

O'Brien, Kathleen. *Happily Never After.* Harlequin Signature Select Spotlight. New York: Harlequin, 2005. (Adult)

Pade, Victoria. "Tidings of Joy." *1993 Keepsake Christmas Stories.* New York: Harlequin, 1993. 263–377. (Adult)

Palatini, Margie. *Bad Boys.* Illus. Henry Cole. New York: Harper, 2003.

_____. *Piggie Pie.* Illus. Howard Fine. New York: Clarion, 1995.

Puttock, Simon. *Big Bad Wolf Is Good.* Illus. Lynne Chapman. New York: Sterling, 2001.

Regan, Dian Curtis. *Princess Nevermore.* New York: Point-Scholastic, 1995.

Roberts, Lynn. *Once Upon a Time: A Modern Fairy Tale.* Philadelphia: Xlibris, 2000.

Rodda, Emily. *Dragon's Nest.* Dragons of Deltora #1. New York: Scholastic, 2003.

_____. *Isle of the Dead.* Dragons of Deltora #3. New York: Scholastic, 2004.

_____. *Shadowgate.* Dragons of Deltora #2. New York: Scholastic, 2004.

_____. *The Sister of the South.* Dragons of Deltora #4. New York: Scholastic, 2004.

Sanvoisin, Éric. *The City of Ink Drinkers.* Illus. Martin Matje. Trans. Georges Moroz. New York: Dell, 2001.

_____. *The Ink Drinker.* Illus. Martin Matje. Trans. Georges Moroz. New York: Dell, 1998.

_____. *A Straw for Two.* Illus. Martin Matje. Trans. Georges Moroz. New York: Dell, 1999.

Smith, Karen Rose. *Once Upon a Baby ...* Silhouette Romance 1737. New York: Silhouette, 2004. (Adult)

Stadther, Michael. *A Treasure's Trove: A Fairy Tale about Real Treasure for Parents and Children of All Ages.* Pound Ridge, NY: Treasure Trove, 2004.

Stewart, Paul, and Chris Riddell. *Beyond the Deepwoods.* The Edge Chronicles #1. New York: David Fickling-Random, 1998.

Straub, Wendy Corsi. *A Thoroughly Modern Princess.* New York: Avon-Harper, 2003.

Stroud, Jonathan, *The Amulet of Samarkand*. The Bartimaues Trilogy Book One. New York: Miramax-Hyperion, 2003.
Thomas, Trisha R. *Nappily Ever After*. New York: Crown, 2000.
Townley, Roderick. *The Great Good Thing*. New York: Aladdin, 2001.
Vande Velde, Vivian. *Dragon's Bait*. New York: Magic Carpet-Harcourt, 1992.
_____. *Heir Apparent*. New York: Magic Carpet-Harcourt, 2002.
_____. *A Well-Timed Enchantment*. New York: Magic Carpet-Harcourt, 1990.
Willman, Marianne. "A Fairytale Season." *1993 Keepsake Christmas Stories*. New York: Harlequin, 1993. 149–257 (Adult)
Wrede, Patricia C. *Calling on Dragons*. New York: Magic Carpet, 1993.
_____. *Dealing with Dragons*. New York: Magic Carpet, 1990.
_____. *Searching for Dragons*. New York: Magic Carpet, 1991.
_____. *Talking to Dragons*. New York: Magic Carpet, 1985.

Film/Video Revisions

There are numerous more film revisions, short and feature-length, than this list contains. For a more information about feature-length films, go to Internet Movie Database <http://www.imdb.com/>, and for more information about cartoons (short or long), go to the Big Cartoon Database <http://www.bcdb. com>.

The Adventures of Cinderella's Daughters. Perf. Shirley Jones and Joe Lando. 2002. DVD. Sand Hill, 2004.
Aesop and Son. In *Rocky & Bullwinkle & Friends Complete Season 1*. 1959–60. 4 DVDs. Ward, 2003.
"Cinderella Blues." 1931. *Aesop's Fables*. DVD. Digiview, 2004.
Barbie As Rapunzel. By Cliff Ruby and Elana Lesser. DVD. Matel, 2002.
The Beautician and the Beast. By Todd Graff. Perf. Timothy Dalton and Fran Drescher. 1997. DVD. Paramount, 2003.
Beauty and the Beast. By Roger Allers. 1991. DVD. Disney, 2002.
"Beauty and the Beasts." *Buffy the Vampire Slayer*. By Marti Noxon. 1998. DVD. Fox, 2003.
Belle's Tales of Friendship. By Michael Ryan et. al. VHS. Walt Disney Home Video, 1999.
"Big Bad Wolf." *Toonerville*. Cartoon Craze Vol. 23. DVD. Digiview, 2004.
"The Big Bad Wolf." *Mutt and Jeff Slick Sleuths*. Cartoon Craze Vol. 22. DVD. Digiview, 2004.
"The Boy Who Cried Wolf." *Muppet Classic Theater*. By Jim Lewis and Bill Brady. Videocassette. Jim Henson, 1994.
"Bugs Bunny and the Three Bears." *Looney Tunes Golden Collection*. By Ted Pierce. Dir. Charles M. Jones. 1944. DVD. Warner, 2000.
Cinderella. By Ken Anderson et. al. 1950. VHS. Walt Disney Home Video, 2005.
Cinderella, Sleeping Beauty, Thumbelina. 1994, 1995, 1992. DVD. GoodTimes, 2003.

A Cinderella Story. By Leigh Dunlap. Perf. Hilary Duff. Warner Brothers, 2004.

Cinderella II: Dreams Come True. By Jill E. Blotevogel et. al. VHS. Walt-Disney Home Video, 2002.

CinderElmo. Perf. Keri Russell and French Stewart. DVD. Sony, 2000.

Cinderfella. By Frank Tashlin. Perf. Jerry Lewis. 1960. DVD. Paramount, 2004.

"Cinderkitty." By Phil Harnage. *Hello Kitty Becomes a Princess.* 1987. DVD. MGM, 2003.

"Duck Amuck." *Looney Tunes Golden Collection.* By Michael Maltese. Dir. Chuck Jones. 1953. DVD. Warner, 2000.

Ella Enchanted. By Laurie Craig et. al. Perf. Anne Hathaway. Miramax, 2004.

"The Elves & the Shoemaker." *Muppet Classic Theater.* By Jim Lewis and Bill Brady. Videocassette. Jim Henson, 1994.

"The Emperor's New Clothes." *Muppet Classic Theater.* By Jim Lewis and Bill Brady. Videocassette. Jim Henson, 1994.

"The Emperor's Nightingale." *Extreme Fairy Tales Featuring the Emperor's Nightingale.* English Narr. by Phyllis McGinley. Narr. Boris Karloff. 1951. DVD. GoodTimes, 2004.

Ever After: A Cinderella Story. By Susannah Grant, Andy Tennant, and Rick Parks. Perf. Drew Barrymore and Anjelica Huston. 1998. DVD. 20th Century Fox, 2002.

"Felix the Cat and the Goose that Laid the Golden Eggs." 1936. *Felix the Cat & Friends: Neptune Nonsense.* Cartoon Craze Vol. 7. DVD. Digiview, 2004.

Fractured Fairy Tales. In *Rocky & Bullwinkle & Friends Complete Season 1.* 1959–60. 4 DVDs. Ward, 2003.

The Frog Prince. By Jerry Juhl. 1972. Videocassette. Jim Henson, 1994.

"Gingerbread." *Buffy the Vampire Slayer.* By Jane Espenson. 1999. DVD. Fox, 2003.

"The Girl Who Cried Wolf." *Care Bears Forever Friends.* 1985. DVD. Sterling, 2004.

The Glass Slipper. Perf. Leslie Caron and Michael Wildling, By Helen Deutsch. 1955. VHS. MGM/ UA Home Video, 1990.

"Greedy Humpty Dumpty." 1936. *Felix the Cat & Friends: Neptune Nonsense.* Cartoon Craze Vol. 7. DVD. Digiview, 2004.

Hansel & Gretel. By Timothy Dolan. Perf. Delta Burke and Howie Mandel. 2002. DVD. Warner, 2003.

Happily Ever After. By Martha Moran and Robby London. 1988. VHS. World-vision Home Video, 1993.

Hey Cinderella. By John Stone and Tom Whedon. 1969. Videocassette. Jim Henson, 1994.

"Hush." *Buffy the Vampire Slayer.* By Joss Whedon. 1999. DVD. Fox, 2003.

Into the Woods. By Stephen Sondheim and James Lapine. Perf. Bernadette Peters and Joanna Gleason. 1990. Videocassette. Image Entertainment, 1990.

Jack & the Beanstalk. By Sue Radley and Martin Gates. Perf. Ben Savage and Sara Gilbert. 2000. DVD. Sony, 2004.

Jack and the Beanstalk. Perf. Abbott and Costello. 1952. DVD. Digiview, 2004.

Jim Henson's Jack & the Beanstalk: The Real Story. By James V. Hart and Brian Henson. Perf. Matthew Modine and Mia Sara. 2001. DVD. Hallmark, 2001.

Jim Henson's The Storyteller. 1988. DVD. Columbia TriStar, 2003.

"Kitty and the Beast." By Temple Mathews. *Hello Kitty Becomes a Princess*. 1987. DVD. MGM, 2003.

"Kitty Locks and the Three Bears." By Jack Hanrahan and Eleanor Burian-Mohr. *Hello Kitty Becomes a Princess*. 1987. DVD. MGM, 2003.

The Little Mermaid. By Roger Allers. 1989. Videocassette. Disney, 1998.

Little Mermaid II: Return to the Sea. By Elizabeth Anderson and Temple Matthews. VHS. Walt Disney Home Video, 2000.

"Little Red Bunny Hood." *Hello Kitty's Furry Tale Theater*. By Jack Olesker, Jack Hanrahan, Eleanor Burian-Mohr, and Phil Harnage. 1987–2003. DVD. MGM, 2003.

"Little Red School Mouse." 1949. *Toonerville*. Cartoon Craze Vol. 23. DVD. Digiview, 2004.

"Old Mother Hubbard."*Twenty/Elmer Fudd: A Corny Concerto*. Cartoon Craze Vol. 21. DVD. Digiview, 2004.

"Once Upon a Time." *Hunky and Spunky & Friends: You Can't Shoe a Shoefly*. DVD. Digiview, 2004.

The Pagemaster. By David Casci et. al. Perf. Macaulay Culkin and Christopher Lloyd. 1994. DVD. 20th Century Fox, 2002.

"The Pied Piper." *Happily Ever After Fairy Tales for Every Child*. By Daryl Nickens. Narr. Robert Guillaume. 1996. DVD. Home Box Office, 2004.

The Pied Piper of Hamelin. DVD. Digiview, 2004.

"Poor Cinderella." 1934. *Betty Boop and Grampy*. Cartoon Craze Vol. 25. DVD. Digiview, 2004.

Prince Charming. By Doug Palau. Perf. Martin Short and Christina Applegate. 2000. DVD. Warner, 2003.

The Princess Bride. By William Goldman. With Cary Elwes, Mandy Patinkin, and Robin Wright. 1987. Videocassette. Nelson, 1988.

"Rapunzel." *Extreme Fairy Tales Featuring the Emperor's Nightingale*. Dir. Harry Hausen. By Charlotte Knight. 1951. DVD. GoodTimes, 2004.

Red Riding Hood. By Carole Lucia Satrina. Perf. Craig T. Nelson, Isabella Rossellini, and Amelia Shankley. 1988. DVD. MGM, 2004.

"Robin Penguin." *Hello Kitty's Furry Tale Theater*. By Jack Olesker, Jack Hanrahan, Eleanor Burian-Mohr, and Phil Harnage. 1987–2003. DVD. MGM, 2003.

Rodgers and Hammerstein's Cinderella. Music by Richard Rodgers. Lyrics by Oscar Hammerstein II. Perf. Julie Andrews. 1957. DVD. Image Entertainment, 2004.

Rodgers and Hammerstein's Cinderella. Music by Richard Rodgers. Lyrics by Oscar Hammerstein II. Teleplay by Joseph Schrank. Perf. Lesley Ann Warren and Stuart Damon. 1965. DVD. Columbia, 2001.

Rodgers and Hammerstein's Cinderella. Music by Richard Rodgers. Lyrics by Oscar Hammerstein II. Teleplay by Robert L. Freedman. Perf. Brandy, Whoopi Goldberg, and Whitney Houston. 1997. VHS. Walt Disney Home Video, 2002.

"Rumpelstiltskin." *Muppet Classic Theater*. By Jim Lewis and Bill Brady. Videocassette. Jim Henson, 1994.

Shrek. By Ted Elliott, Terry Rossio, Joe Stillman, and Roger S. H. Schulman. 2001. Videocassette. DreamWorks, 2001.

Shrek 2. By Andrew Adamson et. al. DreamWorks, 2004.

Sleeping Beauty. By Erdman Penner. 1959. DVD Special Edition. Disney, 2003.
"Sleeping Kitty." By Martha Moran. *Hello Kitty Becomes a Princess.* 1987. DVD. MGM, 2003.
The Slipper and the Rose. By Robert Forbes, Robert B. Sherman, and Richard M. Sherman. Perf. Richard Chamberlain and Gemma Craven. 1976. DVD. Image, 2000.
Snow White and the Seven Dwarfs. 1937. VHS. Walt Disney Home Video, 2001.
Snow White: A Tale of Terror. By Tom Szollosi and Deborah Serra. Perf. Sigourney Weaver and Sam Neill. 1997. DVD. Universal, 2002.
Snow White: The Fairest of Them All. By Caroline Thompson ad Julie Hickson. Perf. Miranda Richardson and Kristin Kreuk. 2001. DVD. Hallmark, 2002.
"Snow White Kitty and the One Dwarf." By Phil Harnage. *Hello Kitty Becomes a Princess.* 1987. DVD. MGM, 2003.
A Tale of Cinderella. By W.A. Frankonis. Mus. by Will Severin and George David Weiss. Perf. Christianne Tisdale and Lorraine Serabian. 1996. DVD. Warner, 2004.
The 10th Kingdom. By Simon Moore. Perf. Ann. Margret, John Larroquette, and Kimberly Williams. 1999. DVD. Hallmark, 2000.
"The Three Bears." *Mutt and Jeff Slick Sleuths.* Cartoon Craze Vol. 22. DVD. Digiview, 2004.
"Three Little Pigs." *Muppet Classic Theater.* By Jim Lewis and Bill Brady. Videocassette. Jim Henson, 1994.
"Tortoise Wins by a Hare." *Looney Tunes Golden Collection.* By Warren Foster. Dir. Robert Clampett. 1943. DVD. Warner, 2000.
"The Ugly Quackling." *Hello Kitty's Furry Tale Theater.* By Jack Olesker, Jack Hanrahan, Eleanor Burian-Mohr, and Phil Harnage. 1987–2003. DVD. MGM, 2003.
"Wolf Wolf." *Mighty Mouse/ Heckle and Jeckle: Wolf Wolf.* Cartoon Craze Vol. 18. DVD. Digiview, 2004.
The World of Hans Christian Andersen. 1971. DVD. Digiview, 2004.

Advertisements

The advertisements listed here represent only those mentioned in the book. There are many more that could be mentioned.

Capital One Credit Card. Advertisement. TBS. 20 Apr. 2005. ["Cinderella"]
H3 [Hummer 3]. ESPN. 11 Sept. 2005. ["Goldilocks and the Three Bears"]
Odor-Eaters Foot and Sneaker Spray Powder. TBS. 22 May 2005. ["Cinderella"]
Quaker Chewy Fruit and Nut Bars Ad. WB. 19 May 2004. ["Goldilocks and the Three Bears"]
ESPN Ad. ESPN2. 12 Mar. 2005. ["Cinderella"]
MassMutual Financial Group. Advertisement. ESPN2. 8 Mar. 2004. ["The Frog Prince"]

Critical Sources and Other Non-Folktale References

Aarne, Antii and Stith Thompson. *The Types of the Folktale: A Classification and Bibliography.* FF Communications 184. Helsinki: Academia Scientiarium Fennica, 1961.

Ashliman, D.L. *Folk and Fairy Tales: A Handbook.* Westport, CT: Greenwood, 2004.

Bacchilega, Cristina. *Postmodern Fairy Tales: Gender and Narrative Strategies.* Philadelphia: U of Pennsylvania P, 1997.

Bascom, William. "The Forms of Folklore: Prose Narratives." *The Journal of American Folklore* 78 (1965): 3–20.

Benson, Stephen. *Cycle of Influence: Fiction, Folktale, Theory.* Detroit: Wayne State UP, 2003.

Bernheimer, Kate, ed. *Mirror, Mirror on the Wall: Women Writers Explore Their Favorite Fairy Tales.* New York: Anchor, 2002.

Bottigheimer, Ruth B., ed. *Fairy Tales and Society: Illusion, Allusion, and Paradigm.* Philadelphia: U of Pennsylvania P, 1986.

_____. "Fractured Fairy Tales." Zipes, *Oxford* 172–3.

Cart, Michael. *What's So Funny?: Wit and Humor in American Children's Literature:* New York: Harper, 1995.

Cashdan, Sheldon. *The Witch Must Die: Hidden Meanings in Fairy Tales.* New York: Basic Books, 1999.

Conrad, Joseph. *Heart of Darkness.* 1899. Clayton, DE: Prestwick House, 2004.

Cox, Ruth. "Fantastical Flights of Fancy." *Emergency Librarian* 25.4 (1998): 53–5. *Periodical Abstracts.* First Search. Lake Superior State U. 22 June 2004 <http://newfirstsearch.oclc.org/FSIP>.

Crew, Hilary S. "Spinning New Tales from Traditional Texts: Donna Jo Napoli and the Rewriting of Fairy Tale." *Children's Literature in Education* 33.2 (2002): 77–95.

Cutler, Blayne. "The Folk Tale Market." *American Demographics* Oct. 1990: 47–. *General Reference Center Gold.* InfoTrac Web. Lake Superior State U. 18 Feb. 2002 <http://infotrac.galegroup.com/>.

Dégh, Linda. "Folk Narrative." Dorson 53–83.

Dorson, Richard M., ed. *Folklore and Folklife: An Introduction.* Chicago: U of Chicago P, 1972.

Doughty, Amie A. "'This Is the Real Story ... I Was Framed': Point of View and Modern Revisions of Folktales." *Journal of American and Comparative Cultures* 25 (2002): 357–62.

Dundes, Alan, ed. *Cinderella: A Casebook.* Madison: U of Wisconsin P, 1982.

_____. "Fairy Tales from a Folkloristic Perspective." Bottigheimer 259–69.

_____, ed. *Little Red Riding Hood: A Casebook.* Madison: U of Wisconsin P, 1989.

Edinger, Monica. "A Cinderella Story." *School Library Journal* 46.11 (2000):30–1. *Periodical Abstracts.* First Search. Lake Superior State U. 22 June 2004 <http://newfirstsearch.oclc.org/FSIP>.

Fleischman, Suzanne. *Tense and Narrativity: From Medieval Performance to Modern Fiction.* London: Routledge, 1990.

Griswold, Jerry. *The Meanings of "Beauty & the Beast": A Handbook.* Petersborough, ON: Broadview, 2004.

Hall, Susan. *Using Picture Storybooks to Teach Literary Devices: Recommended Books for Children and Young Adults.* Phoenix: Oryx, 1990.

Hearne, Betsy. "Swapping Tales and Stealing Stories: The Ethics and Aesthetics of Folklore in Children's Literature." *Library Trends* 47 (1999): 509–28. *Arti-*

cle First. First Search. Lake Superior State U. 22 June 2004 <http://newfirst-search.oclc.org/FSIP>.

Hill, Sandy. "Sanitized Fairy Tales Don't Help Kids Learn to Handle Scary Thoughts." *Knight-Ridder/Tribune News Service* 7 Dec. 1993. *General Reference Center Gold.* InfoTrac Web. Lake Superior State U. 18 Feb. 2002 <http://infotrac.galegroup.com/>.

Hollenbeck, Kathleen M. *Teaching with Cinderella Stories from around the World.* New York: Scholastic, 2003.

Jones, Steven Swann. *The Fairy Tale: The Magic Mirror of the Imagination.* New York: Routledge, 1995.

King, James Roy. *Old Tales and New Truths: Charting the Bright-Shadow World.* Albany, NY: SUNY P, 1992.

La Farge, Benjamin. "Comedy's Intention." *Philosophy and Literature* 28.1 (2004): 118–36.

Lane, Marcia. *Picturing the Rose: A Way of Looking at Fairy Tales.* New York: HW Wilson, 1994.

Lurie, Alison. *Don't Tell the Grown-Ups: The Subversive Power of Children's Literature.* New York: Bay Back, 1990.

Lüthi, Max. *The Fairytale as Art Form and Portrait of Man.* 1975. Trans. Jon Erickson. Bloomington: Indiana UP, 1984.

Malarte-Feldman, Claire. "Folk Materials, Re-Visions, and Narrative Images: The Intertextual Games They Play." *Children's Literature Association Quarterly* 28 (2003–4): 210–18.

Matoush, Toby Leigh. "Whimsy in the Fairy Tale Re-Visions of Anne Sexton and Kurahashi Yumiko." 2003 PCA/ACA Conference. New Orleans Marriott Hotel, New Orleans. 17 Apr. 2003.

Mondloch, Helen. "Folkwisdom: A Global Enchantment — Cinderella's Dance Through Time." *World And I* Feb. 2001: 180- . *General Reference Center Gold.* InfoTrac Web. Lake Superior State U. 18 Feb. 2002 <http://infotrac.galegroup. com/>.

Nikolajeva, Maria, and Carole Scott. *How Picturebooks Work.* New York: Garland, 2001.

Orenstein, Catherine. *Little Red Riding Hood Uncloaked: Sex, Morality, and the Evolution of a Fairy Tale.* New York: Basic Books, 2002.

Peters, Julie Anne. "When You Write Humor for Children." *The Writer* 111.1 (1998): 19-. First Search. Lake Superior State U. 12 Sept. 2005. <http://new firstsearch.oclc.org/FSIP>.

Pizer, John. "The Disenchantment of Snow White: Robert Walser, Donald Barthelme and the Modern/Postmodern Anti-Fairy Tale." *Canadian Review of Comparative Literature* 17 (1990): 330–47.

Propp, Vladimir. *Theory and History of Folklore.* Theory and History of Literatue, vol. 5. Ariadna Y. Martin and Richard P. Martin, trans. Manchester, UK: Manchester UP, 1984.

Rothstein, Edward. "Into the Woods, Children, for Dark Mysteries, Not Simple Lessons." *The New York Times* 7 Dec. 2002. 9 Dec. 2002. <http://www. nytimes.com/>.

Sale, Roger. *Fairy Tales and After: From Snow White to E.B. White.* Cambridge, MA: Harvard UP, 1978.

Schenda, Rudolf. "Tellig Tales—Spreading Tales: Change in the Communicative Form of a Popular Genre." Bottigheimer 75–94.

Schwartz, Alvin. "Children, Humor and Folklore, Part 1." *The Horn Book Magazine* June 1977: 281–7.

_____."Children, Humor and Folklore, Part 2." *The Horn Book Magazine* August 1977: 471–6.

Sellers, Susan. *Myth and Fairy Tale in Contemporary Women's Fiction.* New York: Palgrave, 2001.

Shelley, Mary. *Frankenstein.* 1818. Ed. J. Paul Hunter. Norton Critical Ed. New York: Norton, 1996.

Stein, Mary Beth. "Folklore and Fairy Tales." Zipes, *Oxford* 165–70.

Stephens, John, and Robyn McCallum. *Retelling Stories, Framing Culture: Traditional Story and Metanarratives in Children's Literature.* Children's Literature and Culture vol. 5. New York: Garland, 1998.

Tatar, Maria. *The Hard Facts of the Grimms' Fairy Tales.* Princeton, NJ: Princeton UP, 1987.

Trites, Roberta Seelinger. *Waking Sleeping Beauty: Feminist Voices in Children's Novels.* Iowa City: U of Iowa P, 1997.

Von Franz, Marie-Louise. *The Feminine in Fairy Tales.* Rev. ed. 1972. Boston: Shambhala, 1993.

_____. *The Interpretation of Fairy Tales.* Revised ed. Boston: Shambhala, 1996.

Warner, Marina. *From the Beast to the Blonde: On Fairy Tales and Their Tellers.* New York: Farrar, 1994.

Weinraub, Bernard. "Back to the Woods, with Darker Lyrics and a Dancing Cow." *New York Times* 24 Feb. 2002. 24 Feb. 2002. <htyp://www.nytimes.com/>.

Wloszczyna, Susan. "A fairy-tale bending." *USA Today* 16 Sept. 2003. 22Sept. 2003. <http://www.usatoday.com/life/movies/news/2003–09–16-fairytale_x.htm>.

Wojcik-Andrews, Ian. *Children's Films: History, Ideology, Pedagogy, Theory.* Children's Literature and Culture vol. 12. New York: Garland, 2000.

Wolfson, Nessa. "A Feature of Performed Narrative: The Conversational Historical Present." *Language in Society* 7 (1978): 215–37.

Yolen, Jane. *Touch Magic: Fantasy, Faerie, & Folklore in the Literature of Childhood.* 1981. Expanded ed. Little Rock: August House, 2000.

Zipes, Jack. *Breaking the Magic Spell: Radical Theories of Folk & Fairy Tales.* Austin: U of Texas P, 1979.

_____. *Fairy Tales and the Art of Subversion: The Classical Genre for Children and the Process of Civilization.* New York: Routledge, 1983.

_____. *Happily Ever After: Fairy Tales, Children, and the Culture Industry.* New York: Routledge, 1997.

_____. *Fairy Tale as Myth/Myth as Fairy Tale.* Lexington: U P of Kentucky, 1994.

_____, ed. *The Oxford Companions to Fairy Tales.* New York: Oxford UP, 2000.

_____. *Sticks and Stones: The Troublesome Success of Children's Literature from Slovenly Peter to Harry Potter.* New York: Routledge, 2001.

_____. *When Dreams Came True: Classical Fairy Tales and Their Tradition.* New York: Routledge, 1999.

Index